AGAINST WIND AND TIDE

AGAINST WIND AND TIDE

The African American Struggle
against the Colonization Movement

OUSMANE K. POWER-GREENE

New York University Press
NEW YORK AND LONDON

NEW YORK UNIVERSITY PRESS
New York and London
www.nyupress.org

© 2014 by New York University

Cloth ISBN 978-1-4798-2317-8

For Library of Congress Cataloging-in-Publication data, please contact the
Library of Congress.

References to Internet Web sites (URLs) were accurate at the time of writing.
Neither the author nor New York University Press is responsible for URLs that
may have expired or changed since the manuscript was prepared.
New York University Press books are printed on acid-free paper, and their binding
materials are chosen for strength and durability. We strive to use environmentally
responsible suppliers and materials to the greatest extent possible in publishing our
books.

Manufactured in the United States of America
10 9 8 7 6 5 4 3 2 1

Also available as an ebook

To William and Gwendolyn Greene

If as the friends of colonization hope, the present and coming generations of our countrymen shall by any means, succeed in freeing our land from the dangerous presence of slavery; and, at the same time, in restoring a captive people to their long-lost father-land, with bright prospects for the future; and this too, so gradually, that neither races nor individuals shall have suffered by the change, it will indeed be a glorious consummation. And if, to such a consummation, the efforts of Mr. Clay shall have contributed, it will be what he most ardently wished, and none of his labors will have been more valuable to his country and his kind.

—ABRAHAM LINCOLN, "EULOGY ON HENRY CLAY," 1852

Contents

ACKNOWLEDGMENTS

This book would not have been completed without the support, guidance, wisdom, and patience of numerous scholars, family members, and friends. Manisha Sinha first encouraged me to take up this study of the colonization movement during the antebellum era. For that reason, this book reflects her tremendous wisdom and guidance about how best to write about the colonization movement from the vantage point of black abolitionists and community leaders during that period. John Bracey's patience and enthusiasm for this project had an immeasurable impact on my desire to see it to completion. Like all master teachers, John challenged me on nearly every idea I had on this topic, pushing me to be more clear in my thinking and in the way I expressed my ideas. While I am certain he will find many points I have made in this book worthy of rethinking and further conceptualization, I am thankful for his unquenchable desire to see me do the best work I am capable of doing. Ernie Allen's ideas about African American social and political movements remain a crucial foundation upon which this book has been built. Ernie has been a wonderful mentor, and I am very fortunate to have been encouraged by his example. Bill Strickland's honest, frank criticism of this work has compelled me to remember the big picture and its relevance to the black community. John Higginson provided me with my first lessons of scholarly inquiry a year before I joined the African American Studies Department, and for those formative lessons about writing and research I am extraordinarily grateful. Bruce Laurie's seminar on the abolition movement provided me with early guidance about nineteenth-century history and how best to approach the study of the antislavery movement. My other mentors and teachers at the African American Studies Program at Umass—Michael Thelwell, James Smethurst, Steve Tracy, Esther Terry, Robert Paul Wolff, and Joy Bowman—have offered wisdom and guidance that extend beyond this book, yet remain crucial to its completion. For all of their words of encouragement and advice, I am very grateful.

The graduate program in the W.E.B. DuBois Department of African American Studies at the University of Massachusetts-Amherst provided me an ideal intellectual environment to learn much of what underpins this study. Its broadly trained graduate students, passionate about African American history, culture, and politics as well as the importance of scholar-activism, had an immense impact on my approach to researching and writing this book. While all of my peers have formed a wonderful support network, I am especially grateful for the camaraderie and insights of Shawn, David, Dan, Stephanie, Jen, Rita, Carolyn, W.S., Tkweme, Andrew, Zeb, Sandra, Trimiko, Christy, Karla, Anthony, Allia, Chris, Johnathan, McKinley, Zarrah, Deroy, David S., and David L. Tricia Loveland deserves special mention for her support during graduate school.

My colleagues in the History Department at Clark University have proven themselves to be indispensable allies in my effort to complete this book. Thus, I extend my thanks to Norm Apter, Taner Akcam, Deborah Dwork, Janette Greenwood, Wim Klooster, Nina Kushner, Thomas Kuehne, Doug Little, Olga Litvak, Drew McCoy, Amy Richter, and Paul Ropp. Each of them have in their own way provided me with guidance on how best to negotiate the challenges of teaching history while managing ambitious research projects. I owe a special debt of gratitude to Amy, Drew, Janette, and Wim, who read drafts of the manuscript and offered important insights that helped me make this a stronger book. My students at Clark University have each challenged me with wonderful and at times provocative questions about the study of African American social and political movements, which have compelled me to rethink many of the ideas in this book. While space does not permit me to mention all of them, I am particularly thankful to undergraduates Brady, Frank, Tibby, Natalie, Natasha, Rosaly, Tim, and Stephon, and graduate students Steve, Diane, Lindsay, Chris, Brooks, and Mike.

Those scholars of African American history and culture whom I have come to know over the course of this study have helped me place my work within the broader context of African American history. Special thanks go to Hilary Moss and Amani Whitfield, both of whom read or commented on this work early on. In addition, Winston James provided me with crucial insights about the limitations and possibilities of this project in my effort to make this a worthwhile contribution to the history of the pan-African protest tradition; for his advice and suggestions I am truly in debt. Similarly, I am thankful for the support of scholars Colin Palmer, Fred Opie, Jeffrey O.G. Ogbar, and Amy Jordan, who engaged me in lively discussions about African American history in ways that have shaped this book.

My editor at NYU Press, Clara Platter, had the burden of picking up this project while only having been at the Press for a short time. I am indeed thankful for her patience and her willingness to shepherd the book to completion. Likewise, I'd like to thank her excellent assistant Constance Grady, who has provided me with courteous and gentle reminders about deadlines, documents, and other details needed for the publication of this book. The two blind reviewers at NYU Press have offered the exact sort of critique that a first-time author needs when trying to complete a book with ambitious, far-reaching implications. Although I am certain there are portions of the book that they may find tenuous, I do hope that this study reflects my earnest attempt to make a useful contribution to the study of nineteenth-century African American history. For their advice and support, I am truly appreciative.

I am blessed with a large and incredible family and group of friends who support my work with passion and enthusiasm. My in-laws, Phil and Diana Power, have championed my accomplishments with much enthusiasm, while being there to support me whenever I've needed it. My father and mother, Bill and Gwen Greene, to whom this book is dedicated, did all in their power to allow me to follow my passion for studying African American history and culture. My father offered unwavering support for the project, reading portions of the manuscript from the vantage point of those outside the academy who may not be familiar with the topic. For his eagerness to dive into a subject that he had not previously been familiar with, I am much appreciative. My mother drove from New York to Massachusetts whenever we needed her in order to support my quest for a little bit of quiet time to work on the manuscript. Words cannot fully express how thankful I am for having such a wonderful person in my life. In the final year of the completion of this book, I was fortunate enough to have my brother Maurice Greene nearby to help me work through my arguments and remind me of the importance of my book for artists and intellectuals interested in understanding African American history. Much love goes out to him for those numerous mornings siting at my kitchen table discussing history and politics. I am also very thankful for the support of my sister-in-law Jodi Power who remained always eager to hear about the progress of this work. All of my friends, especially Andy, Hank, Jim, Kevin, Matt, Mike, Rocco, and Stephanie have provided me with very much support throughout the completion of this book. A big thank-you goes out to my Fresh Air Fund coworkers, who have helped me find time to work on this book each of the past eight summers. My sincere gratitude goes out to Kshinte, Akara, Terna, Raphael, Megan, Orien, Dion, Allia, Jonathan, Karolina, Shay, Brandyn, and Max for encouraging and supporting me as I worked through the ideas in the book.

Through the course of the research and writing of this book, my children Kyla, Coletrane, and Imanni have helped me remain grounded by reminding me of the importance of being more than a scholar and professor. Kyla was there from my entrance to graduate school, Coletrane was born when I first started this project, and Imanni arrived just as I began shaping the manuscript into a book. I am very thankful for having such wonderful children in my life. This short space will not allow me to express my thanks adequately to Melissa for doing all those things needed to balance my work with my family duties. To her, I am immensely grateful. This book would not have been possible without her.

PREFACE

On December 21, 1816, Rev. Robert Finley of Baskingridge, New Jersey, gathered together some of the nation's most respected attorneys, businessmen, and politicians at the Davis Hotel in Washington, D.C., to discuss creating an organization dedicated to establishing a colony for African Americans in West Africa. Henry Clay, Speaker of the U.S. House of Representatives, called the meeting to order and then went on to discuss the various ways colonization could benefit America. Like Finley, Clay believed that providing free blacks passage to their "fatherland" was a "just" way to compensate them for being "torn from their kin" in Africa. While Clay shared Finley's emphasis on the importance of Christian charity in this repatriation scheme, he stated bluntly that the organization could not promote emancipation or destroy slavery if it intended to gain broad support. Others at the meeting, such as John Randolph of Roanoke, Virginia, pointed out that many slaveowners would "delight" in this project, since the free black population of Virginia constituted a "nuisance" that destabilized slavery.[1]

One week later, these men met in the House of Representatives chambers to write the constitution of the American Society for Colonizing the Free People of Colour of the United States, better known as the American Colonization Society (ACS), with the express intent of "ridding us of the free people of color, and preparing the way for getting rid of slaves and of slavery." Nevertheless, members of the organization viewed their mission as one that would benefit free blacks living in "a state of hopeless inferiority, and consequent degradation." Since, as they explained, free blacks would never be able to rise from this lowly state of being in the United States, their status had actually caused some of them to "lose the most powerful incitements to industry, frugality, good conduct, and honorable exertion." Over time, they argued, this had caused many to sink "into a state of sloth, wretchedness, and profligacy." It was their belief that only in a "colony composed of themselves" could free blacks "enjoy real equality" be able to "become proprietors of land" and "master mechanics," and learn other dignified professions. Without whites "to remind them of and to perpetuate their original inferiority," African Americans would enjoy "true freedom" and a sense of pride.[2]

This book examines African Americans' struggle against the American Colonization Society and the colony it helped settle, Liberia. Established in 1822, Liberia would become an independent republic in 1847. Although Liberia did inspire nearly 13,000 African Americans to leave the United States to settle there between the founding of the colony and the Civil War, this represented less than 3 percent of the total free black population in the United States during that time. By and large, African Americans did not seek to leave the United States for Liberia, despite the persistent efforts of the American Colonization Society and the handful of notable black Americans who championed colonization in Liberia as a step towards creating a black American homeland.

Interestingly, in this same period African Americans were inspired by the possibility of leaving the United States for Haiti. In fact, over 8,000 black Americans emigrated to settle in Haiti during the 1820s alone. Even though this number is no more impressive than the number of blacks who left for Liberia, free African American spokespersons and leaders seemed much more eager to promote Haitian emigration than colonization in Liberia. Such interest in Haiti actually worked to undermine the American Colonization Society because both Haitian emigration advocates and ACS colonizationists competed for funds and potential recruits in free black communities throughout the nation. While the members of the ACS worked tirelessly to convince black Americans that Liberia remained a better option than Haiti, the "first black republic," black Americans and particularly their leaders championed Haiti while denouncing Liberia. This books seeks to show the reason for that, as well as to explain why the vast majority of free blacks rejected Liberia and the ACS's effort to promote colonization there between the establishment of the ACS in 1816 and the Civil War more than four decades later.

One caveat must be noted at the outset, and it surrounds the terms *colonization* and *emigration*. Scholars have used these two terms rather loosely and at times interchangebly since the publication of P.J. Staudenraus's work on the American Colonization Society in the early 1960s. However, free African American activists, abolitionists, and community leaders in the nineteenth century rarely did so. This is because those who spoke with reverence of Haiti sometimes denounced Liberia, and they sought to dissociate their interest with emigrating to Haiti, and even Canada, from the American Colonization Society's Liberia project. Thus, in this book the terms *colonization, colonizationist,* and *colonizationism* refer to the people and ideas of those who associated themselves with the ACS and Liberia. *Emigrationist, emigrationism,* and *emigration movements,* meanwhile, are associated with the black-led movements that paralleled the colonization movement.

Such narrow usage of similar terms may appear to some as hairsplitting. However, free blacks who promoted emigration would never describe their initiatives as "colonizationist" because that term, to them, was tainted by its association with the ACS's colonization movement to Liberia. In fact, some free black leaders, such as Martin Delany, actually denounced those who called him a "colonizationist" even as he championed emigration during the 1850s. In an effort to offer some clarity for this interconnected story , I describe those who promoted emigration to Haiti, Canada, and West Africa (except to Liberia) as *emigrationists* and those aligned with the ACS and Liberia as *colonizationists.*

Chapter 1 examines how the Haitian emigration movement of the late 1810s and 1820s undermined the American Colonization Society and African colonization. Over eight thousand blacks left for Haiti during the 1820s, and some black spokespersons who denounced Liberia championed Haiti during this decade. By the end of the 1820s, Haiti actually became a more common destination for black emigrants than Liberia.

Chapter 2, "'One of the Wildest Projects Ever': Abolitionists and the Anticolonizationist Impulse, 1830–1840," looks specifically at the role of anticolonization ideology and activism within the abolitionist movement. Black spokespersons convinced William Lloyd Garrison that the ACS was a major obstacle facing those interested in ending slavery immediately, as well as those agitating for black citizenship. Thus, Garrison would follow his African American colleagues' cue and work ardently toward undermining the ACS whenever and wherever possible. Through the pages of Garrison's *Liberator,* African American abolitionists established a clear anticolonization position that would provide

Garrison with the fuel he would need to trounce ACS leaders in the press and on the lecture circuit.

The third chapter, "'The Cause Is God's and Must Prevail': Building an Anticolonizationist Wall in Great Britain, 1830–1850," follows the anti-colonization movement to England, where ACS officials sought financial support for their African colonization project. However, black abolition-ists like Nathaniel Paul joined William Lloyd Garrison to oppose ACS leaders in public debate in an effort to show the British public that black Americans had no desire to leave for Liberia. Thus, anticolonization agi-tation became a centerpiece of the black international struggle against white racial antagonism in the United States.

While the ACS suffered many setbacks during the 1830s, the organi-zation actually had a rebirth in the late 1840s. Thus, the fourth chapter, "Resurrecting the 'Iniquitous Scheme': The Rebirth of the Colonization Movement in America, 1840–1854," examines the way pro-colonization forces, particularly in the Midwest and West, utilized colonization ideol-ogy to undermine black Americans' ability to gain citizenship status in the newly formed states. Anticolonization in this context became central to the struggle against white racist policy. Black American leaders were compelled to accept on some level that the ACS had been weakened by the abolitionists during the 1830s, but not destroyed.

By the 1850s, a shaky political landscape, a black-led emigration movement, and an aggressive ACS bent on shaping national politics forced anticolonizationists to organize with renewed vigor. These cir-cumstances compelled the most famous black abolitionist, Frederick Douglass, to devote increasing time and energy toward calling on black Americans to stay put and expel from their minds any notion that leaving the nation would do anything to end racial oppression and slavery. The fifth chapter charts this development and shows how Douglass conflated emigration and colonization in order to undermine Martin Delany and those "black nationalists" who argued for the creation of a black Ameri-can homeland in Africa, because he feared that such pronouncements aided the colonization movement.

Chapter 6, "'For God and Humanity': Anticolonization in the Civil War Era," examines African American debates over colonization and emigration within the context of the Civil War. Lincoln took a page from Henry Clay and made colonization—in this case, to Latin America—a centerpiece of his gradual emancipation plan. Douglass and other black abolitionists were livid. Even after four decades of anticolonization agi-tation, white American politicians and spokespersons continued to flirt with the idea that colonizing black Americans away from U.S. shores was the only way to proceed in the wake of emancipation.

The epilogue of the book provides a discussion of the legacy of the ACS and how some black Americans would eventually decide that leaving the South was the only alternative after the collapse of Reconstruction. Rather than witness the death of colonization or emigration, black Americans would time and time again consider leaving their communities or even the country when white racial hostility reached unimaginable levels of barbarity. Consequently, those who believed that America could one day live up to its ideals as a land of liberty and justice witnessed violence in the 1870s and 1880s as an ominous sign, and what has been described as the "nadir" in African American history compelled many black Americans to reconsider emigration to Haiti or colonization to Liberia as a last resort.

AGAINST WIND AND TIDE

Introduction

To the Free Colored People
Air-Spider and the fly
Will you, will you be colonized?
Will you, will you be colonized?
Will you be colonized on the African shore?
And my fears will sleep,
And you will rouse them no more . . .

    —A SLAVEHOLDER, "COLONIZATION SONG,"
    IN *THE ANTI-SLAVERY HARP*, 1848[1]

When in early 1817 free blacks in Georgetown, Virginia learned of the creation of the American Colonization Society, an organization established to settle them in West Africa for their own "elevation," they gathered at the house of Nicholas Warner to "shew [*sic*] unto the world at large [their] dislike to colonize in Africa."[2] During the meeting, those present discussed the threat of this new organization, declaring the necessity for "free and independent men of color" to form "a firm and strong social compact" and to agitate against the ACS.

After the meeting, Christopher McPherson, the secretary, sent circulars to black community leaders that called on "Free People of Color" to support "a memorial to Congress, praying for the colonizing of the free people of color on the waters of the Missouri river, and under the government of the United States." It was crucial, McPherson claimed, that free blacks "lose no time in forwarding them to the National Legislature; that the subject may be acted upon during the present session."[3] Nearly a decade before the National Black Convention movement would bring free blacks together to discuss matters pertinent to their communities, African Americans in Georgetown took a decisive step toward unifying blacks across the country against the white-led ACS and what they believed was a threat of mass deportation to Africa.

Organized resistance to colonization began to coalesce immediately after the formation of the American Colonization Society (ACS) in December 1816. Free blacks were disturbed when they heard that some members of the ACS had joined the organization to rid the nation of those free blacks who, they believed, "corrupt[ed]" slaves and "render[ed] them discontented."[4] If American Colonization Society members truly believed in their professed mission to offer free blacks a better life in Africa, then why would members claim that free blacks had a corrupting influence on slaves in the South? Such a position caused many African Americans to distrust the ACS and argue that the organization was really motivated by a belief among white slaveholders that colonizing provided a perfect way to preserve slavery while ridding the nation of an unwanted group of free blacks who were living on the margins of society in the early republic.[5]

There were of course some blacks, such as Paul Cuffe, who shared white colonizationists' notion that the creation of an African American–led nation not on American soil could benefit those individuals and families who left. However, others worried that settlement in Africa or elsewhere would leave enslaved Africans in the South without their most passionate defenders. This viewpoint became popular in the black community immediately after the formation of the American Colonization Society, and from the earliest anticolonization meetings free blacks emphasized this point when confronted by white colonizationists who sought to convince them to form a colony in Africa.[6]

Yet when white colonizationists learned that free blacks viewed the organization and its ideology as antiblack, they were shocked.[7] ACS members refused to accept such an accusation, arguing that anticolonizationists misunderstood their intentions. Once the free black community learned of the colonizationists' noble intent, these same free black adversaries would accept colonization in Africa as the only route to racial advancement. With this reasoning, the ACS set out to build a base of support among free blacks and in turn to convince them that white ACS members only sought their best interests.

Although at times this worked, and several prominent blacks, such as the black editor and intellectual John Russwurm, did change their view of the Society and indeed did leave for Liberia to begin their lives anew, nevertheless between 1820 and 1860 the overwhelming majority of free blacks rejected the Colonization Society and Liberia.[8] Perhaps Frederick Douglass articulated this sentiment best: "Our minds are made up to live here if we can, or die here if we must; so every attempt to remove us will be, as it ought to be, labor lost. Here we are, and here we shall remain. While our brethren are in bondage on these shores, it is idle to think of inducing any considerable number of free colored people to quit this for a foreign land."[9]

This book is about the free black struggle against the American Colonization Society and the colonization movement they led. It examines the efforts of activists and reformers who believed that the colonization movement was one of the greatest obstacles to African Americans' gaining citizenship in the United States. For that reason, many whites and free blacks who took part in the post-1830 abolition movement condemned the ACS and settlement in Liberia for being an impediment to their own efforts to see that blacks were included within the nation. Furthermore, blacks feared that colonization to Liberia would become national policy. Thus, it wasn't enough to ignore the colonization movement: free blacks believed they needed to destroy it.

As this book shows, from the formation of the American Colonization Society in 1816 to Lincoln's colonization plan during the Civil War, the majority of black abolitionists and community leaders believed that the battle against the American Colonization Society and colonization to Liberia was central to their quest for citizenship. Simply put, this was because black leaders believed that colonization in the wake of emancipation—gradual or immediate—would be a cruel fate for a people who had practically built the nation and whose labor had provided the commodity (cotton) that was so crucial to the United States' economic ascendancy during the nineteenth century.

From the Northeast to the "Old Northwest," free blacks wanted more than freedom—they wanted to live in a land without slavery, racial violence, or employment discrimination. Their vision was intertwined with that of the Americans who first struck against British rule in an effort to build a republic based on inalienable rights of land, liberty, and equality regardless of one's station in life. They wanted to be a part of the nation, and they believed that white colonizationists wanted to drive them away. This book shows that in each of the six decades before the Civil War, the struggle against the colonization movement remained a central issue in free black communities, just as it had been a central topic of discussion among white politicians, clergy, and social reformers who failed to see how free or freed black Americans could ever be a part of the national fabric.

Although most free black leaders opposed colonization, they did not necessarily reject all emigration plans. In some cases, free black leaders championed emigration to places such as Haiti because they believed that such initiatives showed African American potential and undermined the colonization movement to Liberia. Emigrationism remained an ideology of empowerment that centered on the notion that a black-ruled nation could provide a refuge for those African Americans who found racism intolerable, and that a powerful black republic could potentially arbitrate on behalf of African people enslaved everywhere.

For several reasons, the study of black emigration to Canada, Africa, and the Caribbean provides a crucial context in which to understand anticolonization discourse and activism. First, African American leaders often considered relocating to a more supportive place to agitate against slavery and white prejudice. Some scholars argue that Liberia also became a crucial refuge for pan-African intellectuals such as John Russwurm, Edward Blyden, and Alexander Crummell, to name a few. However, this study focuses on emigration initiatives and debates that intersected with the struggle against colonization to Liberia, because most black leaders did not share the opinion of Russwurm, Blyden, and Crummell about Liberia. This more narrow approach toward anticolonizationists such as Frederick Douglass and Mary Ann Shadd Cary, as well as black-led emigration movements to Haiti and Canada, seeks to complement the excellent studies of Liberia and black colonizationists who formed a pan-Africanist community in West Africa. Ultimately, this book explains why the majority of free black Americans rejected colonization despite the efforts of those who tried to convince them that Liberia remained their best hope for living their lives in a black-led nation free of racism.

Although historians such as Winston James, Claude Clegg, and Marie Tyler-McGraw have examined African American colonization in Liberia, no work has focused exclusively on those who opposed colonization between the founding of the American Colonization Society and the Civil War. Recent studies of the American Colonization Society, like those published by Eric Burin and Beverly Tomek, reexamine white colonizationists' ideology and intentions within the context of the antislavery movement, particularly in Pennsylvania. Burin's study is especially useful because it offers both the perspective of Colonization Society members and also that of those freed persons who actually left for Liberia. Here, Burin departs from the foundational work of P.J. Staudenraus, which almost exclusively focuses on white colonizationists' efforts to make colonization national policy, by telling the story of the colonization movement as one of elite white males—some southern and others northern.[10]

Beverly Tomek builds on Burin's and Staudenraus's works by framing the colonization movement in Pennsylvania as a legitimate reform attempt which coincided with other humanitarian efforts that strove to better the lives of free blacks. By situating the colonization movement within the context of the activities of white reformers, such as Elliot Cresson, Beverly Tomek shows that those who participated in the colonization movement sometimes had overlapping motives. Often, she writes, these men were "too conservative for the northern reform community even though their antislavery stance made them too radical for the South." Because of this, Cresson and other colonizationists downplayed emancipation as a central tenet of colonization when lecturing to some audiences, while calling colonization a feature of gradual emancipation when describing their plan to other audiences. This sort of "flexibility" may have cost them free black support, and some, such as James Forten, eventually shifted from "guarded optimism" over colonization to firm opposition.[11]

If Burin's and Tomek's work on colonization revises the history of the colonization movement from multiple vantage points, Winston James's study of John Brown Russwurm goes deeper than any other work in exploring the American Colonization Society from the point of view of independent-minded, race-conscious black Americans. Russwurm was not the colonizationist dupe whom Douglass and other abolitionists railed against when condemning the ACS or arguing that those blacks who left for Liberia were ignorant of the organization's "grand design." James shows the importance of Russwurm and other black colonizationists who have been written out of the history of the pan-African struggle against slavery and white supremacy due in large part to historians' inability to place them within the context of the domestic struggle to end slavery and the attempt to build black-led institutions outside the South.[12] James joins Burin and Tomek in trying to enrich our understanding of black and white colonizationsts who never held high-ranking positions in the national organization, and who considered themselves social reformers. Moreover, these three works offer black perspectives on Liberia's potential as a place of refuge for those African Americans who were on the verge of drowning in a tidal wave of racial animosity from the upper South to the Midwest.

This book benefits immensely from these works and other recent scholarship on the colonization movement among whites and blacks who held antislavery beliefs, but who could not envision a nation where whites and blacks lived equally. By taking a long view of the movement against colonization, from the founding of the American Colonization Society in 1816 to the Civil War, this book focuses on black American's struggle *against* the ACS and those who believed that African colonization was the best way to "deal" with free blacks who lived outside the slave South. Thus, this book differs from recent studies of colonization, such as those by Burin, Tomek, and James mentioned previously, by placing African American anticolonizationists at the center of its narrative. This study is the first to focus on the struggle against the colonization movement, and for that reason it offers a fresh perspective for scholars interested in the impact and legacy of the American Colonization Society and Liberia on the free black protest tradition. Even if slavery ended, the anticolonizationists argued, deportation to Africa in slavery's wake remained a serious concern. For this reason, this book shows that free black anticolonizationists regarded their efforts as something both within and beyond the abolition movement.

While scholars writing about colonization and abolition have charted the intersections of both movements in the United States, Richard Blackett's foundational study of black abolitionists abroad points out the important role that anticolonization played in the transatlantic struggle to end slavery. Indeed, black and white American abolitionists arrived in Europe eager to spread both their antislavery message and their anticolonization views. As Blackett has demonstrated, the "antislavery wall" that black abolitionists built was also an "anticolonizationist wall" that sought to stem the flow of philanthropic dollars from Great Britain to the ACS coffers in the United States.[13]

Such a transnational story is central to our understanding of the colonization movement because it places black American activists within the context of nation building and identity formation in the Atlantic world. Because the movement against the American Colonization Society remained an international affair, much like the abolition movement in America, this study traces the arc of free black agitation to Britain, Africa, Haiti, and Canada. Internationalism was crucial for those struggling for black equality during the nineteenth century, and black leaders, from Prince Saunders in the 1810s to Martin Delany in the 1850s, used this well-worn circuit in Britain to raise money as they gained allies in the fight against slavery and colonization.

Scholars who study African American history have long pointed out that many African Americans supported *emigration* while rejecting *colonization*. James and Lois Horton, for example, dedicate an entire chapter of their study of free blacks in the North to a discussion of how truly pronounced the ambivalence over emigration was among free blacks. However, there was little uncertainty when it came to colonization to Liberia. In fact, the Hortons remind readers that "as their direct memory of Africa as a home diminished, and the American Colonization Society was identified with slaveholders' plans to rid America of free blacks, few proponents of African colonization could be found among African Americans in the North."[14] With this in mind, this book builds on the Hortons' observations but moves the debate over colonization and emigration beyond the 1830s, especially within the context of westward expansion, the rise of political abolitionism, and Liberian independence in 1847.[15]

Since Floyd Miller published *The Search for a Black Nationality: Black Colonization and Emigration, 1787–1863* in 1975, scholars have understood emigrationism as an ideology that called on black Americans to create a nation-state or settlement, as opposed to the type of antiblack impulse that underpinned white colonizationist thinking.[16] For this reason, many black Americans who embraced emigrationism rejected colonization to Liberia because they believed colonization ideology undermined black Americans' ability to attain citizenship for those who remained. Emigrationism was more than colonization minus white control. The key issue here was black agency. As the black abolitionist James Forten explained to William Lloyd Garrison, "Colonization principles, abstractly considered, are unobjectionable; but the means employed" were what Forton and other anticolonizationists found so problematic.[17] If blacks were to leave America, he argued, they would do so of their own accord, and thus they had no need for aid from white colonizationists.[18]

Within so much of the documentation of the anticolonization movement gleaned from newspaper editorials, convention minutes, or resolutions from public protest gatherings, the voices of African American women are noticeably faint. Such slim inclusion of black female perspectives should not suggest that black women did not have opinions on the subject, or that they were not present at the same public meetings where black male leaders drafted resolutions or petitions. However, the documents used for this work, and other works on the nineteenth-century black protest tradition, do not offer a diverse representation of black female views on colonization. Black women's contributions to the black freedom struggle were indispensable, even if their specific perspectives on colonization come to us through only a handful of female voices, such as those of Maria Stewart, Sarah Mapps Douglass, and Mary Ann Shad Cary. It is difficult to say with certainty how much the ideas and actions of this minority of black female orators, editors, and organizers represented the majority of black women during the four decades before the Civil War. Still, black women's voices were heard consistently from the 1830s until the 1860s. And by the 1850s, Mary Ann Shad Cary emerged as one of the most important African American anticolonizationists. She had shared Martin Delany's initial disdain for Liberia and his views on the benefits of emigration to Canada before she contemplated leaving for Africa in the late 1850s.

Outside of the male-led American Anti-Slavery Society and its regional affiliates, African American women joined with white women in the mid-1830s to form female antislavery auxiliaries. For example, the black women who helped form the Clarkson Society in Salem, Massachusetts in 1818 did not comment on the American Colonization Society specifically, but these black women must have been aware of the strident anticolonization views of black male spokespersons such as James Forten at this time, because black women lived in communities where debates and discussions about the possible consequences of the ACS-led colonization initiative were found everywhere. Therefore, when these women showed up at meetings of female antislavery societies, they were well prepared to offer important insights about colonization to their white sisters—if, of course, these white women were ready to listen.[19]

While some white women joined benevolent organizations aimed at improving the daily life of free blacks living in cities all across the nation, they also worked to spread colonization societies. Because colonization was a central tenet of gradual emancipation ideology during the late 1810s and 1820s, these white women regarded free black colonization in Liberia as a viable plan for ending slavery and providing Africa with Christian missionaries. As Elizabeth Varon affirms, "For Virginia's most prominent female colonizationists, the conviction that Africa should be Christianized went hand in hand with the conviction that the institution of slavery was sinful and should, on moral grounds, be gradually dismantled."[20] Therefore, these white women founded ACS female auxiliaries and participated in a form of social reform that was more in line with activism that the dominant part of society deemed appropriate for women.

Although sources on anticolonization do not document black female participation in meetings, anticolonization sources do reflect the type of masculinized cultural prerogatives that underpinned black nineteenth-century protest thought. Black male spokespersons challenged the ACS and Liberia in ways that resembled their broader challenge to slavery, kidnapping, race riots, and racial discrimination. Often, such challenges presented black men as protectors of women and children who were prey for slave catchers and colonizationists. If black men, as the argument was framed, could not prevent the kidnapping of northern black women for southern slave markets, or the deportation of free black women and children to Liberia, how would they ever be considered men, and by extension, be worthy of full citizenship in the United States? These notions played on traditional gendered roles and expectations, and this idea of "manliness" was used as a strategy to capture the attention and to solicit the participation of free black men in the anticolonization struggle.[21] While such recruitment rhetoric reinforced gender constructions that we may find problematic today, they were a staple of nineteenth-century male discourse. In short, black spokespersons played on dominant Western notions of "duty" and "honor" as crucial features of masculinity, central to anticolonization writings and speeches.[22]

Given the celebrated political and ecclesiastical figures who had prominent roles in the ACS, African Americans had a mountain of public sentiment to overcome. While anticolonizationists clamored loudly, they most certainly did not have the same access to the public sphere as men, such as Henry Clay, who held elected political positions. Even if, for example, Nathaniel Paul was capable of frustrating ACS agents, his barbs hardly discouraged ACS leaders like Clay, who, even at the end of his life, continued to wield power in Washington and advocate for colonization. To change the "public mind" on colonization remained a major hurdle of the black anticolonizationist struggle. While most whites found the specific plan unrealistic, they still believed that, at its core, colonization was the best way to "deal with" free blacks, and by extension, to ameliorate the great sin of slavery.

African American anticolonizationists also struggled mightily against the general perception among whites that free blacks had no place in America. Even whites who were not "card-carrying" members of the ACS or its state auxiliaries supported removal of free blacks from the United States. Hence, the most frequent cry among anti-abolitionist mobs was for deportation of blacks to Africa. In fact, attempts to exclude African Americans from newly formed states in the Midwest and West reveal the degree to which antiblack ideology coalesced with colonization ideology. Black people, some argued, remained a threat to national identity formation whether they were slave or free—and this mentality was exactly what worried free blacks so much. While Frederick Douglass scoffed at the ACS efforts to revive the colonization movement in the late

1840s, it seems that what the organization lacked in support it made up for with its resolve.

The region where colonizationists had the most success was the South. Most free blacks who left for Liberia came from Virginia, North Carolina, and Maryland. Recent studies of black colonizationists document the circumstances that led them away from these states, as well as from Mississippi. This study, however, focuses instead on anticolonization movements in the northern and midwestern states rather than in the South, because it places anticolonization within the black abolitionist tradition during the four decades leading up to the Civil War.[23] By the time the colonization movement took root in the late 1820s, the abolition movement had shifted to the nonslaveholding states in the North and Midwest. Of course, the most noticeable exception here is Maryland. This study, like others on the black protest tradition, elides traditional southern boundaries, and it treats the "middle ground" state of Maryland within the context of anticolonization and pro-colonization debates in northern, midwestern, and western states.[24]

Although recent studies of black protest thought and activism during the nineteenth century point toward the elite character of the abolition movement, this book focuses instead on the ways anticolonization actually promoted class unity. Those blacks most susceptible to recruitment and deportation to Liberia were often poor. Thus free black elites only had to gaze across the pond to England for a precedent to fuel their concerns. Indeed, Sierra Leone, one of Britain's African colonies, had been populated by London's black poor, as well as recaptured Africans, Maroons from Jamaica, and desperate Canadians seeking to flee horrible conditions near the border of the United States.[25] Blacks with property and standing, such as James Vashon, were well aware that one of the chief arguments the ACS used to gain legitimacy in the eyes of wealthy whites and politicians was that there was an ample supply of poor free blacks eager to leave. While ACS members purported that free blacks were anxious to flee American racism and degradation, free blacks challenged this assertion by writing letters to newspapers and holding public meetings to declare the contrary, and by presenting signed petitions to any and all who would read them. The threat of colonization collapsed class divisions, and as in any crisis, it called on free blacks to join together, or else meet their demise at the hands of colonizationists—some of whom, free blacks often reminded their audiences, owned slaves.

Scholars such as Patrick Rael have shown that the "different measure of oppression" among free blacks of various classes did not necessarily determine how they resisted colonization or other forms of oppression. Instead, Rael contends that black resistance to the white racist assumptions that underpinned central colonizationist tenets came out of "pragmatic concerns" *and* "romantic racialist" notions of black redemption through nation building.[26] Even while members of the black elite pushed for building a black settlement in opposition to slavery and racism, most blacks only supported these plans when they were distinguished from those of the ACS and Liberia. For this reason, class status did not weigh heavily on whether or not a person rejected the ACS and Liberia. One particular case stands as a clear example of this reality.

When free blacks, having heard of the formation of the American Colonization Society, met in Philadelphia in 1817 to formulate a response, their impressions were gathered in the form of a series of resolutions. These resolutions, affirmed unanimously by those in attendance, reflected the attendees' disdain for colonization. While such gatherings continued to occur over the course of the next four decades, it seems that those who wrote down their impressions, circulated petitions, and were elected as spokespersons may have been members of the free black elite. James Forten, for example, had publicly rejected the notion that black people wanted to leave for Africa, while privately he admitted to Cuffe that he supported Cuffe's emigration initiative to West Africa. In this instance, Forten, an established businessman and important black thinker in Philadelphia, had faithfully conveyed the views of the majority, even when his personal opinions differed from those of others less fortunate than he.

Clearly, any study of African American history requires one to consider the ways in which class plays into particular positions regarding race advancement, uplift, or radicalism. But one must also recognize that class distinctions within the black community did not allow for the type of community formation—geographical or otherwise—that would have fostered a rigid class hierarchy in the antebellum North, Midwest, and West in the way that it may have in, say, Charleston or New Orleans. There were few blacks in Boston and New York, for example, and the spaces in which they could conduct their business, entertain themselves, worship, or protest remained sharply constricted. Colonization, understood by Forten and others as a mass deportation scheme to rid the nation of free blacks in the North, would impact all blacks in the North regardless of class status. In addition, wealthy blacks shared poorer blacks' kinship with those still enslaved in the South. Even if only for this reason, they wanted to stay in the United States rather than leave for Liberia.

Although Frederick Douglass and other anticolonizationists continually agitated about the idea that the colonization movement sought to banish free blacks to Liberia, they were not entirely correct. In fact, some ACS members rejected compulsory colonization from the outset. These northern "emancipationists" often clashed with other members of the ACS, particularly those from the South who owned slaves. Since these northern members truly believed that black Americans would never be accepted as equals in the United States, colonization in Liberia seemed to them like a munificent alternative. Nevertheless, they had no intention of driving free blacks from U.S. shores by means of a sort of reverse middle passage. In fact, colonizationists in Massachusetts placed their efforts within the context of prophetic Christianity more often associated with the works of black agitators such as David Walker. For example, Alexander H. Everett rose at a colonization meeting in Massachusetts in 1847 and spoke with contempt about the belief that "the African is a degraded member of the human family." In his view, such statements were nothing less than "miserable heresy," and he argued that those who held that belief needed to "goback to an earlier period in the history of our race. See what the blacks were, and what they did, three thousand years ago, in the period of their greatness and glory, when they occupied the forefront in the march of civilization—when they constituted, in fact, the whole civilized world of their time." Not only did Everett call upon his audience to recognize the glorious history of Africans, he noted that Egyptians were in fact "black," quoting the "father of history" Herodotus, who wrote that "Egyptians were blacks with curled hair." Even though some in the audience disputed his claim, Everett declared: "I cannot believe that the father of history did not know black from white." Thus, Everett asserted that the very civilization that Americans claimed as a testament to white European superiority was actually derived from "these very blacks, whom we are pleased to consider as naturally incapable of civilization."[27]

Furthermore, Everett and others in the room claimed that colonization had the potential to provide the "dark continent of Africa" with missionaries to spread Christianity to the "benighted" Africans, while redeeming free black Americans who had been forced unjustly from their "native land." It would be in Africa, these colonizationists declared, that black Americans could create a home without racial discrimination, and build an equal society where political power and economic independence could finally be attained.

Although Massachusetts's colonizationists placed their argument for colonization within a framework that some free blacks may have found acceptable, most black spokespersons in the North and Midwest could not help but point out that the majority of white colonizationists did not hold such views. In fact, Samuel Cornish, one of the first black newspaper editors, charged white colonizationists with using newspapers to spread negative views of blacks. He believed white colonizationists often highlighted black criminality, drunkenness, and disreputable behavior in an effort to convince elected officials that free blacks were a "public nuisance" and ought to be colonized in Liberia for the good of the nation.[28]

For black spokespersons to convince the broader society that black people, given equal opportunity, were worthy of equal citizenship rights, they needed to shift the conversation from deporting black people to Liberia to a discussion centered on how to provide equal opportunities to African Americans, who faced discrimination and antiblack policies at every turn. Here, then, I suggest that there were important links between anticolonization agitation, blacks' quest for citizenship rights, and the social reform movements of the nineteenth century. Every penny donated to the ACS's brand of "improvement" was one penny diverted from what free blacks and their white allies viewed as extraordinary and pressing concerns in the community, such as education and relief for the poor. The main question anticolonizationists were confronted with in this world of benevolence and charity was: why spend money—state or private—on improving or "elevating" the condition of free blacks in the United States when prejudice and racism stood as a barrier to their ultimate progress?

Furthermore, black anticolonizationists connected immediate abolitionism with moral reform and mass education because they believed that poor, uneducated blacks were most vulnerable to deportation to Liberia and that they provided fuel for antiblack discourse. When whites stopped focusing their attention on driving blacks from the nation, and began supporting reform and uplift efforts at home, they would see that black people were as capable as any other group of contributing positively to the country of their birth.[29]

Anticolonizationists "appealed to the heart" of their white detractors, holding firm to the belief that white Americans would one day abandon their racial animosity and confer social status, political power, and economic opportunities upon black people when they accepted that blacks had shed their blood and sweat to build the nation.[30] Although this seems optimistic, perhaps even utopian (given the rise of King Cotton), free black "founders" like Richard Allen had witnessed emancipation within individual states in the North during the Revolutionary era, and they remained hopeful about the possibility of attaining citizenship and ending slavery during the first few decades of the 1800s. Nevertheless, black activists and intellectuals such as David Walker understood that this would not come easy. By writing pamphlets, essays, and letters to the editors of white newspapers, black leaders refused to be silenced, or to allow pro-colonization, antiblack articles or essays to go unanswered. This bustling print culture had the dual intention of proving black intellectual capabilities and arousing blacks, as Richard Newman explains, to "build a public protest movement to overwhelm white apathy" through mass action.[31]

Free African Americans were nearly as deathly afraid of mass deportation to Liberia as they were of being kidnapped and forced into slavery. Even while the prospect of slavery being reinstated in the North or spreading into the old Northwest seemed unlikely, the fact that well-positioned businessmen, clergy, and politicians met annually to discuss how to convince the federal government and wealthy elites to fund free black colonization in Liberia was disturbing, to say the least. Thus, the struggle against colonization could only be won if free blacks obtained recognition as legitimate, hence *equal*, citizens in the nation. Without citizenship, they believed, they would always be threatened by what they deemed to be a mass deportation movement akin to the Cherokee removal of the 1830s.[32]

This study argues that anticolonization discourse and activism actually reaffirmed African Americans' faith in republican and democratic ideals, even in the face of colonizationists' systematic assault against their quest for citizenship. It was through anticolonization agitation that the African American protest tradition found fertile soil, with free blacks in the North recognizing colonization as a threat to their ultimate goal.

This debate over the fate of free blacks originated during the Revolution. By the end of the war, white leaders in both the North and the South contemplated African American colonization as a feature of their emancipation plans. Since "whiteness" became one of the most important criteria of citizenship, many white reformers considered free blacks unqualified for such status.[33] White public officials such as Thomas Jefferson claimed colonization was the most effective way to promote emancipation on a national level.[34] Others claimed that individual manumission and colonization in territories outside U.S. borders, especially in Africa, would offer slaveholding whites a realistic way to end slavery gradually without the prospects of having to live amongst the newly emancipated ex-slaves who, they believed, constituted their greatest enemy.

When white state representatives met behind closed doors in Philadelphia in the late 1780s, African Americans asserted their American identity through petitions and letters to state legislatures, arguing that they had just as much right to live in the new nation as whites. These petitions claimed that slavery violated the principles of the Revolution, and their authors wondered how a nation proclaiming that all men were equal could continue to be built upon the backs of enslaved Africans. Through their words black petitioners hoped to demonstrate their humanity and point out the contradiction of a Christian nation enslaving fellow human beings.[35]

Slavery cast an ominous shadow over the new nation, pushing the Founding Fathers to contemplate ways to deal with the inherent contradiction of holding humans in bondage while charging British authorities with treating colonists like "slaves." Although questions surrounding slavery dominated this discussion, those who met in Philadelphia struggled to come to a consensus about the status of free blacks within the new nation. What rights did free blacks have? How should individual states deal with these "public nuisances" who threatened the institution of slavery in the South and the social order in the North? Did free blacks, as slaveholding whites argued, jeopardize slavery by providing enslaved Africans with a group of coconspirators prepared to partake in a cataclysmic insurrection that would sink the newly formed republic? Such concerns were very much on the minds of those who, nearly thirty years later, organized the American Colonization Society.

Although most New England states began abolishing slavery within a decade after the Revolutionary War, the nationwide temperament of white supremacy remained boundless. Blacks in major cities, such as Boston, Providence, and New Haven, confronted equally oppressive and disturbing patterns of racial exclusion that functioned to perpetuate white power and to maintain pre-emancipation social, political, and economic relationships. While whites in New England sought to "disown slavery," they used various practices and methods to force blacks into segregated communities, and, if possible, they hoped to push them out of the nation.

Colonization was the culmination of the "erasure" of people of color that commenced soon after the Revolution was won and emancipation began in northern states such as Massachusetts. Historian Joanne Pope Melish identifies this process as two-pronged. First, whites represented blacks in print media as "absurd" and "threatening" as a strategy to undermine their efforts to attain citizenship rights.[36] Second, whites used episodic violence against black people to reinforce racial bound-aries, and when individual blacks behaved in ways that whites viewed as unbecoming, they lashed out at them. Both collective violence and individual acts of terror were actually an expression of the type of white attitudes that underpinned colonization ideology, even if some coloniza-tionists did not necessarily condone these actions. However, both those who espoused colonization ideology and members of the ACS agreed that Africa remained the best place for free black Americans.[37]

The ACS united northern clergy and humanitarians opposed to human bondage as well as southern politicians and planters invested in slavery. While these may seem like strange bedfellows, their alliance demonstrates the important way the construction of a national citizen-ship had been predicated on a notion of "whiteness" that became manifest in the African colonization movement from its earliest manifestations. For this reason, the organization assembled a diverse coalition of whites who viewed both free blacks and those still enslaved as an impediment to national unity and to the future of a white republic.[38] Thus, free blacks came to regard their struggle against colonization within the context of the abolition movement and their efforts to attain citizenship in the nation. After all, as the anticolonizationists contended, what would freedom mean if the end of slavery were followed by the colonization of emancipated blacks? As historian Eric Foner explains, "In an era of nation-building, colonization formed part of a long debate about what kind of nation the United States would be. . . . At mid-century, the pros-pects of colonizing American slaves probably seemed more credible than immediate abolition."[39] For this reason, black Americans believed that their quest for equality and citizenship depended on ending slavery and proving to those in power that free black colonization in Liberia would betray a people who had struggled since independence for a place at the American table.

1 / "The Means of Alleviating the Suffering": Haitian Emigration and the Colonization Movement, 1817–1830

On December 11, 1818, Prince Saunders, the influential black educator and secretary of the African Masonic Lodge in Boston, stood before white antislavery leaders at the annual meeting of the American Convention for Promoting the Abolition of Slavery to rebuke the means and ends of the American Colonization Society. In his speech, he explained how the Colonization Society had encouraged congressional and state officials to fund an effort to drive free African Americans out of the United States and "back" to Africa. This colonization project, Saunders argued, was creating a "frenzy" among free blacks fearful of a mass deportation across the Atlantic Ocean reminiscent of the Middle Passage. As an alternative to colonization in Africa, Saunders requested that the delegates consider funding African American emigration to the first black republic, Haiti. Saunders described Haiti as a "magnificent and exstensive [sic] island," which travelers had labeled the "paradise of the New World." "If the two rival governments of Hayti [sic] were consolidated into one well balanced pacific power," he asserted, "there are many hundreds of free people in the New England and middle states, who would be glad to repair there immediately to settle."[1]

Like Paul Cuffe and other black leaders in the early nineteenth century, Saunders praised Haiti as an example of African potential, providing Africans in the diaspora with a point of reference when they challenged the racist assumptions that underpinned white supremacy in the United States. By defeating one of the most powerful nations in

Europe and shaking free the fetters that bound them, Haitians had demonstrated their willingness to use any means available to them to achieve their freedom. Such a demonstration of African agency and self-determination inspired more than eight thousand black Americans to leave the United States for the small, newly independent Caribbean nation during the 1820s.[2]

Whether or not Haiti truly represented the best of African potential remained open to debate, yet it continued to inspire black Americans, encouraging some free blacks in the North to join Haitian emigration societies as a sign of solidarity, while others went ahead and packed up their belongings and emigrated there.[3] This upsurge in pro-emigration sentiment in the black community was far from universal: most African Americans had no intention of leaving. The primary reason for this was the rise of the American Colonization Society (ACS) and its African colonization project. By the end of the 1810s, free blacks had become concerned that the ACS sought, in fact, to drive them to Africa. For this reason, pro–Haitian emigration advocates had to convince free blacks that Haitian emigration would actually undermine the ACS, while affirming blacks' potential for self-governance. Thus, those who embraced Haitian emigration dismissed colonization to Liberia and were compelled to make their argument clear and persuasive if they were to succeed.[4]

Indeed, several of the most prominent black Americans of the era took up the task of challenging the ACS while endorsing Haitian emigration. James Forten, the Philadelphia sailmaker and abolitionist, for example, played an important part both in leading the struggle against the colonization "scheme" hatched by the Colonization Society, and in urging black Americans to consider Haitian emigration.[5]

But was Forten's support of Haitian emigration incompatible with, or contradictory to, his denunciation of colonization? Why did some black leaders, like Forten, protest the American Colonization Society's colonization plan while championing Haitian emigration? This chapter outlines the rise of the Haitian emigration movement in the late 1810s and the 1820s, demonstrating that emigration (to Haiti) and colonization (of Liberia) were far from synonymous, and that black leaders utilized a transnational network of social reformers as a means to undermine colonization, on the one hand, and to fund Haitian emigration, on the other. Furthermore, it explains how black leaders used the rhetoric of nationalism as a discourse that linked the formation of an African diasporic identity through nation building in Haiti with the struggle against white supremacy in the United States and abroad.

Black leaders certainly did envision Haitian emigration in nationalistic terms, which collided with their quest for racial uplift and "respectability" in the United States.[6] While northern black leaders spoke publicly of Haiti's greatness as a rhetorical strategy for urging racial unity and challenging white racist ideology, in reality, Haiti had yet to emerge as a stable nation.[7] However, as early as 1815 Prince Saunders called on blacks to turn towards the "slumbering volcano" in the Caribbean in order to start anew and cast their lot with other Africans building a nation free of slavery and racial prejudice.[8] Born in Connecticut, Saunders interacted with free blacks from Philadelphia to Boston early in his career as an educator in the African school in Colchester, Connecticut, and Boston's African School. As a teacher at the African School, Saunders lived amongst Boston's "Brahmins," meeting Paul Cuffe, the wealthy black ship captain, and most certainly winning his approval, and then developing a relationship with Cuffe's daughter. In 1811 these ties allowed him to rise to the role of secretary of the African Masonic Lodge, alongside Baptist clergyman Thomas Paul. As a member of the Lodge, Saunders first began to consider joining with Paul and others to organize a Haitian emigration movement.[9]

While traveling with Paul on a fund-raising effort to Britain in 1815, Saunders learned about the Haitian project from British dignitaries who had applauded Cuffe's efforts a few years earlier to settle black Americans on the coast of West Africa.[10] Perhaps because of Haiti's instability during its first fifteen years of statehood, Cuffe had instead placed his hopes in a new African colony to be founded near British Sierra Leone.[11] But Paul and Saunders had sailed to Britain to try to convince antislavery activists and politicians that black Americans were just as eager to relocate to Haiti as they were to Sierra Leone or anywhere else in West Africa.[12] Even if Paul and Saunders had shifted their plans from Africa to Haiti, they still built upon Cuffe's previous efforts to unify British and American abolitionists interested in destroying the transatlantic slave trade and ending the oppression of Africans in the West. As it turned out, several leading British abolitionists agreed that Haiti remained an apt site for black American settlement. According to a newspaper account of the meeting with British abolitionists, Saunders and Paul listened to William Wilberforce praise "Christophe, the black king of Hayti," for having "every princely quality." Wilberforce declared that Christophe had "a right more legitimate than the ex-emperor of France, or the kings of Spain and Naples . . . besides being the Farther [sic] of his people." In addition, Christophe was, in Wilberforce's view, "a patriot, liberator, and hero . . . and pious christian . . . [who] wanted nothing but Bibles, prayer books, implements of agriculture, and information respecting the arts, sciences, and humanity of Europe."[13] Evidently, Thomas Clarkson and William Wilberforce succeeded in confirming Prince Saunders's view about Haiti, leaving Saunders with the intention to sail to the island and learn more about King Christophe's plan for African American emigration.

King Henry Christophe had risen to power in Haiti after the previous ruler, Dessalines, was murdered near Port-au-Prince on October 17, 1806.[14] Christophe, described as "a fine portly looking man . . . quite black, very intelligent, pleasant, and expressive," had a domineering personality that was "useful on the battlefield, but a liability as a political leader."[15] Soon after he became king, he found himself faced with opposition from Alexandre Pétion, the leader of the "mulatto faction" who sought to impose upon Haiti an executive system based on the national assembly of representatives from different regions. Christophe, upon learning of Pétion's manipulation of the Assembly, rushed towards Port-au-Prince prepared to do battle with Pétion and his men. After two days of combat, Pétion's army stood its ground, and Christophe retreated to the north. Thus, in 1807, Haiti remained a divided nation, with Christophe in control of the North Province and the valley of the Artibonite in the West Province, and Pétion commanding most of the west and the South Province.[16]

While Pétion struggled to maintain his command in the south and west, and to begin engaging in negotiations with the French, Christophe sought English support and guidance. Ever fearful of a French invasion, Christophe forged ties with England and declared English to be Haiti's official language and Protestant Christianity its state religion. Hoping that English abolitionists would use their influence to help Haiti create diplomatic ties with England, Christophe reached out to William Wilberforce and Thomas Clarkson. In 1814 Wilberforce commented, "I am very sure I should not lose a day in embarking for Hayti. To see a set of human beings emerging from slavery, and making most rapid strides towards the perfection of civilization, must I think be the most delightful of all food for contemplation." Wilberforce embraced Christophe and Haiti, sending financial assistance, plows, and farmers to teach Haitians English methods of agriculture.[17]

Like Wilberforce, Thomas Clarkson, the famed abolitionist who rose to public attention when he became one of the original members of the Committee for the Abolition of the Slave Trade in 1787, took to Christophe's vision as well, and he became his adviser in Europe. Clarkson kept Christophe informed about the probability of French invasion, and more generally of French and English opinions about Haiti, while offering him advice about his policies—especially the nature of his military rule. When a friend described to Clarkson the American Colonization Society–inspired movement to colonize African Americans in West Africa, Clarkson sent word to Christophe that he ought to reach out to African Americans interested in leaving the United States. Clarkson mentioned to him the advantages of black American emigration to Haiti, explaining, "Such persons would be very useful to your Majesty. They would form that middle class in society which is the connecting medium between rich and the poor and which is the great cause of prosperity in Europe, but which cannot at present have been raised up in your Majesty's Dominion." Clarkson hoped that Christophe "would of course give to each family a few acres of land."[18]

African American emigration from the United States to Haiti, Clarkson believed, was good government policy. He explained to Christophe that an African American presence in Haiti could compel the United States to recognize the new republic. Clarkson, however, was not fully aware that southerners in the United States opposed Haitian independence, and this stood as a major obstacle to such a plan. Not until the Civil War, four decades after Christophe's death, would the United States ultimately recognize the black republic as an independent nation.[19]

Christophe embraced Clarkson's African American emigration plan, offering an initial donation of $25,000 for those free black Americans who were interested in resettling in Haiti.[20] Learning of this financial allocation, Saunders traveled to Haiti to meet Christophe and provide help for his emigration project. When Christophe and Saunders first met, each seemed impressed by the other. Saunders praised Christophe's vision for Haiti as expressed in his "Manifesto of the King," in which Christophe proclaimed, "True to our oath, we will sooner bury ourselves beneath the ruins of our native country, than suffer an infraction of our political rights."[21] Christophe delighted in meeting a man with such pronounced "African features," refined manners, and high intellect. Christophe immediately appointed Saunders his "official courier," hoping that Saunders could help him gain diplomatic recognition from Britain.[22] With letters and documents from the king, Saunders traveled to London to meet with British abolitionists and London's high society to further such ends.

When Saunders arrived in London he established himself as the principal African American advocate of Haitian emigration in Europe. Upon publication of *The Haytian Papers*, a series of documents related to Haiti, he had impressed British dignitaries so favorably that he became the "darling of British royalty." At a party thrown by Countess of Cork, for instance, his eloquence and refined manners served him well as he dined with members of the English court and London's social elite. So well did Saunders ingratiate himself with the English upper crust that word of his "flamboyant lifestyle" got back to Christophe, who recalled him to Cap-Henri, Christophe's capital.[23]

When Saunders returned to Haiti in 1816, he brought two English teachers familiar with the Lancastrian method, a technique employed in England that included "mechanical teaching devices, and used advanced children to monitor the work of beginners."[24] His confidence in his "official courier" restored, Christophe named him his minister of education, and Saunders organized several schools and introduced vaccination in Haiti.[25] Over several years, Saunders traveled back and forth between the United States, England, and Haiti, attempting to gain support and to convince other African Americans to emigrate there. Recognizing the linkages among the abolition of slavery, black self-determination, and international recognition of Haiti as the first black republic established in opposition to slavery, Saunders hoped to persuade free blacks in the North that Haiti could provide them with an asylum from American racial oppression.[26]

Before Saunders returned to Boston in 1818, the mainstream press had already set the stage for his Haitian emigration plan. One article in the *New England Palladium* in 1817 championed Haiti as an ideal location for black emigration, preferable to an African colony such as Sierra Leone. The article proclaimed that "a land of promise nearer our doors" seemed a more likely location than Africa. The author of the article reminded free blacks that, in Haiti, "the same constitution that excludes the white man, invites the black."[27]

Soon after Saunders arrived in the United States, he published a second edition of *The Haytian Papers* for an American audience. These documents, according to Saunders, proved that black people were capable of self-rule and were endowed with "natural intelligence," falsifying the assertions of prejudiced whites who "have endeavoured to impress the public with the idea that those official documents, which have occasionally appeared in this country, are not written by black Haytians themselves."[28] Saunders's respect for Haiti and King Christophe stemmed in no small part from the "Code Henri," and Saunders asserted that "nothing that white men have been able to arrange is equal to it."[29] Saunders presented Haiti's legal code and portions of the "Deliberations of the Consuls of the Republic" to demonstrate African resourcefulness and intelligence. Ultimately, he hoped to gain white financial support for African American immigration to Haiti, and impress upon black Americans the potential for a better life in a nation free of racial prejudice and slavery.[30]

In September 1818, Prince Saunders left Massachusetts for Bethel Church in Philadelphia to make an address for the Pennsylvanian Augustine Society in regard to his Haitian emigration plan. His address called for black education and self-determination, and he suggested to the African American audience that they consider taking their intelligence and Christian virtue to Haiti. He explained: "Perhaps there never was a period, when the attention of so many enlightened men was so vigorously awakened to a sense of importance of a universal dissemination of the blessings of instruction, as at this enlightened age, in this, in the northern and eastern sections of our country, in some portions of Europe, and in the island of Hayti."[31] By the meeting's end, Saunders had convinced prominent African American leaders such as James Forten and Russell Parrott, who had condemned colonization soon after the formation of the American Colonization Society in 1817, that emigration to Haiti and colonization to Africa were rooted in two quite different and discrete notions.

It appears that Parrott and Forten were persuaded by Saunders's speech, and this may have planted the seed of interest in emigration to Haiti that grew among free blacks in the North during the 1820s. Although historian Arthur O. White characterizes Saunders's address as an "ironic moment," where the "foremost black colonizationist" lectured an anticolonizationist audience about educational uplift and Haitian emigration, the evidence suggests that free blacks in Philadelphia distinguished the emigration proposals initiated by blacks from those of the white-led African colonization project.[32] The Haitian emigration movement, he insists, differed from the ACS-derived colonization movement to Africa. Thus, Saunders's goal was to convince his audience that black Americans had the chance to lead a transnational movement against slavery, the slave trade, and nation building on a grand scale.

As the idea of Haitian emigration gained popularity throughout the North in the 1820s, some black Americans, such as a man named James Tredwell, wrote directly to Haitian officials to inquire specifically about the benefits of leaving the United States for Haiti. The secretary general of Haiti, Joseph Inginac, responded that "the men of color, who may desire to become Haytians, will find but little difference in our manner of living from that of the places they shall leave. . . . Men of all arts, of all trades—smiths, braziers, tinmen, ship and house carpenters, millwrights, caulkers, coopers, cabinet makers, boot and shoemakers—can earn in this place from six to twelve dollars per week, and even more, according to their talents and activity."[33]

While this letter reads like an advertisement for Haitian emigration as an alternative to living "under the dominion of a barbarous prejudice" in the United States, Secretary General Inginac expressed his sincere desire to see African Americans enjoy the fruits of liberty in a way that reflected his sense of African diasporic unity. For example, he wrote that "this message, sir, could not but be received with the greatest satisfaction by those who have sacrificed twenty-eight years of their life, in order to efface the traces of a yoke to which other men, who pretend to virtue and justice, had long enchained them." The secretary-general deliberately and explicitly framed Haitian independence within an oppositional tradition that linked emigration to Haiti with the black American struggle against slavery in the South and racial discrimination in the North.[34]

After gaining support from prominent blacks from Boston to Philadelphia, Saunders shifted his appeal to the mostly white antislavery organization, the American Convention for Promoting the Abolition of Slavery and Improving the Condition of the African Race. In 1818, just over a year after the formation of the American Colonization Society, colonization was at the center of debate at the American Convention's annual meeting, the largest gathering of American Convention members in its history. It was here that Saunders read his "Memoir," based upon his experience in Haiti, in an effort to build a network of white American philanthropists with the financial wherewithal to fund African American emigration to Haiti. Saunders also utilized this opportunity to differentiate between colonization and emigration, and he expressed to the delegates the general fear among free blacks that a large-scale colonization scheme had been hatched to expel them from the United States. In his conclusion, he explained that a movement encouraging free black emigration to Haiti would undermine the American Colonization Society, while providing blacks with a new home.[35] Saunders read his "Memoir" to show these antislavery reformers that Haitian emigration was a more realistic alternative than African colonization. While it is unclear how influential Prince Saunders's presentation of his "Memoir" was to the members, the outcry against colonization among some of the delegates compelled the Convention's leadership to establish a committee to investigate colonization.[36] This committee was also instructed to investigate Haitian emigration within the context of the ACS's African colonization project.[37]

After deliberating on the merits of colonization, the American Convention's committee reported back that it found the ACS's plan unrealistic, and that it would neither improve the lives of African Americans nor eradicate slavery in the United States. The committee determined that the $82,000,000 in estimated expenses was too costly, and the fact that most African Americans rejected colonization only further compromised the ACS in their eyes.[38] While committee members believed that colonization and emigration would benefit *some* free blacks, they declared that ultimately both the ACS colonization plan and the Haitian emigration movement would undermine universal emancipation, which many wholeheartedly supported.[39] Thus, little enthusiasm for either colonization to Africa or Haitian emigration took root among white American Convention members in the late 1810s.

Although the committee rejected colonization or emigration schemes, it did recommend, instead, a black settlement west of the Missouri River, which would allow benevolent whites to support resettled blacks as they lifted themselves from their "degradation."[40] This, the committee argued, would benefit the nation because these industrious African Americans were capable of populating the western frontier with upright, Christian communities that would resemble the ones they would leave in Philadelphia, New York, and Boston. By spreading Christianity to indigenous tribes who viewed the United States and Western culture with disdain, African Americans had the potential to serve as intermediaries for those native peoples on the outskirts of American civilization.[41] The committee's recommendations were included in the American Convention's annual statement, which was mailed out to abolition societies across the nation.

Although these recommendations reflected white American Convention members' generally positive attitude about black potential, they were also worded in a way that illustrates the paternalistic attitude of white reformers of the time. For example, the committee believed neither African colonization nor resettlement in Haiti had any chance of succeeding on the grounds that African Americans were unprepared for self-rule. Of course, James Forten and Prince Saunders must have balked at such conclusions, even if they were well intended. What made the committee's recommendations particularly irksome to free black leaders were the specific comments that sounded nearly identical to the types of racialist comments made by members of the American Coloni-zation Society. For example, William Rawle, the president of the Penn-sylvania Abolition Society and a member of the American Convention, opposed colonization yet agreed with one of the main colonizationist tenets: White racial hostility and African American poverty were major obstacles for assimilating blacks within northern cities.[42] Even so, Rawle was well aware of free blacks' animosity toward colonization, and for this reason he supported the idea of settling free blacks in the West. Fearful perhaps that Rawle's comments sounded too much like those of colonizationists, other members reminded him that the Convention's constitution forbade supporting such a plan, and this may have halted further efforts that year to promote the creation of an African American settlement in the West.

However, this did not end the debate over colonization.[43] When the American Convention met for its next annual meeting in 1819, some members arrived still determined to discuss colonization further. In fact, some of them had heard of blacks who were indeed considering colonization to West Africa, and this contingent called on their peers to reopen debates about colonization and the ACS. These members pointed to a report from the Kentucky Abolition Society affirming that a group of blacks in Kentucky had written to both the American Colonization Soci-ety and its Kentucky state auxiliary to request passage to Africa. Thus, they called on their American Convention colleagues to take a closer look at colonization and not dismiss it outright without a more thorough examination of its potential benefits. But as historian Beverly Tomek has shown, in the end the majority of American Convention members held firm in their rejection of colonization as a waste of resources that could better be used for other humanitarian purposes.[44]

While the Convention had moved on, Prince Saunders toured north-ern cities in the late 1810s, promoting Haitian emigration and struggling against such skepticism. He hoped his close ties with British abolitionists would help persuade people that his Haitian emigration plan had merit. As he had done in the preface to his *Haytian Papers*, Saunders frequently reminded white audiences that he was "personally acquainted" with Wilberforce and Clarkson, and that he had their unwavering support for "any object, which might serve to advance the great cause of African improvement and happiness."[45] Such references to distinguished English abolitionists, esteemed in the minds of American Convention mem-bers, suggest that Saunders understood emigration to Haiti as part of a larger human rights struggle transcending national borders and ethnic particularities. Rather than present emigration as an isolated phenomenon, Saunders connected Haitian emigration with the global movement against slavery, the slave trade, and African oppression. Like Olaudah Equiano, Paul Cuffe, and Prince Hall, Prince Saunders understood that his fight for African American self-determination and improvement had a transnational context.[46]

Saunders returned to Haiti in August 1820, but violence erupted shortly after he arrived there. Before long, King Christophe died and Saunders fled the country aboard a ship bound for Philadelphia. His troubles were far from over: before his ship left the port it was hijacked, and the robbers who boarded the vessel took Saunders's clothes and other possessions, leaving him at the mercy of Christophe's successor, President Jean-Pierre Boyer. Upon meeting Boyer, Saunders faced the task of convincing him to embrace the American emigration plan, arguing that a unified Haiti under Boyer would inspire African Americans seeking refuge from racial oppression in the northern United States. For this reason, he explained to President Boyer, thousands of African Americans would immigrate to Haiti if Boyer were to bestow his blessings on the project and back up such support with the financial means necessary to make it happen. Boyer, however, seemed indifferent, and Saunders left the island for Philadelphia believing that Boyer was "possessed of very little ability to govern" and that he was "prejudiced against blacks."[47]

Despite what Saunders thought about him, Boyer actually did acknowledge the benefits to Haiti of black American immigration.[48] Because Boyer sought the United States' recognition, he thought that an African American presence in his country would boost its appeal in the eyes of American statesmen. He also recognized that Haiti would benefit from skilled African American artisans and agricultural laborers.[49] As for those emigrants recently manumitted in the United States, Boyer hoped to entice them with an offer of free land in Haiti, and soon enough this became a major feature of Boyer's recruitment efforts. Boyer also sought to undermine the American Colonization Society's African colonization plan by demonstrating Haiti's advantages over those of West Africa.[50]

Even though Saunders was frustrated with Boyer's lack of cooperation, other black leaders continued to advocate Haitian emigration during the mid-1820s. Thomas Paul returned to his role as chief advocate of Haitian emigration just as Saunders faded from the picture.[51] Paul frequently reminded audiences that "having been a resident for some months in the Island of Hayti, I am fully persuaded that it is the best and most suitable place of residence which Providence has hitherto offered to emancipated people of colour, for the enjoyment of Liberty and equality with their attendant blessings." Furthermore, he claimed that "a country possessing an enterprising population of several hundred thousand of active and brave men, who are determined to live free, or die gloriously in the defence of freedom, must possess advantages highly inviting to men who are sighing for the enjoyment of the common rights and liberties of mankind."[52]

Blacks in Philadelphia shared Paul's interest in Haitian emigration, and in July 1824, some of them met to consider President Jean-Pierre Boyer's invitation to resettle in the nascent black republic. To clarify their position on colonization, they began the meeting by denouncing "any measures which may be taken to transport them to the coast of Africa." According to one account, "The free blacks of Philadelphia have unanimously protested against the execution of the plan to colonize them in Africa; and have expressed their determination to discountenance it. Their attention, it appears, is turned to Hayti." The meeting continued with discussion about the "favorable climate, a fruitful soil and a free government [where] they may acquire all the privileges which the most favored Whites of the most favored country can enjoy. . . . blacks and mulattoes are continually leaving this country and taking advantage of the invitation of the Haytians."[53]

Philadelphia blacks were not alone in their interest in the Haitian emigration plan. In fact, free blacks in Maryland came under the influence of Haitian emigration when an elected agent, George McGill, returned from Haiti excited about President Boyer's support for African American immigration. McGill shared with the audience his opinions about Haiti as a location for resettlement, reading a letter he had from Secretary General Inginac. In this letter, Inginac explained that "His excellency has been charmed to hear that the decendants [sic] of the African, form the project of coming here and carrying their industry into a free country, which guarantees to them an honorable existence under the protection of a constitution." This sense of shared racial identity between African Americans and Haitians reinforces the notion that a sense of African diasporic unity underpinned the Haitian emigration movement. Secretary General Inginac proclaimed, specifically, that Haitians were "interested more than any other in the fate of the descendants of the Africans, whose blood runs in their veins," and hoped to provide blacks in America with an opportunity to help "the Haytiens form at this time a society whose end is to favour the emigration of our American brethren into the Republic."[54]

Individual accounts of life in Haiti also encouraged black Americans to seek Haiti as a refuge from the American racial caste system. According to one newspaper account, John Lewis, "a respectable man of colour," spent several years in Haiti and then returned from the nascent republic "perfectly satisfied with the stability of the government there established." Upon returning to the United States, the article claims, Lewis made plans "to remove his family there for a permanent residence." These accounts broadened the appeal of Haitian emigration, and enticed some blacks to seek Haiti rather than to continue "like wander[ing] Israelites, without a tabernacle and without a home."[55]

As the idea of Haitian emigration gained momentum in the 1820s, the American Colonization Society acknowledged the threat that Haitian emigration posed to their own African colonization plans, even as colonization societies proliferated throughout the nation. In fact, ACS auxiliaries and "Committees of Correspondence" had sprouted in New York, Maryland, Vermont, Virginia, Connecticut, North Carolina, Pennsylvania, Georgia, Tennessee, and Kentucky.[56] Virginia boasted twenty-one auxiliaries, thus establishing it as the epicenter of colonization sentiment in the South, while New York's six auxiliaries led all northern states. State auxiliaries represented an extension of the larger national organization, which operated out of Washington, D.C.[57]

The ACS's broad base of support and its distinguished membership came with benefits and drawbacks. Agents of state auxiliaries often cited the membership of esteemed statesmen such as Henry Clay as a way to gain financial support and recruit new members from the white population of towns and cities. At times, though, the national affiliation proved to be a burden for agents in the Northeast who had joined the colonization movement to support what they believed were the organization's benevolent intentions. In their effort to unite southern and northern interests, the members of the parent organization shied away from any overt declaration that the organization supported gradual emancipation, and instead claimed only that it "encouraged" free blacks to leave America for their West African settlement. This did not bode well for those members and agents interested in colonization as a tool for the emancipation of Africans enslaved in the South, or as a means to offer free blacks an alternative to living in a society rife with rampant "Negrophobia."

For this reason, Prince Saunders and his ally, the Reverend Thomas Paul Sr., exploited the ACS's ambiguous stance on emancipation in order to undermine the ACS and African colonization. Some ACS agents reported meeting blacks who were openly hostile to colonization, yet supportive of Haitian emigration. When, for example, Loring Dewey, an agent of the American Colonization Society and the New York auxiliary, attempted to recruit new members, he found that black people's unfavorable view of the ACS did not mean they were opposed to leaving the United States. From the hamlets in the Hudson Valley to the outskirts of New York City, he noted, "a preference of Hayti over Africa was frequently expressed." Among those whites sympathetic to the plight of free blacks in the North, Dewey discovered that "there was not only an opposition to colonization in Africa manifested by many, but an assurance given of their ready aid to promote emigration to Hayti." Taking these views into consideration, Dewey wrote to the American Colonization Society in the hope of gaining support for Haitian emigration as well.[58]

As he waited for a reply, Dewey shared his idea with his colleagues who, as it turned out, were not at all enthusiastic about Haitian emigration. General Robert G. Harper even chided Dewey about it, explaining that Haitian emigration would not serve the interest of the larger organization.[59] This did not deter Dewey, who, on his own, wrote to President Jean-Pierre Boyer inquiring about African American emigration. When the managers of the New York Auxiliary Society learned of Dewey's correspondence with President Boyer, a special meeting was called to discuss his actions. White slaveholding members, and their sympathizers in Virginia and Washington, D.C., viewed Haiti with scorn, and many of them believed that a free black emigration movement to Haiti would threaten the perpetuation of slavery in America. Thus, the New York auxiliary was compelled to rebuke Dewey for his actions. On April 1, 1824, the New York Colonization Society Board of Managers claimed that "colonization is the only 'remedy' for slavery, the mighty 'evil' of our country. . . . Hayti, which at first would seem to offer great advantages, is found, by examination, to be encumbered with difficulties, which will probably for a long time prevent colonization there to any considerable extent."[60] This mild statement was soon followed up with a more forceful comment in the press, rejecting Dewey and his Haitian project. By May, the New York Colonization Society went on record to declare, "The New York Auxiliary Colonization Society has officially disavowed the proceedings of Mr. Dewey, the agent, in opening a correspondence with President Boyer, of Hayti, for the establishment of colonies in that Island, and recommended the removal of Mr. Dewey from this agency."[61]

The New York Colonization Society accepted this recommendation for Dewey's dismissal when they met in July. According to one account, "certain resolutions were passed disclaiming the correspondence of Mr.

Dewey, and denouncing the plan of emigration to Hayti as contrary to the known wishes and interfering with the great national objects of the American Colonization Society."[62] Accordingly, Dewey was dismissed as an agent of the American Colonization Society. However, a representative of the parent organization stepped forward to establish a new society "to promote the emigration of the Blacks to Hayti." Twenty-five members were appointed to create a committee to call for a closer look at black Americans' interest in leaving for Haiti. In an unusual turn of events, these ACS members organized a "Haytian Emigration Society" of their own, perhaps to co-opt the movement.[63] However, it took almost two months for the committee to establish the society and to begin recruiting blacks to emigrate to Haiti. It is unclear to what degree these efforts worked to undermine "legitimate" Haitian emigration efforts by free blacks or to stifle critics of the ACS who claimed that the organization needed to accept black interest in Haiti within the broad parameters of colonization. West Africa, after all, was not the only place to resettle the few blacks who sought to leave America.

Even if the New York Colonization Society had missed its opportunity to shape the destiny of Haitian emigration, the dismissed New York Colonization Society agent, Loring Dewey, met with others to consider President Boyer's overtures towards black Americans. After discussing business matters, a Dr. J. Wainwright put forth a resolution recommending that "a Committee of Nine be appointed to take into consideration the documents submitted to this Meeting in relation to the Emigration of Coloured Persons to Hayti, and report to an adjourned meeting, to be held on Friday the 25th."[64]

Peter A. Jay, the son of Founding Father John Jay and an active member of the New York Manumission Society, and eight others met to discuss the free and enslaved black population of the state, and the July 4, 1827, termination of slavery in New York.[65] They wondered whether African Americans in the state would "cheerfully embrace any opportunity that may present to place the descendants of Africa in a situation which will furnish them with more powerful motives, than are offered among ourselves, to respectability of character, and intellectual improvement." The goal, though, was still to convince free blacks to leave, whether to Africa or Haiti. Historian Leslie Harris explains that in 1826, delegates from the New York Manumission Society were perhaps influenced by this goal, and they called on members of the American Convention to promote "the transportation of the whole coloured population, now held in bondage, to the coast of Africa, or the island of St. Domingo.[66]

After discussing the prospects of Haiti as a suitable location for black emigration, the committee resolved "that it is expedient to form a Society, to be called 'The Society for promoting the Emigration of Free Persons of Colour to Hayti.'" They established the price of subscriptions and membership, and their desire to create a board of directors. Before the meeting closed, Chairman Thomas Eddy read an "interesting communication" that described a meeting among notable African Americans, including Peter Williams and Samuel E. Cornish, that discussed President Boyer's proposition as well as black interest in such a venture.[67] Members also pointed out that African American "excitement" over Haitian emigration was intertwined with their anticolonization sentiment. Whites had come to believe that emigration to Haiti demonstrated black agency, and African Americans' desire to participate in the success of a black republic that represented black people's abilities and potential. This of course did not mean that the majority of free blacks felt so inclined to leave. However, for those free blacks who had come to the conclusion that New York City would never be a place where blacks could live in safety from white violence or discrimination, Haitian emigration seemed a much better alternative than the ACS's Liberia colony.

When Loring Dewey sailed to Haiti toward the end of 1824 to gain a firsthand impression of the island, he was well aware that this would aid his recruitment campaign when he returned to the United States. By January 10, 1825, having arrived safely in Samaná, located in a part of eastern Hispaniola that had recently been occupied by Haitian troops, Dewey sent a letter back to the United States describing his experience and encouraging the continuation of the recruitment efforts of Haitian emigration societies. One hundred twenty free blacks sailed to Haiti with Dewey, and upon arrival they bore witness to what Dewey called the "abundance and luxuriance of the foliage of the trees and plants." "I know no part of the new countries of our land," he claimed, "from the earliest settlement till the present time, that presented to settlers so *great and immediate advantages* as are here offered to our emigrants." He described the large plantations, which had been abandoned by Spanish residents after the area was occupied by Haitian troops, claiming that, with only seven hundred inhabitants, there would be plenty of room for African American settlers, since at one time the peninsula had provided space for thirty thousand residents.[68]

Such an account must have enraged his old colonizationist colleagues. By this point, nearly all members of the ACS believed that Haitian emigration threatened to destroy the project of African colonization because it shifted free blacks' attention closer to home. In addition, African American emigration to Haiti seemed to stir up southern slaveholders' fears that such a movement would unsettle their slaves, given Haiti's radical legacy.[69]

The conflict between Dewey and the New York Colonization Society illustrates two important points about the colonization movement in the 1820s. First, individuals came into the colonization movement with diverse motives, creating a fragile alliance among whites from North and South who supported the ACS. Second, the Dewey-NYCS dispute shows the limits of the national ACS's ability to monitor local auxiliaries from its national headquarters in Washington. Considering the range of backgrounds and interests among ACS members, and the different perspectives about the efficacy of West African settlement versus Haitian emigration, it's little wonder that the state affiliates began to pull away from the national organization and act independently during the following decade.

As white colonizationists tried to undermine Dewey and others, black people met to organize a group to sail to Haiti and investigate the possibilities for black emigration there. On August 7, 1824, free blacks in New York gathered at the African Baptist Church to hear a report about Haitian emigration and President Boyer's offer. One account of the meeting in the *Columbian Star* claimed, "The Committee reported the expediency of forming a Society in that city, for the general object of promoting emigration to Hayti . . . [and] having been read, it was unanimously voted to form a society."[70] Those in attendance moved quickly to select twenty people to form a board of managers to run the society. It appears that Thomas Paul, "a missionary from the Baptist Missionary Society" in Haiti, made a positive impression on the gathering. When he spoke to the group about his conversation with President Boyer, the audience seemed even more confident than before that the island was a suitable location for resettlement.[71]

President Jean-Pierre Boyer's agent, "Citizen" Jonathan Granville, attended a meeting of New York black leaders and expressed "satisfaction" about free blacks' efforts to initiate a Haitian emigration movement in New York.[72] Described in the mainstream press as "a man of respectable talents and acquirements, possessing all the finer feelings of men in polished society, and exhibiting the elevated deportment of a gentleman," Granville explained that Boyer had offered to "defray part of the expense of the transportation of the colonists."[73] Furthermore, Granville claimed to have the authority to arrange for six thousand black

American emigrants to set sail to Haiti. Once they arrived, according to Granville, they would be provided with land, citizenship, and temporary provisions.[74]

In Baltimore, white antislavery newspaper editor Benjamin Lundy had been following Granville's recruitment efforts in northern cities, writing in one editorial that "it is now supposed, that between four and five thousand coloured persons have already embarked for Hayti, or will have done so before the end of this month, under the direction of citizen Granville, whose arrival in New York was announced on the 13th day of June last."[75] Black American interest in Haiti encouraged Lundy and reinforced his belief that "the prejudice of the white people, against the blacks, operates as an almost insurmountable barrier to the progress of emancipation." This conviction motivated Lundy to put all his efforts behind Haitian emigration. Some whites with power and influence joined Lundy's Haitian emigration cause, and, according to a report describing a meeting of the Baltimore Emigration Society on September 4, 1824, "the Board proceeded to the election of officers, when the honorable Edward Johnson, Mayor of the city, was chosen President... [and] Citizen Granville, Agent from the Haytien [sic] was then introduced to the Society, and explained in a very lucid manner the object of the Government of the Hayti, in sending him on his present mission." The previous day, the article stated, Baltimore's "respectable men of colour" met with Granville at the Bethel Church to discuss President Boyer's offer and African American interest in Haitian emigration. According to an article in the *Genius of Universal Emancipation*, those who gathered resolved "That we highly appreciate the liberal offers of President Boyer, and that we will use all honourable means to procure a speedy and effectual emigration of the free people of colour ... [and] That Robert Cowley be appointed to take the names of persons disposed to emigrate, to whom application may be made as early as possible, at the African Bethel Church, in Fish street."[76]

In New York, Peter Barker wrote a letter to Lundy explaining that he planned to travel to Haiti as a representative of the Haytien Emigration Society of New York. The letter claimed that he intended to "make definitive arrangements with president Boyer for the future transportation of coloured persons to Hayti." Prominent African American leader Peter Williams joined Barker "as agents of this Society, to confer with President Boyer on this important subject of Emigration, investigate the situation of the emigrants, and settle upon a solid basis the order and arrangement of our future transactions."[77]

By January 1825, African American emigrants living in Haiti had begun to send letters describing their experiences to family and friends in the United States. While, according to Lundy, "they are generally well pleased with their new situation," and although "the government has completely fulfilled the reasonable expectations of all who have thus sought an asylum from the tyranny of prejudice under the fostering wing of its protection," nevertheless, rumors were circulating in the United States that African American emigrants were miserable in Haiti. Lundy seemed relieved that the most recent letters he had received "contain a complete refutation of many of those rumors," which he felt should put to rest potential emigrants' fears about embarking on a voyage to the Caribbean island. One letter from a black man from Baltimore claimed, "I like the place much; we have been sick, but are all well at this time. It is much better here than I expected to find it." In another letter, an emigrant remarked, "The district is well watered by numerous streams, and seems only to require the art and industry of man." He concluded that "it appears that our choice of this place was wisely directed."[78]

Lundy believed that the negative rumors he had encountered only reflected a growing resentment from certain segments of the nation that did not want to see Haitian emigration succeed. According to Lundy, "Late accounts from every quarter, in fact, tend to corroborate the sentiment expressed in the last number of this work, viz. that the unfavourable reports respecting the situation of the emigrants to Hayti, were circulated by persons unfriendly to the removal of our coloured people to that island."[79] This group, he deduced, represented slaveholding interests and others who simply failed to understand the great benefit of Haitian emigration. Lundy explained that "there are, it is true, some honest well-meaning persons who are conscientiously scrupulous as to the propriety of it; but these are, comparatively, few in number; and I hesitate not to believe that their doubts arise from a want of the necessary information."[80]

Lundy's argument in favor of Haitian emigration was, of course, taken as a challenge to those who favored African colonization, and this led to a counterattack against Lundy in white pro-colonization newspapers. One supporter of the ACS wrote a letter to Lundy claiming that Lundy's "interesting paper, endeavours to prejudice your readers against the members of the American Colonization Society, by remarks, as unfounded as uncharitable ... [and] there has been no opposition of any description, to the emigration to Hayti, of such free blacks, as may prefer the government of President Boyer." According to the letter, the American Colonization Society applauded President Boyer's offer regarding African American emigration to Haiti. Furthermore, it stated that "what has been denominated 'strenuous opposition' was in fact, applause for the object of President Boyer: but a persevering adherence to the ends, which the Colonization Society have kept steadily in view; the formation on the coast of Africa, of a line of colonies already existed in Sierra Leone . . . the advocates for African colonization have never opposed the wishes of any, but their own members, to aid by money, or moral influence, the emigration to Hayti."[81]

In his defense, Lundy explained that "In the first place, I have ever been aware, that a considerable portion of its [the ACS's] members were averse to the abolition of slavery in this country. This has been admitted by one of the managers. Secondly, although many of them desire the riddance of the whole of the black population, it appears very unwise to choose a situation for that purpose, so far distant, that it will be almost *impossible* to effect the object."[82] Certainly Lundy's abolitionist network provided him with inside information about the Colonization Society. As an advocate of gradual emancipation, Lundy had supported the principles behind colonization, yet he believed that the ACS was controlled by southern slaveholders. In his response to one claim that the ACS never discouraged blacks from Haitian emigration, he asked with a hint of sarcasm, "Why did an influential member of the Society aforesaid, from Virginia, repair to New York, and 'strenuously' oppose the emigration to Hayti, in a meeting [not of the Auxiliary Colonization Society, but] of the citizens generally, who had assembled for the purpose of considering the propriety of seconding the propositions of President Boyer?"[83]

This conflict between Lundy and the American Colonization Society foreshadowed the battle between the ACS and William Lloyd Garrison, Nathanial Paul, and other advocates of "immediate" emancipation in the early 1830s. And, like other well-known white abolitionists, Lundy's opinions mirrored those of black leaders who often voiced their anticolonization views at public meetings or, after 1827, in *Freedom's Journal.*[84] Lundy challenged ACS members to prove that their mission on the coast of West Africa sought to end the illegal practice of trading slaves nearly two decades after Great Britain and the United States had banned it in 1807 and 1808, respectively. He also doubted the credibility of colonizationists who claimed to share anti–slave trade beliefs, arguing that they only "talk loudly" about their efforts to end the slave trade "now as [the slave trade] has become unpopular." Lundy argued: "Even those among them who are opposed to emancipation, make [the slave trade] the frequent theme of declamation . . . because the measures adopted for its annihilation do not prevent them from procuring as many slaves as they desire."[85]

Colonizationists refused to give up, and they continued to mail Lundy letters defending the ACS, which Lundy regularly published in the *Genius of Universal Emancipation*. One letter claimed that "the Colonization Society have expended more money, out of their private funds, in behalf of this unfortunate race among us, than all the emancipation societies put together." Meanwhile, some of the letters used African American emigration to Haiti as an indication that black Americans supported colonization. This interest in Haiti, they argued, proved that blacks would leave America if they had the means to do so. Of course, this argument was nothing new, and when ACS members gathered at their ninth annual meeting, William H. Fitzhugh from Virginia asked his colleagues to "recollect the recent emigration to Hayti when invited to that Island: six thousand coloured persons in a few weeks were ready to embark. Let the arm of our government be stretched out for the defence of our African Colony, and this objection will no longer exist."[86] Although African Americans frequently declared their disapprobation of African colonization, members of the ACS used black interest in Haiti as a stepping-stone toward the means and ends of the organization.

Before the end of 1825, Haitian President Boyer had grown weary of American settlers' complaints, and he was convinced that an African American emigration agent had stolen a significant portion of the money set aside to aid black American immigration to the island.[87] In response, President Boyer ceased providing land for American settlers and officially withdrew financial support for African American emigration in April of 1825. This forced Lundy and others to take on the burden of raising money for the transportation expenses, which proved daunting. Lundy left his newspaper, the *Genius of Universal Emancipation*, under the direction of Daniel Raymond, and he sailed for Haiti in an attempt to persuade the government to change its policy.[88]

When Lundy met with Haitian officials, they explained that almost one-third of the six thousand black Americans had returned to the United States, and many of those who remained were proving burdensome. Desperate to salvage the movement, Lundy petitioned the Haytian Philanthropic Society for financial support for African American emigration. Although the members vowed to pay 150 dollars for the transportation of each black American émigré, those who accepted their offer would have to agree to repayment by laboring for three years and turning over one-half of their produce to the Society.[89] After only a brief stay in Haiti, Lundy returned to the United States and arranged for a ship to transport African Americans to Haiti in February of 1828. Those who arrived in Haiti with Lundy soon realized the Haytian Philanthropic Society's terms were absurd.

Ultimately, Haiti did not become the "promised land" that African Americans had anticipated, and some complained, among other things, about the derisive way in which Haiti's new black elite treated American settlers. The climate was unsuitable for some immigrants, and others were frustrated by the language barrier and different religious practices.[90] According to one account, black Americans were "infinitely worse off than the natives, having no commanity [sic] of language or feeling with them."[91] The Haitian government had promised to protect black American newcomers, yet, as this letter explained, "The fact, lamentable as it is, ought not to be disguised, that the American emigrant is not sure of protection, either in life or property in that island, under its present unquiet state."[92] And, for those black Americans eager to return to the United States, "the policy of the government there prevents their embarkation under severe penalties." As far as this emigrant was concerned, Haiti had failed to live up to his expectations, and he called out to his African American brethren: "We trust for humanity's sake that any further emigration of the free people of color to that island will be sedulously discouraged."[93]

While Haitian emigration petered out towards the end of the 1820s, African Americans and their white allies began to move in new directions. The Haitian emigration movement forced Lundy to recognize the limitations of antislavery agitation in the South. As his hope for a massive emigration of blacks to Haiti dimmed, he abandoned the project altogether, claiming that slaveholders and their sympathizers were uninterested in any program, however benign it might be, which benefited blacks. Lundy's views about abolitionism in the South reflected what historian Merton Dillon observes as "an ultimate shift in the geographical base of the antislavery movement from South to North, with a consequent increase in sectional antipathy."[94]

Lundy lamented how few whites seemed interested in emancipation and expatriation, and he began to accept that, since slaveholders and planters profited—financially, materially, and socially—from slavery, any program designed to threaten those benefits would be met with scorn, and even, if necessary, force. Many slaveholders shuddered at the thought of the Haitian Revolution, and they feared an African American emigration movement could lead to unrest among slaves in the American South.[95] Still, Lundy remained intent on developing a plan with economic incentives that would end slavery without violence and would provide for a settlement of manumitted African Americans in Haiti. In his view, freed blacks would work more efficiently than those enslaved, and through an experimental community in Haiti, he hoped to prove that there would be a financial benefit to slaveholders if they embraced the idea of freeing their laborers.[96]

Although the Haitian emigration movement of the late 1820s may have seemed a failure to some, such as Lundy, it did succeed in derailing the American Colonization Society, leading to what historian P.J. Staudenraus identifies as "a crisis" within the Colonization Society. The issue of Haitian emigration divided whites within the American Colonization Society over how best to deal with competition from Haitian emigration. This prompted managers of the ACS to send two agents, Dr. Eli Ayres of Baltimore and Reverend George Boyd, an Episcopal rector of Philadelphia's St. John's Church, into the North to recruit free blacks to leave for their settlement in West Africa. Through touring New York, Philadelphia, and some New England cities, they found that Haitian emigration overshadowed African colonization, and that many free blacks were hostile to the ACS program. Nevertheless, the two agents established "Corresponding Committees" in Boston and Providence, even though they had learned that many whites in the North hesitated to donate money to the colonization cause until the ACS could garner federal support for African colonization. Also, some whites claimed that they would not support the ACS until southerners took the initiative, since, as they argued, free blacks caused more problems in the South than they did in the North. With their small African settlement in Liberia struggling to create a viable presence in West Africa, the American Colonization Society remained stymied at home as a consequence of ideological rifts and a lack of clarity over the organization's motives.[97]

Regardless, Haiti remained a symbol for African Americans, much to the dismay of southern planters and some white northerners. Black Americans continued to proclaim that Haiti illustrated African potential for nation building rooted in self-reliance, individual elevation, and racial progress. These were attributes that African American leaders believed were key for African progress in the United States and the world.

Such grandiose notions of Haiti as a potential crucible for African redemption became a cornerstone of John B. Russwurm's own racial awakening as one of the few black students in American colleges or universities in the 1820s.[98] When Russwurm gave the 1826 commencement speech to his white peers and their families at Bowdoin College, his address, entitled "The Condition and Prospects of Hayti," extolled the first black republic, acknowledging "the irresistible course of events that all men, who have been deprived of their liberty, shall recover this previous portion of their indefeasible inheritance."[99] Russwurm argued that Haiti demonstrated the capacity of black men to rise from the depths of oppression to the heights of liberty—an overt challenge to prevailing racial assumptions. Concluding his speech optimistically, Russwurm explained to the audience that "We look forward with peculiar satisfaction to the period when, like the Tyre of old, her [Haiti's] vessels shall extend the fame of her riches and glory, to the remotest borders of the globe; to the time when Hayti, treading in the footsteps of her sister republicks, shall, like them, exhibit a picture of rapid and unprecedented advance in population, wealth and intelligence." With these final words, the audience exploded "with hearty applause" at what one newspaper reporter claimed "was one of the most interesting performances of the day."[100]

While Russwurm's words illustrate his awareness of the historical significance of Haiti in his own time, they also show the transnational character of the black protest tradition. Since his childhood Russwurm had been on the move, developing a pan-African identity. Born in Jamaica from a liaison between a white Virginian merchant and an African slave, Russwurm moved with his father to Quebec in 1807, and then to Maine in 1812. Although his mother's African origins most greatly limited his life opportunities, it was his father's liberality that enabled him to live in a manner few African Americans would ever know.[101] Aware that his mother's status, rather than his father's, determined the types of obstacles he would face in the predominantly white New England community where he lived, he never lost his sense of being an African, and he cast his lot with his fellow blacks from Boston to Port-au-Prince to Liverpool.[102]

Russwurm did consider joining the wave of emigrants leaving for Haiti. Winston James points out that Russwurm, having graduated from Bowdoin, planned on leaving for Haiti, yet by October 1826 he still remained in America. He travelled initially to Boston to work at the African Free School, but there was no position for him. Some tried to entice him to travel to Liberia under the ACS banner, but he turned down the offer. Soon he left Boston for New York and the opportunity to join the community of abolitionists seeking to respond to antiblack attacks in newspapers in advance of the forthcoming 1827 emancipation decree in New York State.[103]

In the fall of 1827, Russwurm took command of the *Freedom's Journal* when Samuel Cornish resigned to direct the African Free School and work as an agent for the New York Manumission Society. When Russwurm began to publish both pro- and anticolonization views in the paper, some free blacks became alarmed. At the time, Russwurm had not made public his drift away from his anticolonizationist stance and toward joining the American Colonization Society's Liberian colony.[104] Yet free blacks in New York and other parts of the North held such negative impressions of the ACS that Russwurm's inclusion of pro-colonization views raised the suspicion that he had become sympathetic to the Colonization Society. By February 1829, Russwurm did indeed announce his support for the ACS, explaining to his readers that his decision to leave for Liberia had come after prolonged contemplation. Regardless, Russwurm was attacked viciously by his former anticolonization peers in public meetings and in letters to the newspaper.[105]

One interpretation of Russwurm's shift suggests that he came to believe that Liberia was becoming a place where African Americans could build political and social institutions that would challenge white assumptions about black inferiority. Others argue that Russwurm accepted ACS secretary Ralph Gurley's offer to join him in his colonization mission because Russwurm believed that emancipation would never take place unless "blacks already freed could move to Liberia." Historian Sandra Sandiford Young argues: "Russwurm's drive to establish himself in the absence of business opportunities and his abhorrence of the violence perpetuated against free blacks were the likely catalysts for his decision."[106]

Regardless of the reason, some African Americans viewed Russwurm's shift in sentiment as treasonous.[107] Before leaving the paper he did attempt to explain his change of heart through a series of editorials. In the first of these, on February 14, 1829, Russwurm announced, "As our former sentiments have always been in direct opposition to the plan of colonizing us on the coast of Africa: perhaps, so favourable an opportunity may not occur, for us to inform *our* readers, in an open and candid manner, that our views are materially altered." By March, he explained that "The change in our views on colonization seems to be a 'seven days wonder' to many of our readers. But why, we do not perceive: like others, we are mortal like them, we are liable to change."[108] Russwurm argued that Liberia offered African Americans fertile soil, liberty, and opportunities denied them in America. As for the trials and tribulations that black colonists had endured in Liberia, Russwurm viewed them as analogous to the trials and tribulations of the first American colonists in Roanoke and Plymouth. Even so, some African Americans were unconvinced.

Although the opportunity to castigate Russwurm presented itself, Samuel Cornish, Russwurm's former coeditor, passed on the chance. When addressing "the sudden change of the late Editor of 'The Freedom's Journal,' in respect to colonisation," Cornish wrote that he would only say a few words about it "and I am done." In brief, he acknowledged that "to me the subject is equally strange as to others," and he placed it "with the other novelties of the day."[109] Choosing not to attack Russwurm personally, Cornish ended his editorial by stating that

> ... my views, and the views of the intelligent of my brethren genne-
> rally, are the same as ever in respect of colonisation; we believe it
> may benefit the few that emigrate, and survive, and as a mission-
> ary station, we consider it as a grand and glorious establishment,
> and shall do all in our power to promote its interests. ... But as it
> respects three million that are now in the United States, and the
> eight millions that in twenty or twenty five years, will be in this
> country, we think it in no wise calculated, to meet their wants or
> ameliorate their condition.[110]

The American Colonization Society wasted little time publicizing Russwurm's "Candid Acknowledgment of Error" in the *African Repository and Colonial Journal,* where an editorial explained that "The Editor of *Freedom's Journal,* Mr. Ruswurm [*sic*], who has for several years, been decidedly and actively opposed to the Colonization Society, in his paper on the 14th of February, candidly and honourably confesses that his opinions in regard to our Institution, have become entirely changed." There is little question that Russwurm was welcomed as an important ally for the ACS, and his support must have boosted the spirits of many colonizationists.[111]

What led John Russwurm to shift from interest in emigration to Haiti and anticolonization beliefs, toward supporting the American Colonization Society and colonization? According to his editorial on February 21, 1829, Russwurm explained, "We have generally wrong ideas of the society and the members thereof. ..." After reflecting on the successes of the ACS in southern manumissions, he came to believe that "The society have done much in favor of emancipation; for it is a fact, that there are many in the colony, who are indebted for that liberty which they now enjoy to the door which the establishment offers to liberal and humane slave holders to emancipate their slaves." Regardless of how many ACS members held firm in their opposition to interfering "with the legal rights and obligations of slavery," Russwurm observed that "as we well know, there are four or five hundred slaves now waiting [for want of funds] to be landed on the shores of Liberia, to become freemen."[112]

When one considers the plight of African Americans in bondage, it should not be too surprising that some would support colonization as a condition of freedom. Russwurm's account of blacks waiting for passage to Liberia, having never lived as free men and women in territories or states where slavery was illegal, failed to convince the vast majority of northerners that Africa generally, and Liberia specifically, offered more opportunity than Haiti or Canada. Thus, even while some black anti-colonizationists recognized the benefit of forming a separate nation or colony outside of U.S. borders, they stood in firm opposition to an organization so closely aligned with slaveholders.

What complicates the matter is that Russwurm's positions on slavery and emancipation differed from those of many white colonizationists. While some ACS members believed that colonization must never be allowed to threaten the existence of slavery, Russwurm and his white northern emancipationist associates viewed gradual emancipation as one of the most important reasons to support the ACS. Several notable antislavery advocates came to regard gradual emancipation and colonization as the only realistic way to promote their cause. So he concluded, "As the work of emancipation has thus commenced under the immediate auspices of the society, we cannot consider it out of the natural course of things to conclude that as the means and patronage of the society extend, this great and glorious work will also advance in the same ratio, until the blessed period come, so ardently desired by the Friends when the soil of this happy land shall not be watered by the tears of poor Afric's sons and daughters."[113] Russwurm continued to argue in favor of colonization after he moved to Liberia and became the editor of the *Liberia Herald*. Besides, within the ACS there were people pushing its other members to move beyond their evasive stance on emancipation.[114]

John Russwurm's transformation from advocate of Haiti to colonization to Liberia demonstrates the complexity of black emigrationist and colonizationist thought during the 1820s. Once Russwurm decided he was going to "quit America," the next question centered on where he should go. Haitian emigration remained an option, yet, as Sandra Sandiford Young points out, "the collapse of the Haitian emigration venture and the severely limited opportunities for black economic advancement posed a serious dilemma" for Russwurm. Liberia, while tainted by the antiblack views held by many ACS members, still had potential. However, Russwurm was well aware that the decision to leave America for Liberia meant the loss of his esteem among black leaders in the United States. In the eyes of free blacks whose respect he had earned, he was abandoning not only America but also the community that had acknowledged his leadership. Soon, James Forten and others would claim that Russwurm's support for colonization would add credence to the view of some white state officials that the colonization of free blacks in Liberia remained a viable and desirable plan.[115]

The African American–led Haitian emigration movement of the 1820s illustrates several crucial points about early anticolonization agitation. First, it pioneered a tradition of African American internationalism as a feature of the struggle for black rights in the United States and against African colonization. Second, it showed the ACS that those few thousand blacks who wanted to leave had shown a preference for Haiti over Liberia. Through this Haitian emigration movement, black Americans forged a transnational alliance with venerated abolitionists willing to lend support. For the next three decades, black Americans would travel to Britain for a variety of causes, seeking support in their attempt to demonstrate that African-descended people were as capable as Europeans of building a great nation. This nation-building project sought to undermine one of the chief justifications—that is, black inferiority—for maintaining slavery in the U.S. South.

The Haitian emigration movement also highlighted how far blacks would go to attain citizenship and live in a place where racial prejudice was not the central obstacle to personal advancement. While those free blacks who remained in America continued to fight against racial inequality, those who left for Haiti hoped they had finally found a way to transcend it. Over the next three decades, African American community leaders, activists, and journalists continued to regard the first black republic as a symbol of African-descended people's potential, a symbol particularly potent for black Americans struggling against slavery and for equality in a nation that questioned their humanity and whether they had the prerequisite abilities ever to contribute to the nation equally with whites. Even for those with no intention of leaving for Haiti, the Caribbean nation continued to be a point of reference in their struggle for equal rights and against white supremacy in the United States.

Although African Americans and white antislavery advocates failed to initiate a widespread movement to Haiti, the movement did present an alternative to colonization in Africa. When recruiters spoke in churches and halls to discuss the benefits of emigration to Haiti, they used this as an opportunity to condemn Liberia and to argue that the American Colonization Society posed a serious threat to black advancement in the United States. In a way, the Haitian emigration movement spread anticolonization ideology due in large part to the advocacy of its chief promoters, men such as Prince Saunders.

However, the American Colonization Society would not give up in the face of this concerted challenge to their African project. When it came down to it, the ACS had the resources to provide a better alternative for black Americans who wanted to leave. John Russwurm remained the pro–Haitian emigration contingent's greatest loss. Having spoken of Haiti in glorious terms, and having actually tried to raise funds for those who sought to leave for Haiti, John Russwurm chose instead to "quit America" and sail for Monrovia, Liberia, in the fall of 1829. This was obviously a major blow to anticolonizationists.

Just as the Haitian emigration movement died out, a new brand of antislavery activism took root throughout the North. By the end of 1820, the majority of the American Convention's antislavery activist members had come to embrace colonization. Yet a new sort of antislavery advocate emerged, making the anticolonization sentiments widely held in black communities throughout the nation a cornerstone of their ideology. These men and women heeded the argument that ending slavery was not enough. As David Walker explained in his *Appeal to the Coloured Citizens of the World*, those who battled against slavery needed also to combat the "wretchedness in consequence of the colonizing plan" if they hoped for justice and equality in the United States. Soon the man most associated with the "immediatist" strain of antislavery advocacy, William Lloyd Garrison, would work to organize a regional and national antislavery society that called for the immediate end to slavery, equality for black Americans, and the destruction of the American Colonization Society.[116]

In February of 1833, Maria Stewart stood before a group of people gathered at the African Masonic Hall in Boston to condemn the ACS for its goal of "influencing us to go to Liberia." Rather than donate money to fund black colonization in Liberia, these "real friends" of African Americans, Stewart urged, should use those funds "which they collect, in erecting a college to educate her injured ones in this land." Stewart explained that the colonization movement was siphoning off funds to educate and care for free blacks in the North, while doing little to change the circumstances in this country that stifled black progress. "The unfriendly whites first drove the native American from his much loved land," she argued, and then brought Africans to America, "made them bond-men and bond-women," and now sought to "drive us to a strange land." It is for this reason, as Stewart explained, that "African rights and liberty is a subject that ought to fire the breast of every free man of color in these United States."[1]

This was not the first time Stewart lectured on colonization, marshaling various arguments that were common among anticolonizationists in the early 1830s. Through these lectures Stewart demonstrated her intellectual merit, poetic gift, and ability to analyze the contradictions she found central to colonization ideology, which she also had published in the *Liberator*. "I observed a piece in *The Liberator* a few months since," she explained, "stating that the colonizationists had published a work respecting us, asserting that we were lazy and idle." This was simply untrue, she explained. Even if there were some in Boston "who never were and never will be serviceable to society," she asked, "have you not a similar class yourselves?"[2] If whites had been placed under the burden of racial prejudice and slavery, they too would struggle to display qualities associated with Christian virtue and social respectability. This was not about African depravity, Stewart explained; this was about education and uplift.[3]

From the Mid-Atlantic to New England, African Americans gathered in churches, halls, and public spaces to express their disapproval of the views of the ACS. In January 1831, for example, black leaders in New York City called a meeting in Prince Hall Mason's Boyer Lodge (named after Jean-Pierre Boyer, the fourth president of Haiti) to express their outrage at the "proceedings of an association under the title, 'New-York Colonization Society.'" Those in attendance condemned the organization for "vilifying us" and attempting to promulgate the notion that blacks represented a "difference of species." Such notions were unfounded, they argued, because "Our structure and organization are the same, and not distinct from other men." With this in mind, the group claimed to be "content to abide where we are," rather than leave for Liberia as wards of the ACS. Although colonizationists attempted to convince the general public in the United States and Britain that racial distinctions presented an intractable barrier to free blacks seeking acceptance in American society, African Americans in New York asserted, "We do not believe that things will always continue the same," arguing that the day would come when black Americans would be vindicated, and "when the rights of all shall be properly acknowledged and appreciated."[4]

As the antislavery movement shifted toward immediate abolition, black American leaders convinced white abolitionists, most notably William Lloyd Garrison, that colonization undermined both the cause of ending slavery and free blacks' efforts to gain rights in the North. Most importantly, Stewart showed, colonization became linked to antiblack policies, race riots, and employment discrimination in the states where slavery had been outlawed. Unfortunately for black abolitionists and anticolonizationists, white abolitionists often shared the same racialist attitudes as those most hostile to the cause, and the movement to end slavery needed to be linked with a movement for black equality and citizenship in the North.[5] For this reason African Americans who worked against slavery and colonization also struggled to destroy the pervasive view among whites that black Americans were inherently unequal.

By the 1830s, African Americans had argued for a decade that the American Colonization Society and its auxiliaries discredited, smeared, and undermined African Americans' efforts to obtain equal rights and citizenship in America. For this reason the colonization movement became a central topic of discussion among blacks attending conventions and participating in newly formed antislavery societies and colored associations. This "new breed" of abolitionists had, as Richard Newman points out, "revolutionized" the tactics of the movement against slavery in America by 1830, and this pushed white reformers to act with a sense of immediacy toward ending slavery and overwhelming the American Colonization Society and its agents.[6]

Had it not been for free blacks such as William Watkins and David Walker, William Lloyd Garrison might have continued to hold colonization sympathies as well as his view that "immediate and complete emancipation is not desirable."[7] African Americans' opinions about the American Colonization Society were widely known. Few expressions of black protest against colonization so influenced Garrison to take a different path more than the anticolonization ideas presented in David Walker's infamous *An Appeal to the Coloured Citizens of the World*. Born in Wilmington, North Carolina, Walker had left for the North soon after Denmark Vesey's plot in South Carolina in 1822, which made whites even warier about free African Americans' presence in the slave South. Arriving in Boston in 1825, Walker became a member of an outspoken community of African Americans struggling against colonization.[8] He joined Prince Hall's well-known African Lodge No. 459, and participated in the formation of the first black American association, the Massachusetts General Colored Association. This network of black community leaders afforded him the opportunity to associate with many people involved in the Haitian emigration movement and other timely issues within the black community of Boston.

David Walker used his *Appeal* to rail against the colonization movement, displaying "a vehemence and outrage," biographer Peter Hinks argues, "unprecedented among contemporary African American authors."[9] While one can only speculate about the degree to which Walker's *Appeal* influenced the intellectual maturation of any one abolitionist, what we do know is that Garrison was deeply moved by it. In fact, in the summer of 1830, when Hezekiah Grice, a black community leader in Baltimore, met with William Lloyd Garrison to discuss the idea of a national black convention, Garrison seemed more interested in discussing the *Appeal to Coloured Citizens*. According to Grice, "Mr. Garrison took up a copy of Walker's *Appeal*, and said, although it might be right, yet it was too early to have published such a book."[10]

It may well be that Article IV of Walker's *Appeal*, entitled "Our Wretchedness in Consequence of the Colonizing Plan," is what persuaded Garrison to see the connection between colonization and antiblack violence in the North and the system of racial oppression that stifled free blacks and barred them from a life consistent with the American creed. At the outset of his section on colonization, Walker charted the origins of the ACS among the power brokers of the nation, noting the influential role of Henry Clay in promoting the colonization "scheme." By citing the black community's immediate and unequivocal rejection of the formation of the ACS, Walker placed this anticolonization sentiment within the framework of the black protest tradition. Likewise, Walker applauded the role of *Freedom's Journal* and *The Rights of All* in providing blacks with a forum for expressing their disapproval of colonization, a realm in which African Americans could demonstrate their understanding of the various dimensions of what he perceived as the ACS's mass-deportation scheme.

Walker's condemnation of colonization was grounded not only on the belief that black progress in the North depended on striking down colonization. He argued as well that the fate of Africans held in bondage in the South also depended on putting an end to colonization schemes. "Do they think to drive us from our country and homes," he wondered, "after having enriched it with our blood and tears, and keep back millions of our dear brethren, sunk in the most barbarous wretchedness, to dig up gold and silver for them and their children?"[11] By connecting his plight with that of his southern brethren, Walker established one of the main underpinnings of anticolonization rhetoric: colonization would sever the bond between Africans enslaved and those free. Throughout the antebellum era, black leaders used such arguments to persuade audiences of the detriment of colonization, and this became central to black abolitionists' anticolonizationism.

Like other African Americans writing against the ACS, Walker acknowledged that at least a few whites who supported colonization were "friends of the sons of Africa." Nevertheless, he believed that those white reformers, "laboring for our salvation," had been duped into "this plot" and needed to "see if the end which they [had] in view [would] be completely consummated by such a course of procedure."[12] Walker expressed "with tenderness" that he "would not for the world injure their feelings," but hoped that his words would lead them to realize that "the plot is not for the glory of God, but on the contrary the perpetuation of slavery in this country forever, unless something is immediately done."[13]

Ultimately, like many other black leaders, he argued that "This country is as much ours as it is the whites'; whether they will admit it or not, they will see and believe it by and by."[14] With the completion of the *Appeal*, Walker challenged many white abolitionists to rethink gradual emancipation and colonization, which had been among the most common antislavery ideologies before the 1830s.

When Garrison did change his mind about colonization, he decided that his first step on the road toward convincing the nation to embrace "immediatism" was a thorough indictment of the American Colonization Society, colonization ideology, and Liberia. He would soon follow in Walker's footsteps and complete his anticolonization treatise, *Thoughts on African Colonization*. Animated with Garrison's penchant for polemics, the volume made American intellectual history by making blacks themselves central to the struggle, demonstrating black agency during a time when most whites believed they themselves knew what was in blacks' best interest. Anticolonization became the foundation upon which "Garrisonism" was built. It was the "key transitional topic" for those who considered themselves disciples of Garrison, and who vowed to fight slavery.[15]

Even though Garrison's New England Anti-Slavery Society canvased the Northeast with lectures calling for an immediate end to slavery, black Americans had been waging an intellectual battle on two fronts: one against slavery and the other against colonization. This led them to hold conventions during the first half of the 1830s to discuss the cause of freedom in ways that departed from the previous generation's effort to "appeal to the heart" of white reformers, as well as gradualists who embraced colonization. As William Hamilton explained, "However pure the motives of some of the members of that society may be, yet the master spirits thereof are evil minded towards us. They have put on the garb of angels of light. Fold back their covering, and you have in full array those of darkness."[16]

Historians have established that African American conventions in the early 1830s became a venue for free blacks to challenge white people's declarations of racial supremacy.[17] Like *Freedom's Journal*, public conventions offered masterful oratorical performances crucial to demonstrating black American intellectual acumen and self-advocacy. Consequently, blacks used conventions as yet another public space in which to express their anticolonization views. Aware that they were "being watched," free black convention-goers spoke with eloquence, intelligence, and passion in their attempt to counter colonizationists' claims that black people lacked the prerequisite traits to warrant citizenship in the United States.[18]

From the inaugural Black Convention held in Philadelphia in September 1830, black Americans declared that these conventions could work to combat the "various ways and means [that] have been resorted to; among others, the African Colonization Society is the most prominent."[19] Even if some delegates believed that Canadian emigration, or emigration to Haiti, had the potential to aid those who had been ensnared in specific assaults on their livelihood, Liberian colonization, in their eyes, worked against race advancement and the destruction of slavery.[20] As would be the case at subsequent conventions, the resolutions at the inaugural convention made clear that free blacks did not doubt the "sincerity of many friends who are engaged in that cause," but still affirmed their anticolonizationist stance.[21]

Nevertheless, blacks who gathered at these conventions were at times willing to listen to agents of the ACS, who sought to set things straight with free black male leaders who, in turn, seemed certain that colonization represented an evil only surpassed by slavery itself. In 1832, for example, ACS secretary Ralph Gurley attended the Second Annual National Black Convention in Philadelphia to convince African Americans that the ACS only sought to ameliorate the condition of free blacks who lived under an oppressive racial order in the United States. Black leaders "patiently listened" to Gurley, allowing him to speak "in behalf of the doings of said Society" so that those assembled could "arrive at truth" in a way that "seldom has been witnessed" during a meeting in which the majority had been decidedly against the ideas set forth by a speaker. Still, when Gurley finished his "eloquent arguments," black leader John Vashon stood to denounce the American Colonization Society's project, reminding delegates that the Colonization Society sought only to secure slavery by deporting free blacks to Africa. After both sides had had their turn, the delegates voted. A majority came out against the ACS, proclaiming that "the doctrines of said Society, are at enmity with the principles and precepts of religion, humanity and justice, and should be regarded by every man of color in these United States, as an evil of magnitude, unexcelled, and whose doctrines aim at the entire extinction of the free colored population and the riveting of Slavery."[22]

Such an unequivocal statement against colonization may have discouraged Gurley, but he did not blame black convention attendees. Instead he focused his contempt upon Garrison for "poisoning their minds with Anti-Colonizationist ideology." Ever since Garrison had first published the *Liberator* in 1831, Gurley had regarded Garrison's invective against the ACS as the root cause of the negative opinions of the ACS held in black communities in the northeastern and mid-Atlantic states. But Gurley actually had it backwards: black leaders in Baltimore had first pushed Garrison to renounce the colonization ideology espoused by the ACS and fight against slavery and colonization. Garrison had himself been "poisoned" by black anticolonization.

Scholars for years have pointed out that Garrison's popularity among black leaders was directly related to his stance on colonization. This popularity translated into subscriptions to Garrison's *Liberator* newspaper, which by the early 1830s supplanted *Freedom's Journal* as the most important newspaper for the cause of freedom in the North. While some blacks pooled their money for subscriptions, African American supporters with wealth and prestige sent large donations to fund the paper. James Forten, for example, paid for twenty-seven subscriptions and sent Garrison many words of encouragement. In fact, scholars note that white subscribers only comprised one-fourth of the *Liberator*'s readers, and Garrison actually ceased looking toward the white community for support. "Our white people are shy of the paper," Garrison bemoaned in a letter to Simeon Jocelyn. "This ill success," he explained, "is partly owing to colonization influence, which is directly and actively opposed to the *Liberator*."[23]

It is very likely that Garrison was correct about Colonization Society members' disdain for him, his paper, and the ideas he so freely shared with any audience that would invite him to speak. In fact, in issue after issue, the *Liberator* published anticolonization letters and essays by black people attacking the American Colonization Society, its local auxiliaries, and the principles that underpinned colonization. Often these letters were in response to pro-colonization editorials, or had been published in other newspapers and reprinted in the *Liberator* so that Garrison could alert his readers to the ongoing debate over colonization appearing within the pages of mainstream papers.

Some of these letters assailed colonization for unabashedly disregarding natural-rights philosophy. Other letters pointed to the un-Christian message implied in pro-colonization rhetoric. A contributor named Garner Jones, for example, called on the colonizationists to "do unto you, do ye even so unto them," and wondered about blacks, "as Americans, ought they not to enjoy the same privileges as white Americans?" In addition, Jones turned the ACS's justification for deporting black Americans to Africa on its head. "Why remove the blacks to Africa? Will it be replied, 'For the purpose of bettering their condition?' Why not better their condition here, where there is abundance of opportunities for instruction, where we are blessed with republican institutions, security, peace, and plenty?"

Jones also rooted his critique in what he deemed to be the impracticality of the colonization "scheme." In his estimation, the American Colonization Society had sent, on average, 150 Africans per year to Liberia between the early 1820s until the 1830s, while the increase of population among African Americans was 56,000 during the same period. Furthermore, as he explained, it would cost approximately $1,120,000 per year to transport all black Americans to Liberia. Jones's calculations sought to demonstrate that the ACS plan for African colonization was nothing short of fantasy. Such money and manpower could be used in much more constructive ways, such as building schools in black neighborhoods and providing blacks with training in skilled trades.[24]

ACS leaders claimed that letters such as these, published in the *Liberator*, undermined their organization's attempt to recruit black members. They were probably correct. In fact, Garrison's central claim had been that the letters he published in the *Liberator* were a true representation of black attitudes about colonization, and that this had compelled him to abandon colonization and move toward immediate abolition. Soon Garrison would call upon black American supporters to submit to him their own perspectives for inclusion in his book *Thoughts on African Colonization.*

Rather than position himself as the "voice" of black people, Garrison used *Thoughts* to acknowledge African Americans' ability to agitate on their own behalf. Since the *Liberator* had been a vehicle for African Americans to express their own attitudes about slavery, racial prejudice, and colonization for over a year, *Thoughts* brought together those essays, petitions, and letters that dealt specifically with colonization. For this reason, Garrison's *Thoughts* forced white philanthropists, journalists, and reformers to bear witness to blacks' intellectual acumen. Moreover, such a gesture represented a distinct turn from previous social reform and antislavery organizations, which frequently excluded African Americans and had no problem reminding blacks that white reformers knew what was best for them.[25] Considering that many whites who engaged in social reform regarded Africans in the United States and throughout the diaspora as their intellectual inferiors, Garrison's inclusion of black perspectives dovetails with his evolution toward embracing a kind of humanism that affirmed the equality of all races and even the genders.

(*Thoughts*'s one glaring point of neglect in this regard is the lack of black female voices in the text, even if this work did inspire black women such as Maria Stewart.)

Garrison began *Thoughts* confessing that "I would premise, that, like many others, I formerly supposed the Colonization Society was a praiseworthy association, although I always doubted its efficiency." Those opinions, he explained, had been "formed for me by others, upon whom I placed implicit confidence: it certainly was not based upon any research or knowledge of my own." In fact, he had not at that point "perused a single report of the society," and this negligence was "the offspring of credulity and ignorance." This "credulity and ignorance" would be challenged through informal conversations with black leaders, letters mailed in to the *Liberator*, and the presentation of resolutions at black conventions. Soon, he had come to view the ACS and the colonization movement from a wholly different perspective. Once he had seen the light, there simply was no turning back.

African Americans embraced *Thoughts*, and some treated the work as an anticolonization textbook capable of persuading the black community to reject colonization once and for all. John Vashon purchased several copies, and Garrison reminded him that "upon its sale depends in a measure the life of *The Liberator*." This was no exaggeration. Soon after Garrison returned to the *Liberator* office from a trip to Maine, his copublisher informed him that the over one thousand unsold copies of *Thoughts* had drained the paper of finances needed to continue publication. In desperation, Garrison sent letters to the Tappans, Fortens, and other wealthy supporters, and soon the entire lot of unsold *Thoughts* had been purchased. While Garrison mailed *Thoughts on African Colonization* to his faithful supporters in Philadelphia, New York, and Boston, he also shipped copies to Great Britain so that antislavery companions abroad, such as British antislavery activist George Thompson and black abolitionist Nathaniel Paul, could spread the word about the threat that colonization posed to the abolition movement in the United States and Europe.[26]

As Garrison traveled throughout the Northeast recruiting followers for his new abolition organization, colonization and its ill intent became a central part of his lectures. Soon he converted many men and women to the cause of anticolonization and immediate abolition. Abby Kelley Foster, for example, heard Garrison lecture, pondered the ideas Garrison put forth, reconsidered her support for colonization, and renounced her allegiance to the ACS; she would eventually dedicate her life to the cause of immediate abolition and anticolonziation.[27] Kelly Foster was not alone, and other women contemplated the benefits and drawbacks of both colonization and immediate emancipation when pushed to consider the potential consequences of advocating for an organization led by slaveholders with a vested interest in ridding the nation of free blacks. Women in Augusta, Maine, for example, held debates over colonization and immediatism. By the end of these debates, immediatism and anticolonization won many adherents, and soon a female abolition society was born.[28]

Like Abby Kelly Foster, Lydia Maria Child was converted to anticolonization by Garrison's influence. While Child did not relinquish her pro-colonization stance at once, by the time she began writing her classic antislavery work, *An Appeal in Favor of That Class of Americans Called Africans*, she had come to accept much of Garrison's anticolonization ideology. In her view, racial prejudice caused the perpetuation of slavery in the United States. "The very existence of the [Colonization] Society," she argued, "is owing to this prejudice," and such prejudice must be linked with the impulse to prevent educating blacks. Without education, free African Americans were forced to the margins of society. "[W]e are constantly told by this Society, that people of color must be removed," but the supposed need for this removal was only due to prejudice born out of centuries of slavery. Child continued, "We made slavery, and slavery makes the prejudice," and thus if the nation would only remove slavery and provide blacks with education, the prejudice would subside. She wondered, "And why should they be removed? Labor is greatly needed, and we are glad to give good wages for it. We encourage emigration from all parts of the world: why is it not good policy, as well as good feeling, to improve the coloured people[?]"[29]

Sarah H. Southwick, on the other hand, shifted her position on colonization while listening to a debate in Boston between British abolitionist George Thompson and Ralph Gurley, the secretary of the American Colonization Society. Having moved to Massachusetts in 1834, Southwick came into the abolitionist movement after her first trip to Boston to attend the first antislavery fair, held on Washington Street. Within a year, Southwick's family relocated to Boston and became fully engaged in the abolition movement. As she recalled, "African colonization was held at that time, by many well-wishers of the black man, to be the best way to abolish slavery, and was considered by Mr. Garrison the most dangerous obstacle to the spread of the anti-slavery movement."[30]

Women living in the Hudson Valley region just north of New York City came to denounce colonization and embrace immediatism in a similar way. Having come under the spell of Maria Stewart, those women who organized the Female Anti-Slavery Society (FASS) of Hudson, New York, believed anticolonization was a crucial ideology for those who battled against racial prejudice and slavery. Like Stewart, these women argued that the money whites donated to the Colonization Society would be better spent on educating free blacks in America and raising them to a middle-class level of respectability.[31]

Black women, who also sought to be accepted on equal terms with white women as well as white and black men, more often found their ideas to be crucial to these debates, even if they had no real vehicle with which to express these views. Without a newspaper, or a black female convention, Maria Stewart was a rare exception, lecturing to male audiences and writing letters to the editors of abolitionist newspapers.[32] In the late 1820s and early 1830s, black women rarely entered the public arena to challenge slavery, racial prejudice, and colonization because of the "double burden" of race and sex.[33] Despite Samuel Cornish and other black male leaders' criticism, Stewart boldly stepped out of the private sphere to express her views when and where she could, from Massachusetts to New York.

Outside of Boston, an interracial group of female abolitionists called the Female Anti-Slavery Society of Salem, came to regard racial uplift to be the chief component of abolitionism in Massachusetts. Historian Julie Roy Jeffrey explains, "These women appeared most interested in combating the prejudice that adversely affected the lives of Salem's free blacks." Central to their concern was the American Colonization Society's "ungenerous scheme of African colonization," which had helped to foster "the monster prejudice" in the minds of whites in Salem.[34]

Nearly five years later, women met at the first Anti-Slavery Convention of American Women in May 1837 and expressed similar sentiments. On the second day of the convention, Anne Weston of Boston put forth a resolution declaring "that we feel bound solemnly to protest against the principles of the American Colonization Society, as anti-Republican and anti-Christian." In step with Child's arguments in her *Appeal*, Weston's resolution linked the "prejudice against our oppressed brethren and sisters" with colonization, claiming that it only caused "the free man, persecution or banishment." When Weston finished reading the resolution, those gathered proceeded to express a variety of opinions about colonization. According to the convention minutes, delegates heard several "touching appeals from the colored members of the Convention."[35] Ultimately, the resolution was adopted. While few specific comments of African American women are recorded in the minutes, black female activist Sarah Pugh recalled that "they spoke with earnestness" when the issue of colonization came up.[36]

Although Garrison had ignited a conversion experience among white female abolitionists, most black women had already been exposed to anticolonization ideology early in their lives. Susan Paul, for example, came from a family in Boston with deep roots in the anticolonization tradition.[37] Her father, Thomas Paul, a Baptist minister, had worked with Prince Saunders in the late teens to oppose colonization and promote emigration to Haiti. Susan Paul's uncle, Nathaniel Paul, traveled throughout Europe during the early 1830s as a representative of the Wilberforce settlement in Canada, which had been established in 1829 when blacks were driven from Cincinnati. For this reason it seems plausible that Susan Paul shared these impressions with white women who participated with her in forming the Boston Female Anti-Slavery Society.[38]

As black women pushed their white sisters to reject colonization, toward the end of the 1830s several prominent white male abolitionists also came to the same conclusions. In fact, Gerrit Smith attributed his own move away from colonization to his interaction with blacks and the realization they were no different from himself or any other white person, except for their "darker hue."[39] For years Smith had believed that the American Colonization Society's call for gradual emancipation and repatriation was a progressive and benevolent enterprise. Yet the rise of radical abolitionism, as well as the numerous debates between ACS officials and abolitionists, caused Smith to rethink his position on colonization and colonizationists' commitment to the cause they advocated.

Some of Smith's frustration with colonization stemmed from the Seventeenth Annual American Colonization Society meeting in 1834. After waiting patiently for others to describe the progress of the organization in various parts of the country, Smith stood and began what would turn into a lecture on the current practices of his colleagues within the Society. Smith started by explaining that "the Society has been made, either by its own fault, or the fault of others, or partly both, to appear to be friendly to slavery" and "an obstacle of emancipation." The abolitionists, as Smith argued, had successfully cast the colonization movement in negative terms, and this stood as the most formidable obstacle to recruiting black emigrants to Liberia. In this sense, Smith admitted that "the Anti-Slavery Society has greatly wronged us," although he still believed the Colonization Society could defend its venture against those charges if it changed its opinion about emancipation. Smith also explained that "[o]ur society is extensively lamentably deficient in the love to that class of our coloured brethren whose condition it seeks to meliorate." This "love," in his view, was crucial for an organization claiming to work to benefit African Americans. Thus, Smith asserted, "we must greatly increase our love to the people for whom we have undertaken to provide a home," if colonizationists were to counter anticolonizationist influence among the masses of free African Americans.

Some of his colleagues certainly must have gasped at Smith's statements, but he did not stop there. He pressed on, claiming that he would stop "this ungracious fault finding" and take his seat once he broached an even less popular topic: dues. "The friends of this Society do not give enough money," Smith proclaimed. "There is a great deal of talking . . . but very little giving to it." He presented a resolution to raise $50,000, claiming "Let us, Sir, not only pass the resolution which I hold in my hand . . . but let us before the present week is closed, or better still, before we leave the room," gather that sum. Such bold proclamations must have unsettled ACS members and hastened Smith's retreat from the organization after 1835, when he cast his lot with the American Anti-Slavery Society.[40]

Recruited to the antislavery cause by Alvin Stewart and Beriah Green, Smith experienced the consequences of joining the abolition movement soon after he left the ACS. When Smith and his wife Nancy attended the inaugural state antislavery society meeting in Utica in October 1835, a mob led by some of the city's leading citizens attacked an antislavery meeting, forcing a state convention to end abruptly.[41] While Smith's early opinions about abolition have been characterized as mild, by 1838 he would fully embrace the cause and become an important leader in advocating for the immediate end of slavery through moral suasion. However, his faith in Garrisonian moral suasion was short-lived, and when Smith witnessed the passage of antiabolitionist legislation he became convinced that he could never change the minds of slaveholders through the apolitical, moral suasionist abolitionism advocated by William Lloyd Garrison. Soon he cast his lot with political abolitionists who were working toward forming an antislavery political party.[42]

When, in 1839, Gerrit Smith joined the Liberty Party's efforts to run a candidate for the 1840 presidential race, he gained a bit of notoriety by publicly encouraging whites and blacks to break the law and aid fugitive slaves.[43] By 1842, Smith went so far as to call on slaves in the South to steal if necessary in order to escape, and encouraged northern abolitionists to travel south to help runaways.[44] This brand of radical abolitionist rhetoric stood in direct opposition to Garrison's call for noninterference and passive resistance. It seems evident that this brand of radical posturing attracted the attention of black leaders such as Henry Highland Garnet and David Ruggles, who grew to embrace self-defense against slave catchers and called on slaves to use all means available—even violence—to free themselves.

But perhaps Gerrit Smith won his greatest victory in the black community when he saw to it that African Americans were given the necessary resources to become eligible to vote in New York. Having inherited a fortune from his family's dealings with "the peculiar institution," Smith decided to allocate nearly 140,000 acres for blacks to establish farms in upstate New York. At the 1847 National Black Convention, members of the Committee on Agriculture resolved, "That this Convention do express its deep thanks to Gerrit Smith . . . for his splendid donation to the cause of God and humanity."[45] Such an act of true benevolence went a long way in demonstrating his sincerity and strengthening the bond between black and white leaders.

While men such as Frederick Douglass stood in opposition to third-party politics in the early 1840s, it seems that the work of New York radical political abolitionists, such as Gerrit Smith, led Douglass to acknowledge the advantages of their cause. And even though the rising Free Soil Party had expressed little sympathy for the plight of free blacks in the North, black leaders at the 1848 National Convention nevertheless resolved that "we heartily engage in recommending to our people the Free Soil movement." However, those convened maintained their dissatisfaction, asserting that "we claim and are determined to maintain higher standard and more liberal views" than those of Free Soilers.[46] Since the rise of both the organized abolition movement and the black convention movement in the early thirties, most black leaders agreed with Garrison's moral suasion doctrine, which rejected the use of politics as a means to end slavery. Garrison helped to convince many blacks that white politicians would only support emancipation without mass deportation if they believed slavery and racism were immoral, un-Christian, and counter to democratic ideals. Thus, the success of the Liberty Party or the Free Soil Party mattered less to Garrison than the creation of a social revolution that would lead whites to embrace blacks as "men and brothers." However, African Americans in Massachusetts worked closely with Liberty Party members such as Elizur Wright in the 1840s to challenge specific laws, such as the interracial marriage ban, Jim Crow railcars, and school segregation. They were with Garrison in theory, but locked arms with Wright and Henry Bowditch in practice.[47]

For some black Americans like William Whipper, the personal was indeed political. By the end of the 1830s, Whipper and others came to regard moral reform and temperance as important tools to combat proslavery and pro-colonization sympathies in the North. In fact, most black leaders who considered themselves abolitionists and anticolonizationists saw the need, first and foremost, for a commitment to dealing with the conditions faced by black people in the North. While free blacks abhorred slavery, colonization, and racism, many of them argued that black people bore the responsibility of proving they deserved freedom and equality. While they did live in a racist society that erected systems bent on undermining their ability to thrive, they clung to the notion that each individual had an obligation to do all in his or her power to live virtuously, temperately, and respectfully for the betterment of the race.

In one sense, Whipper's American Moral Reform Society championed a sense of self-help and individual accountability that appears both practical and pressing. On the other hand, blacks were no more likely to live intemperate lives, scorn formal education, or flout middle-class social practices than were, say, Irish immigrants or other working-class whites. Of course, Whipper believed that the consequences of living in such a way were much greater for blacks than for white immigrants or the white poor.[48]

Only a few radical black abolitionists, such as David Ruggles, pressed forward with a more confrontational style of "practical abolition" that dealt specifically and directly with the reality of kidnapping and white violence. Ruggles argued, "let us in every case of oppression and wrong, inflicted on our brethren, prove our sincerity, by alleviating their sufferings, affording them protection, giving them counsel, and thus in our individual spheres of action, prove ourselves practical abolitionists." Inspiring a generation of black abolitionists such as Frederick Douglass, Ruggles's career at the end of the 1830s provides a contrast to the type of moral uplift emphasis common among black leaders like Whipper.[49] By and large, the quest for respectability within the black community stemmed from the notion that whites would come to accept blacks as equals if free blacks in the North behaved in ways that defied the negative stereotypes that underpinned white pro-colonization and proslavery sentiment.[50] Gerrit Smith's conversion away from colonization and towards the quest for equal rights for blacks in America illustrates the success of this view. As historian Bruce Laurie notes, "Gerrit Smith believed that if he had had the opportunity to get to know African Americans personally he would never have succumbed to racism for so long."[51]

Black leaders agreed with Smith's emphasis on interracial association to combat prejudice, but they knew that only "upstanding" free blacks had such a power to change whites' impression of the race. Thus, they shifted attention towards teaching poor and uneducated black people to behave in ways that defied white stereotypes, such as by abstaining from "spirituous liquors" and the afflictions associated with drunkenness.[52] When African Americans walked, talked, and prayed like middle-class whites, so the argument went, they would be accepted by whites on equal terms and this would undermine the colonization cause. Of course, no such thing had occurred, and African American abolitionists such as Ruggles contested this point of view.

While some free blacks sought to inspire their peers to embrace behaviors and ideas that had been important features of middle-class respectability, others like Ruggles understood that the struggle against slavery and colonization required direct engagement. These black abolitionists, as Graham Gao Russell Hodges points out, were indeed "radical" insofar as they believed racial equality and justice would come to black Americans only through agitation—against slavery and colonization.[53] Still, many black leaders shifted their attention away from abolition and anticolonization, and toward moral reform, as the best way to combat pro-colonization ideology. This, however, would prove futile, and by the end of the 1840s pro-colonization sentiment would only grow in the Midwest and West.[54]

From the beginning, an anticolonizationist stance was one of the new abolition movement's ideological cornerstones. Not only had black Americans pushed white antislavery advocates beyond a call for gradual emancipation, they had also convinced them that the American Colonization Society and colonization ideology remained potent adversaries. Furthermore, these African American leaders formed interracial alliances with white abolitionists committed to the notion that freedom from slavery was only part of what was needed. African Americans wanted full citizenship in the United States, and those whites who considered themselves allies for freedom needed to accept this fact. For that reason, black and white abolitionists worked tirelessly to change the minds of the majority of white antislavery advocates about colonization. By the time the American Anti-Slavery Society was formed, those who considered themselves abolitionists were compelled to place anticolonization next to immediatism, interracial brotherhood, and citizenship among the goals of freedom.

The abolitionist assault of the 1830s took its toll on the American Colonization Society: by the middle of the decade, most social reformers scorned the idea of colonization. The ACS faced dwindling relevance among progressive reformers in the Northeast, and to make matters worse, mismanagement and infighting nearly destroyed the national organization. Nevertheless, all their hopes were not yet lost. Ralph Gurley and other leaders within the Colonization Society seized upon the possibility of raising money and building a support base in Britain to off-set the ACS's waning influence in the United States. This led ACS leaders to travel abroad in an effort to build a transnational coalition to rescue the organization, and these efforts compelled black and white abolition-ists to confront colonizationists on foreign soil.

3 / "The Cause Is God's and Must Prevail": Building an Anticolonizationist Wall in Great Britain, 1830–1850

Studies of the abolition movement have often highlighted the importance of the transnational nature of the antislavery and anticolonization struggles.[1] When abolitionists traveled overseas to argue for their antislavery cause, they quickly recognized that the battle for public support in Britain rested on their ability to undermine the American Colonization Society agents struggling to procure financial and legislative support in Europe. ACS agents courted British antislavery leaders, presenting colonization as if it were popular among blacks in America. Consequently, William Lloyd Garrison, Nathaniel Paul, and fellow American abolitionists traveled to the British Isles throughout the 1830s and 1840s to challenge Elliot Cresson and other colonizationist agents for philanthropic dollars and public sympathy. Most historians point to Garrison's success, yet these confrontations with American colonizationists and their British allies tested American abolitionists' resolve, compelling them to prove to the British public that black Americans' best interest was not at the heart of the ACS crusade to resettle African Americans in West Africa.[2] This chapter examines the anticolonization crusade in Britain between the founding of the *Liberator* in 1831 and the Compromise of 1850.

In December 1831, Nathaniel Paul left Wilberforce, Canada, in search of understanding philanthropists interested in funding causes dedicated to racial justice. Like his brother, the Boston-based Baptist minister Thomas Paul, Nathaniel Paul was one of several African American leaders during the antebellum era who utilized the transnational alliance of abolitionists and social reformers to garner support for the struggle against slavery and colonization. Paul was a gifted public speaker who had been a minister in Albany, New York, prior to joining the second wave of settlers who arrived in the Wilberforce settlement in Canada nearly two years after pioneers from Cincinnati had established roots there.

Soon after Paul arrived in Britain he realized that ACS agents had already worn a trail through British philanthropic circles, posing as if their movement shared the abolitionist spirit of African American uplift. Such deception, as Paul would describe it later, led him to conclude that his greatest obstacle in Britain remained the colonizationists. Paul, one of the leading American abolitionists in England in the early 1830s, put aside his original purpose of raising money in Britain for a fugitive slave colony in Wilberforce, Canada, and instead took on ACS agent Elliot Cresson, who was working to gain allies abroad.[3]

As an African American, Paul quickly gained the attention of the British public through his arresting lectures and vivid descriptions of racial violence in the American North and slavery in the South.[4] "My lectures have been numerously attended," Paul explained in a letter to Garrison, by "from two to three thousand people, the Halls and Chapels have been overflown [sic], and hundreds have not been able to obtain admittance."[5] Perhaps interest in Paul's message remained secondary to white British fascination with Paul's anatomy. One British Abolitionist admitted that "the color of [Paul's] skin was an excellent introduction," and British obsession with his physical presence earned him invitations from British philanthropists, nobility, and others who apparently found his African features of great interest.[6] After several months in Britain, Paul seemed to have used all of this to his advantage in his efforts both to raise money and to increase British awareness of the relationship between racial animosity in America and the rise of the ACS. Still, as his trip went on he encountered the extraordinary degree to which Cresson and his pro-colonization allies worked to undermine him.

As Paul sailed to Great Britain, slaves in Jamaica were on the verge of violent insurrection.[7] The day after Christmas in 1831, African-born and locally born slaves ravaged Jamaica in the largest slave rebellion in the colony's history and indeed all of British colonial history. Researchers suggest that almost 20,000 slaves took part in the rebellion, and 226 estates were damaged. The impact of such a major revolt on the consciousness of British reformers and sympathetic members of Parliament is incalculable. Historian Gad Heuman argues that "The Jamaican slave rebellion made it clear to many in Britain that slavery could not continue."[8] And it was the sheer intensity of this rebellion that pushed antislavery reformers to call for an immediate end to slavery throughout the empire.

A few months earlier, whites in South Hampton, Virginia, had been shocked when Nat Turner led more than fifty slaves in rebellion against whites in an effort to spark a massive insurrection in Virginia and, perhaps, North Carolina. After a month on the run, Turner was caught and executed. His death, however, did not assure whites that others would not follow his lead.[9] This gave some whites grave concerns about the institution of slavery and whether or not the dangerous black population needed to be emancipated in order to protect the general public from a catastrophic insurrection. Within the context of the insurrections in both Virginia and Jamaica, black and white abolitionists seized the opportunity to advance their cause with renewed vigor. Certainly, this moment provided Nathaniel Paul with an attentive audience in Britain for raising awareness and funds to support his settlement in Canada and to gain adherents in the movement against slavery and colonization.[10]

When Paul arrived in Great Britain in 1831, old-guard British abolitionists such as William Wilberforce were on the cusp of urging Parliament to abolish slavery throughout the empire and bringing their half-century crusade against slavery to a victorious conclusion. British humanitarians had successfully agitated for the end of the Atlantic Slave Trade in 1807 and had organized the Anti-Slavery Society in the spring of 1823 to push for gradual emancipation and to improve slaves' living conditions, which were poor and had led to high mortality rates in the British West Indian colonies.[11] The struggle to reform slavery was not easy. Caribbean planters balked at new regulations or "suggestions" that they treat their slaves better, and their reluctance to accept reform measures prompted some British antislavery advocates to embrace the doctrine of immediatism, which had spread in the United States after 1831.[12]

Nathaniel Paul had shown considerable respect for the work of Clarkson, Wilberforce, and other British reformers even before he met them in person. On July 5, 1827, a few years before Paul arrived in Europe, he delivered a speech on the day after New York officially abolished slavery, and thanked "the indefatigable exertions of the philanthropists" in England who worked to end slavery "in their West India Islands." Such bold and courageous actions, Paul explained, illustrated that "The recent revolutions in South America, the catastrophe and exchange of power in the Isle of Hayti, [and] the restless disposition of both master and slave in the southern states" all showed that the wheels of oppression could only turn for so long before African-descended people rose up against those who held sway over their lives.[13] While he may have overstated the role played by British reformers in pushing Parliament to legislate against slavery and the slave trade, he did place the struggle against slavery within a transnational context.

In his lecture Paul also acknowledged the relationship between the perpetuation of slavery and the colonization of free blacks to Liberia, both being expressions of racial prejudice in the American North. After nearly a decade, the American Colonization Society had neither encouraged slaveholders to emancipate their slaves nor offered a successful method for dealing with white racial prejudice. Paul asserted, "That prejudices do exist is too obvious to be denied, and that these prejudices are extensive and deeply rooted is equally true." Yet in his estimation colonization was "utterly chimerical and absurd" because it would require nearly $28,000,000 to remove the free people of the United States.[14] "I am free to admit that a well regulated colony upon the western coast of Africa will be productive of great good.... [However,] I can yet see no just cause why we should leave this country." The members of the ACS were hypocrites, said Paul, and their plan was a cruel attempt to place the burden of encouraging an end to slavery on the shoulders of a small number of oppressed black Americans with little political or economic power.

Having agitated against colonization in the United States for years, Paul had no trouble outlining its flaws to a British public ripe with interest in a black perspective on issues related to abolition and the slave trade. He often employed the same methods he had used as a minister in Albany by affirming his commitment to doing God's work on earth, and acknowledging that he and his white audience were united in Christ. Then he moved on to argue that slavery was a universal wrong regardless of whether it took place in the Caribbean, Latin America, or the United States. Having linked slavery in the British colonies with slavery in the United States, Paul detailed different aspects of slavery and emphasized its inherent brutality. Such treatment of human beings, he argued, violated the principles of Christianity and natural-rights philosophy. Paul explained to a crowd in Glasgow that "for 15 years ... he had been devoted to the cause" of antislavery and "the relief of his suffering fellow-creatures," a mission that fit squarely with the ideals of the American Founding Fathers and British philanthropists on "whose political hemisphere the sun of liberty pours forth his refulgent rays, around which dazzle the star like countenances of Clarkson, Wilberforce, Pitt, Fox, and

Greenville, Washington, Adams, Jefferson, Hancock, and Franklin."[15] These icons, he explained, served as the foundation for his mission, and the legacy of such men depended on an immediate end to slavery.

Several months into his British campaign, Paul was pleased to report Britons' great interest in regard to abolition and the anticolonizationist cause. In July 1832, for example, Paul bragged about having collected 150,000 names for an antislavery petition to be sent to the United States Congress. He wrote to Garrison, "Allow me then to say, sir . . . that the people of this country are alive to the cause of abolition," and he noted that the uprising in Jamaica had caused nearly 300,000 Britons to appeal to the House of Commons to abolish slavery.[16]

Once Paul gained the attention of British reformers, he was able to use those connections to meet William Wilberforce, the namesake of his settlement in Canada. Twice Paul ate breakfast with Wilberforce, boasting that "I have a letter in my pocket that I received from him, a few weeks since, which I would not take pounds for." He also claimed that he had "been in the company of the patriotic Clarkson."[17] And soon after a meeting at Exeter Hall in London on July 13, 1833, Paul gained the support of the famous Irish radical Daniel O'Connell.[18]

While the value of these allies' support in the abolition cause was incalculable, Elliot Cresson and the ACS continued to pose a threat to Paul's efforts. Paul kept coming across Cresson's supporters as he toured through Britain, and he sent word to Garrison that "your *Thoughts on Colonization* are the thoughts of the people here," and also that "[Garrison's book] has done much good. . . . I only regret that your book had not come sooner." He described Cresson's success to Garrison but claimed to feel confident that "the people have their eyes open," and that the majority of British abolitionists seemed to be coming around. "Extracts from your book are published in several of the most respectable periodical publications," Paul reported, and he argued that the tide had begun to turn against Elliot Cresson and the ACS. "I have met with but one gentleman who did not regret that they ever countenanced his cause."[19]

Even with Paul's condemnation, Cresson did succeed in gaining an audience with members of the British Anti-Slavery Society. During this meeting Cresson defended colonization against what he described as abolitionist distortions. Cresson's method was simple. He wrote letters to newspapers describing the ACS as the premier antislavery organization in the United States, while championing Liberia's growing commercial activity. Referencing Paul Cuffe as a forerunner of the ACS movement,

Cresson argued that his mission was one of rectitude and had the support of African Americans.

In this battle over the hearts and minds of the British public, the ACS had struck the first blow by winning approval from British abolitionists under the impression that the principles of the ACS coincided with their own work to end slavery and to ameliorate the condition of Africans held in bondage.[20] Cresson laid colonization roots among British philanthropists and political officials, pushing his agenda each time an opportunity presented itself to him. Cresson also advised ACS officers to cease publishing articles or letters in organizational materials that suggested slaveholder support for colonization. Instead, he suggested that the organization publish statements supportive of free blacks and encouraging colonization for the benefit of Africa.[21] As historian Richard Blackett points out, "The significance of Cresson's visit cannot be overestimated, for it set the international stage on which the battle between colonizationists and abolitionists would be fought."[22].

Although Nathaniel Paul had compelled many leading British abolitionists to view the ACS as misguided, Cresson painted a very different picture of his British endeavor to ACS officials. "It will give this meeting pleasure to know," the American Colonization Society board of managers announced at their fifteenth annual meeting, "that the statements of Mr. Cresson have been well received, and that he has been assured of the cordial support of many eminent friends of Africa and mankind." Thrilled by Cresson's report, ACS officials gloated about the success of the mission, applauding the "liberality of English friends" and Cresson's ability to let their cause be known in "many English Journals."[23] While the board of managers seems to have trusted Cresson's report of his mission's success, a $2,000 donation from the Society of Friends in London, which had been mailed to the North Carolina auxiliary of the ACS, added credence to his boast.

Further, Cresson managed to secure the endorsement of Thomas Clarkson, one of the best-known and most respected antislavery advocates in the world. When the board read the letter aloud during the fifteenth annual meeting, they noted with pride that Clarkson considered the ACS mission and the colony of Liberia "truly astonishing." Clarkson declared in his letter: "No sooner had your Colony been established on Cape Monteserrado, than there appeared a disposition among the owners of slaves to give them freedom voluntarily and without compensation, and to allow them to be sent to the land of their Fathers, so that you have many thousands redeemed, without any cost for their redemption."

Without concrete evidence or any analysis of the consequences of colonization ideology for free blacks in the United States, Clarkson placed the ACS's colonization plan within the context of previous resettlement missions initiated in Britain and America since the American Revolution. But colonizing free black Americans in Liberia would not end slavery in the United States, and Cresson knew it. Since the ACS had sent just over three thousand African American emigrants to Liberia in the 1820s, they could hardly assert that their plan was responsible for affecting slavery on a grand scale. (It was not until the late 1840s and early 1850s that African Americans left for Liberia in any large numbers. In its best year, the ACS sent around seven hundred African Americans to Liberia, some of whom had become dissatisfied with their opportunities for success in America.[24])

Nevertheless, Cresson won Clarkson's support by convincing him that the Colonization Society sought the emancipation of American slaves and their relocation to Liberia as a means for civilizing Africa and stifling the slave trade along the West African coast.[25] In Clarkson's letter to the American Colonization Society, he imagined the ACS project leading to a string of colonies in Africa that would cultivate agricultural goods and provide an alternative income for African rulers dependent on slave trading. By encouraging the growth of schools and churches in these communities, Africans would improve their character and moral worth, and would stop the barbaric practice of trading in humans.

Only an endorsement from William Wilberforce could garner more respect than that of Thomas Clarkson. Cresson therefore sought philanthropists with the clout to arrange for him to meet with Wilberforce. This worked, and Cresson managed to spend a whole week with Wilberforce, discussing the American Colonization Society's mission and trying to win Wilberforce's approval. When this was finally achieved, he wasted no time alerting ACS board members of his success. Cresson shared a letter he had received from Wilberforce that expressed support for the ACS's colonization plan. "You have gladdened my heart," Wilberforce explained, "by convincing me, that as sanguine as had been my hopes of the happy effects to be produced by your Institution, all my anticipations are scanty and cold compared with the reality. This may truly be deemed a pledge of Divine favor, and believe me, no Briton, I had almost said no American, can take a livelier interest than myself, in your true greatness and glory."[26]

When members of the ACS board learned that Cresson had secured both Clarkson's and Wilberforce's endorsements, they were astonished.

As far as the ACS board of managers was concerned, Cresson's mission to England was just what the organization needed to combat the anti-colonizationist attacks that had become the hallmark of the abolition movement. Nevertheless, events unfolding in Britain, beginning with the arrival of Paul, would shatter Cresson's apparent victory, and shake ACS Secretary Ralph Gurley's confidence. As it turned out, British abolitionists like Charles Stuart had read Clarkson's letter endorsing the ACS and colonization ideology, yet they had not read much if any of the anticolonization literature available in the United States. Consequently, when British antislavery advocates read Garrison's classic anticolonization text *Thoughts on African Colonization* and heard Nathaniel Paul ridicule the ACS, they publicly deplored what they believed to be Cresson's duplicity. Charles Stuart, James Cropper, and Zachary Macaulay took action, challenging Cresson to a public debate on the merits of colonization. Cropper wrote an open letter to Thomas Clarkson, stating: "It caused me deep regret to see thy name amongst those many long tried friends of humanity as supporters of the American Colonization Society." Cropper explained that slaveholders would never give up their property and send them to Liberia. "[T]he free people are opposed to this scheme," he explained, and told Clarkson that he had unwittingly sent a message to "these sorely persecuted and oppressed people [that] the philanthropist of England" did not stand behind them.[27]

Cropper's colleague Charles Stuart seconded his analysis, and within two years Stuart published at least four pamphlets analyzing the American Colonization Society in ways that echoed Garrison's *Thoughts on African Colonization*. Stuart linked the American Colonization Society with "Negrophobia," and he attempted to show the negative consequences of colonization both in principle and in practice. Through these pamphlets Stuart countered the views Clarkson had expressed in his letter endorsing the ACS by highlighting evidence of proslavery sentiment in the ACS Annual Reports and *The African Repository*.

Cresson was outraged. He railed against the British Anti-Slavery Society for taking Garrison's anticolonizationist views as fact and for falling under the spell of Garrison's influence. He even went so far as to call Charles Stuart a "2nd Garrison" for the way he excoriated him and the colonization movement in the media and through his pamphlets. Prompted by his anger, Cresson agreed to debate Stuart on colonization and immediate emancipation. Regardless of the outcome of the debate, Cresson blamed Garrison in his reports to ACS secretary Ralph Gurley for what amounted to a public humiliation and his growing inability to cast the ACS in a positive light.[28] While he had tried to present the colonizationists' gradual emancipation and colonization plan as squarely within the transatlantic antislavery movement, the anticolonizationists like Paul continued to hound him.

Soon Cresson would have more than Stuart to contend with. William Lloyd Garrison joined Paul's effort to stifle Cresson's endeavors when he arrived in England in May 1833.[29] While it is unclear to what degree Paul influenced Garrison's decision to travel to England, Paul's letters to Garrison sounded an alarm, calling for reinforcements in the struggle against the ACS in Great Britain. In his report to the board of managers of the New-England Anti-Slavery Society, Garrison alerted his abolitionist peers that "an agent of the American Colonization Society has been traveling nearly three years in its behalf, and by his misrepresentations had extensively succeeded in making the British public believe that his primary object was *the emancipation of all the slaves in the United States.*" This "misrepresentation" had led many British reformers to contribute money to the ACS, further enriching the organization and threatening the success of immediatism and universal emancipation in the United States. According to Garrison, the British public needed "a living agent, speaking by authority and clothed with official power . . . to insure the triumph of TRUTH AND HONESTY OVER FALSEHOOD AND FRAUD."[30] In Garrison's view, "no one was better acquainted" with the machinations of the ACS and the various arguments colonizationists used to justify their cause than he was, and thus he felt obliged to volunteer his talents and to meet the colonization threat in Britain head-on.

Arriving in Great Britain, Garrison called upon James Cropper to assess the situation and provide him with contacts in London who could help him organize a series of lectures and interviews with newspaper reporters. Cropper welcomed Garrison and introduced him to other antislavery reformers who had descended on London because Parliament was gearing up to debate an abolition bill. On one occasion Cropper and Garrison visited a coffeehouse frequented by many social reformers and abolitionists, and they initiated a discussion regarding colonization. Several in the room informed Garrison that Cresson was currently in London, and Garrison went into a rant about the ACS, calling it "corrupt and proscriptive in its principles." He charged Cresson with "abusing the confidence and generosity of the philanthropists of Great Britain," and he challenged Cresson to "meet [him] in public debate in this city."[31]

As Garrison recalled, he had sent a letter to Cresson in hopes of scheduling a public debate. "To prevent any miscarriage of my letter," Garrison explained, "I entrusted it to my esteemed friend Mr. Joseph Phillips." When Phillips approached Cresson with the letter, Cresson, "in the most offensive manner, refused to receive it from Mr. Phillips." This response did not discourage Garrison, and he called upon William Horsenail to deliver the letter. This time, when Cresson turned the letter down, he explained to Horsenail that he and several British colleagues had already made arrangements to meet with Garrison. Horsenail returned the letter to Garrison, who then put the letter into the hands of Jeremiah Barret. Again Cresson refused it. Finally, Joseph Phillips approached Cresson again, and this time, with two respected philanthropists at his side, Cresson was finally compelled to accept the letter. After reading it, Cresson wrote a note to Garrison explaining that Dr. Thomas Hodgkin and J.T. Price had recommended he not respond but instead wait to speak to him at a meeting they would organize. This compelled Garrison to write directly to Hodgkin and Price, telling them that he waited "to learn the course which you may recommend Mr. Cresson to adopt, as to my proposition to him for a public discussion." Hodgkin and Price replied with a letter to both Garrison and Cresson, inviting the rivals to a private meeting among "a few friends impartially chosen" so that both men could voice their opinions without fear of public humiliation.

Yet Garrison turned down the private meeting because, as he recalled later, "I saw it was a mere ruse on the part of Mr. C. and his friend Dr. Hodgkin, to obviate the necessity of a public meeting," and also that "[his] business was exclusively with the British people, and with Mr. Cresson in his public capacity as the Agent of the American Colonization Society." Garrison baited Cresson by mailing a letter to the *Times* of London that charged the ACS with fraud and misrepresentation. Next, Garrison held several public lectures on the Colonization Society designed to provoke a response from Cresson or from those who favored the ACS's views.[32]

Garrison, sure enough, would have his chance to get at Cresson. The moment arrived on June 10, 1833, when Cresson appeared in the audience during one of Garrison's gatherings. Just as James Cropper introduced Garrison, he spotted Cresson and called on him to come forward to refute Garrison's previous allegations. It was "a grave charge to bring against a man," Cropper explained, and he offered Cresson an opportunity to set the record straight. As Cresson sat silently, Cropper continued to bait him, asking him if he was aware that Garrison had said such "things," and acknowledging that "this is not a meeting for discussion; but [he] thought it fair that Elliott Cresson should be allowed to rebut the charge if he thought it false."

Obviously annoyed by Cropper's attempt to draw Cresson out, one of the men in Cresson's party shouted that "this [was] calculated to cause a discussion" when they had come to hear a lecture on colonization. Cropper responded, "I wish, when a charge is fairly brought against an individual, to give him an opportunity of denying it, if he can. . . . Therefore, if Elliott Cresson wishes for discussion, we will have a meeting for that purpose, and we will hear what he has to say." Cresson continued to hold his tongue, and soon Cropper relented and introduced Garrison to address the audience.[33]

Although Garrison failed to push Cresson into open debate that evening or any other evening, he continued his tour throughout Great Britain. Eager to meet the legendary Wilberforce, Garrison traveled to Bath, nearly 100 miles outside London. Although Garrison really wanted to discuss the reason Wilberforce had endorsed the Colonization Society, Wilberforce's wife and son urged Garrison to speak about prejudice against free blacks in the United States. Garrison entertained this discussion for a while, but eventually he shifted it back to Wilberforce's colonization sympathies. Wilberforce claimed that "his commendation of the enterprise had been restricted to the colony of Liberia" and that it "[relied] upon the information which Mr. Cresson had given him respecting the flourishing condition of the colony." With regard to the treatment of free blacks in America, Wilberforce told Garrison that he had found Cresson's argument that blacks could not be elevated to an equal place with whites to be "fundamentally false and unchristian." Furthermore, Wilberforce "expressed much anxiety to learn how far Cresson had made use of his name to give currency to the Society."[34]

The next day Garrison returned to Wilberforce's home, ate breakfast with his family, and spoke with Wilberforce again for nearly five hours. During the course of this second visit, Garrison reported, "I impressed upon his mind, tenderly and solemnly, the importance of his bearing public testimony against the American Colonization Society," and he put into Wilberforce's hands the Fifteenth and Sixteenth Reports of the Colonization Society for him to read with his own eyes the opinions of those who led the organization. This effort to persuade Wilberforce resembled Garrison's approach in *Thoughts on African Colonization*— quoting prominent members of the ACS to refute those who claimed the organization remained committed to antislavery. Thus, Garrison argued that the ACS could not claim to be antislavery in nature. By the end of the discussion, Garrison believed he had persuaded Wilberforce of his position.

When Garrison returned to London, James Cropper organized a meeting at Exeter Hall, explaining to the audience that "the objective of the present meeting [is], the exposition of the real character and design of the American Colonization Society." After Garrison had said a few words, Nathaniel Paul was called to speak, as an African American seeking equality in the United States, about his impressions of the American Colonization Society.

Paul began by praising Garrison's work, reminding the audience that "Mr. Garrison has, for many years past, devoted himself exclusively to the interests of the slaves and the free people of color in the United States of America." In Paul's opinion, such actions warranted "no commendation" from Garrison, and he explained that one need only look at the sacrifices Garrison himself had made on behalf of African Americans for proof of his loyalty to the cause. Furthermore, Paul asserted, "it is not merely the sacrifice that Mr. Garrison has made, or the rigid system of economy that he has adopted, that speaks on his behalf; but the sufferings that he has endured likewise recommend him to the attention of every philanthropist." While Paul compared Garrison's activism to that of a saint, he also used Garrison's experiences at the hands of white proslavery men and colonizationists to show the relationship between advocating slavery and advocating colonization, explaining that both contradicted the "principles of human nature."

Paul argued that "instead of the [American Colonization Society] being the enemy of slavery; instead of its being formed for the purpose of annihilating the system; its object is to perpetuate it, and render more secure the property of man in man."[35] Paul repudiated Cresson's work in England, calling it a deceptive attempt to prey on the sympathies of a British audience "seeking the liberation of slaves." He charged the ACS with cruelty, arguing, "If I am asked why is it cruel? I answer, in the first place, because it undertakes to expel from their native country hundreds of thousands of unoffending and inoffensive individuals."

Paul mocked the ACS and chronicled the ways in which the ACS stood as an obstacle to ending slavery or securing human rights for African Americans, explaining to the crowd that the ACS "professes to be the friend of the free people of color, and to pity their present condition," yet "both in public and in private, it calumniates and abuses [blacks] in the most extravagant manner, as its reports will abundantly show." Presenting himself as the ambassador of black people in America, Paul proclaimed, "I will venture to assert that I am as extensively acquainted with them, throughout both the free and slave States, as any man in that country; and I do not know of a solitary colored individual who entertains the least favorable view of the American Colonization Society; but, in every way they possibly could, they have expressed their disapprobation of it."[36]

As Paul told the audience about the frequent black American anticolonization meetings in the United States, the famed Irish lawyer and Parliament member Daniel O'Connell sat attentive, taking in Paul's words and preparing for his turn to speak. When Paul sat down, O'Connell took a turn rebuking the ACS, calling its campaign in Europe deceitful. He claimed that the organization had duped European reformers into believing that the ACS "aimed at the destruction of slavery." O'Connell admitted they had tricked him as well because he "took them at their word." Yet, as he explained to the audience, "I had not then read the real history, nor the real character of the Society." Upon examining the ACS periodical *The African Repository*, O'Connell told the crowd that the ACS admitted that it was no Abolition Society, yet its representatives had the "insolence to come before the British public, and represent itself as an instrument of humanity!" "It is the most ludicrous Society that ever yet was dreamed of," O'Connell proclaimed, and then asked the crowd to join him in opposition to the ACS in Britain. "In the name of justice," O'Connell averred, "I stand before you as arraigning, above all, the American Colonization Society, as ludicrous and absurd, and as diverting from their legitimate course those streams of benevolence which flow around us in such munificent splendor." When O'Connell finished, the crowd burst into applause. Paul and Garrison could not have overstated the value of O'Connell's support or the impact such support would have on Cresson's credibility in Britain.[37]

Having succeeded in gaining the support of O'Connell and Wilberforce, both Paul and Garrison sought out Thomas Clarkson as well, since he had previously claimed to have supported Cresson's mission. The two Americans were well aware that gaining Clarkson's approval would be no easy task. Nevertheless, Garrison and Paul rode to Ipswich to meet with Clarkson to try to bring the antislavery legend into their crusade against colonization. In Ipswich, Garrison recalled, "It happen[ed] that the individual, who, of all others in England, exerts the most influence over Clarkson's mind, was the main pillar of Mr. Cresson's support—namely Richard Dykes Alexander" —was there with Clarkson. Since Elliot Cresson had convinced Alexander that the ACS was a noble organization, Alexander had in turn persuaded Clarkson to endorse it. Naturally Garrison had much to be concerned about, and he hoped Alexander would not prevent him from meeting with Clarkson. But Alexander had no intention of impeding Paul and Garrison from speaking with Clarkson, and "he offered to postpone another engagement, which he had made, and accompany us in his carriage," Garrison wrote. When Garrison and Paul finally met Clarkson, the sage took Garrison's hand, saying, "I cannot see your face—I have now wholly lost my sight—but . . . I believe I have lost it in a good cause." This impressed Garrison, and he recalled being silenced by the presence of one of the greatest advocates on behalf of the antislavery movement.

As the men discussed the colonization movement in America, Clarkson amazed Garrison with "a vividness of memory." According to Garrison's account of the meeting, Clarkson did not at first understand why the ACS had been deemed such a threat. Its colonizing mission, in Clarkson's opinion, was a useful enterprise for promoting emancipation among whites. Garrison "listened to him with becoming deference," but when the opportunity presented itself, he proceeded to explain to Clarkson that the ACS only served to impede the struggle for immediate abolition in which Garrison and Paul were engaged. Also, Garrison pointed out that "both in England and in the United States" the ACS had used Clarkson's reputation to bolster the colonization movement. Even though Clarkson claimed to be neutral, Garrison argued that "until he publicly requested to be considered neither approving or opposing the Society, he could not possible be neutral in this great controversy."[38]

Clarkson was still unconvinced by Garrison's assertions, so Nathaniel Paul took his turn. Paul explained why African Americans rejected the ACS, and according to Garrison, he claimed that blacks in America believed the ACS was "operating to their injury." Although Paul's words seemed to affect him, Clarkson maintained his neutral position, calling on Paul and Garrison to fight it out with Cresson and the ACS without his support. It wouldn't be until after 1833 that Clarkson would completely renounce the ACS, due in no small part to the pressure of abolitionists.[39]

According to historian Henry Mayer, Clarkson met later with Cresson and told him that he was unconvinced by Garrison and Paul's arguments against the ACS. However, in 1840 Clarkson wrote to Garrison and renounced his association with the ACS. In this letter Clarkson claimed, "You will see in this narrative my reasons for patronizing at first the American Colonization Society, and my reasons, also, for having afterwards deserted it." Like many others, Clarkson came to regard colonization as "impracticable" and newly emancipated blacks as unqualified to "civilize others who wanted civilizing themselves." Also, Clarkson explained that "two American gentlemen of the very highest moral repu-tation [told me] . . . that the cause of it was not a *religious feeling*, as I had been led to imagine, by which the planters had been convinced of the *sin of slavery*, but a base feeling of fear, which seemed to pervade all of them, and which urged them *to get rid of the free people of color* by sending them to Africa."[40]

When Garrison returned to the United States, he brought good news to abolitionists with regard to their anticolonization struggle. As abolitionist Samuel May explained in his memoir, "The success of Mr. Garrison's labors in England, in opening the eyes of the British philan-thropists to the egregious imposition which had been put upon them by the Colonization Society, the protest of the sainted Wilberforce and his most illustrious fellow-laborers, the stinging sarcasms of O'Connell, the champion of Ireland and of universal freedom, were working like moral blisters."[41] The news of Garrison's victory came in the form of a signed protest by prominent British abolitionists that claimed the following:

> Our objections to [colonization] are therefore briefly these—while we believe its pretexts to be delusive, we are convinced that its *real* effects are of the most dangerous nature. It takes its root from a cruel prejudice and alienation in the whites of America against the colored people, slave or free. This being its source, the effects are what might be expected; that it fosters and increases the spirit of caste, already so unhappily predominant; that it widens the breach between the two races; and finally, is calculated to swallow up and divert that feeling which America, as Christian and a free country, cannot but enter-tain, that slavery is alike incompatible with the law of God and with the well being of man, whether the enslaved or the enslaver.[42]

After the British Anti-Slavery Society published this "Protest," Cresson's British allies, such as the duke of Sussex, Lord Buxley, and the archbishop of Dublin, Richard Whately, acknowledged it as a devastating blow.[43] "Cresson burned with rage and frustration," historian Staudenraus explains, and "vented his anger in long, painful letters to Secretary Gur-ley . . . [blaming Gurley entirely for his humiliation before Garrison, for the secretary had neglected to send him the newest issues of the *African Repository*."[44] Perhaps Cresson's "rage and frustration" stemmed from the ambitious goals he had set for himself when leaving the United States for Britain. Even though Cresson established a British Colonization Society and raised £2,246 for the ACS while in Britain, he still failed to attract, and retain, the type of support he had hoped for.[45] Furthermore, when speaking with reformers who in some cases had played a role in establishing Sierra Leone, Cresson and other ACS agents were unable to convince them that the ACS was an authentic defender of freedom and a champion of liberty.[46]

Public humiliation aside, Cresson did score one key victory when Thomas Hodgkin, a British physician who had published several pamphlets between 1832 and 1833, defended colonization and supported Cresson's mission. Yet Hodgkin's views on colonization were more closely aligned with those of northern philanthropists than those of southern planters who supported colonization. Like Benjamin Lundy, Hodgkin championed gradual emancipation with expatriation because he believed this was the only realistic plan to end slavery in the United States. Moreover, Hodgkin argued that such a colonization plan needed to focus on enslaved African Americans rather than free blacks. He also repudiated forced expatriation, and he advised the ACS to renounce slavery publicly if it were ever to achieve any broad appeal in Great Britain. This, of course, had been rejected at the organization's inception, even if some whites in the organization agreed with Hodgkin's position.[47]

By 1834, the ACS was in financial trouble, and it appeared that Garrison's antislavery movement had undermined its ability to raise money among benevolent whites in the North. Meanwhile, Americo-Liberians suffered from crop failures, and the colony struggled to survive.[48] The ACS's internal division over its stance on emancipation, coupled with the popularity of immediatism, had frustrated northern colonizationists and increased tension within the organization. Some white northern colonizationists began to challenge ACS leaders who refused to support gradual emancipation outright.[49]

However, even as the American Colonization Society struggled to raise money, pro-colonization ideology flourished among working-class whites who unified with "gentlemen of property and standing" to destroy the abolition movement and to deny blacks access to schools or jobs. While many of the "toughs" who stood in the crowds at antiabolitionist rallies did not belong to any colonizationist auxiliary, they spewed pro-colonization rhetoric while hurling rocks.[50]

Few examples of the association between pro-colonization and anti-abolition mob action are more instructive than the incident that took place upon William Lloyd Garrison's return to New York from Great Britain. Apparently, Elliot Cresson and other colonizationists had written to the New York press that Garrison was slandering the United States during his trip overseas. Cresson and his colleagues spent weeks spreading these negative impressions, so that when Garrison returned he would be regarded as a traitor. The tactic worked. Garrison's meeting with Lewis and Arthur Tappan, two prominent New York antislavery advocates and businessmen, and with other New Yorkers was disrupted by reports of an antiabolitionist riot. As the mob approached, candles were dashed out and the meeting ended. The New York abolitionists quickly found another location, and, as Garrison stood unrecognized on the outskirts of a crowd, they met in a chapel on Chatham Street. Meanwhile, unable to accost the abolitionists at the original location and disrupt their meeting, leaders of the mob held a mock abolitionist meeting in which an effigy of Arthur Tappan was tossed around and resolutions were passed that reinforced their racist views of African Americans and their rejection of abolition.[51]

When Nathaniel Paul learned about the near riot over Garrison's arrival, he wrote a letter to Garrison expressing his condolences. In the letter, Paul shared with Garrison accounts of the threats he had endured in Europe, commenting that "I, too, may expect to be marked a victim of satanic fury on my return to my native country!!" However, he reassured Garrison that "to slander America, with regard to her treatment of her slaves and free colored people, would be tantamount to slandering his satanic majesty, by calling him wicked!" For Paul, those American antiabolitionist mobs had done more harm to the nation's image by "tarring and feathering abolitionists" than all the speeches and editorials Garrison had ever made. As he reflected on the deeds of the ACS and its proslavery supporters, Paul claimed that America would be able to "raise her flag of liberty, and spread it out unstained and uncontaminated, for the world to look upon and admire" —but only when she stopped persecuting her African children. Then, and only then, would the world cease looking upon the nation in a negative light.[52]

Even though colonizationists spread rumors about Garrison, they could not prevent other anticolonizationists from striving to destroy the colonization movement in Europe.[53] Robert Purvis, one of three African Americans to attend the first meeting of the American Anti-Slavery Society in Philadelphia, arrived in Britain in 1834 to continue where Nathaniel Paul and Garrison had left off. For Purvis, speaking out against the colonization society was nothing new. Just before his trip to Europe, Purvis lectured an audience at Bethel Church in Philadelphia, using "bold and impressive" language which, according to one observer, "was chaste and eloquent" in its condemnation of colonization. At the meeting, Purvis extolled those British abolitionists who rejected colonization, exclaiming that he was proud to hear that they were pre-pared to solicit "the liveliest sympathy for the oppressed, and to kindle a spirit of indignation towards the oppressors."[54] Purvis, an abolition-ist and faithful ally of Garrison, was light-skinned, and according to Samuel J. May, "He was so nearly white that he was generally taken to be so. . . . But, rather than forsake his kindred, or try to conceal the secret of his birth, he magnanimously chose to bear the unjust reproach, the cruel wrongs of the colored people. . . ." In Britain, when he was introduced to Daniel O'Connell, who was unaware that Purvis was an African Ameri-can, O'Connell at first "declined taking my hand; but when he under-stood that I was not only identified with the Abolitionists, but with the proscribed and oppressed colored class in the United States, he grasped my hand, and warmly shaking it, remarked—'Sir, I will never take the hand of an American, nor should any honest man in this country do so, without first knowing his principles in reference to American Slavery, and its ally, the American Colonization Society.'"[55] As he had previously called the American Colonization Society's plan "a wretched delusion," O'Connell's opinion would have assured Purvis that he had a core of dedicated allies in Britain.

Even as the anticolonization adventures abroad demonstrated that American abolitionists, black and white, were unified by the threat of the American Colonization Society, events at home began to splinter the American Anti-Slavery Society, and African American leaders found themselves in the middle. While Garrison's domineering personality posed one set of problems, three specific issues threatened to tear the abolitionist movement apart. First, Garrison's stance in favor of female participation at the convention caused some abolitionists tremendous frustration. Second, his anticlerical position and the harshness with which he railed against organized religion alienated others. Finally, Lib-erty Party advocates found themselves at odds with Garrisonians over the use of mainstream politics to challenge slavery. Despite the inter-necine battle, African Americans remained loyal to Garrison, even if they did not embrace all of his views. Most African Americans found the issue of women's role in the movement to be secondary to the destruc-tion of slavery.[56]

As the abolition movement splintered after 1840, the ACS continued to seek support in Europe. Former ACS secretary Ralph Gurley set sail for England with the financial backing of the New York Colonization Soci-ety in one more effort to win support for the colonization cause. Gurley remained focused on the goal of unifying British colonizationists with members of the African Civilization Society, a British-based organization that appeared to support the ACS plan. Soon after arriving, Gurley set to the task of persuading Sir Thomas Fowell Buxton, the author of two new works, *The African Slave Trade* and *The Remedy*, to speak out in favor of the American Colonization Society. Having previously met with Elliot Cresson, Gurley believed that Buxton's books had expressed "the principles and policy which had for twenty years been adopted and pursued by the American Colonization Society."[57] Furthermore, Buxton had a "distinguished reputation" as an author. He was an "intimate associate of Wilberforce in the war upon the slave trade" because of the books he had written condemning the African slave trade and suggesting the creation of communities of distinguished West Africans capable of teaching advanced methods of agriculture and spreading the Christian Gospel.[58]

Through the guidance of the African Civilization Society, Buxton hoped the British Parliament would seek to gain treaties from African leaders permitting the British to hold exclusive trading rights along the West African coastline. He called upon British officials to send teachers into the hinterlands to instruct Africans about new methods of agriculture and the production of goods that could be shipped to Europe for sale. Gurley believed that Buxton's plan coincided with the goals of the American Colonization Society, and he hoped it would revive the ACS among Britons and Americans interested in forming independent colonies with the support of ACS auxiliaries. Considering the desperate state of affairs among the board of directors of the American Colonization Society, as well as Gurley's waning influence in the organization, it should not be surprising that Gurley would jump at the opportunity to rush off to Europe to link Buxton's African Civilization Society with the ACS's mission.

Arriving in England on June 28, 1840, Gurley learned from Dr. Thomas Hodgkin that Buxton was "absent, for two or three days," but one of Gurley's allies informed him that the American abolitionists had garnered support from British antislavery leaders during the World Convention, and that certain leaders, such as Henry Stanton and James Birney, "took occasion, not only to cast reproach upon their own country, but also to attack with vehemence the American Colonization Society." Certainly, Gurley believed his presence in Europe was crucial to changing such negative sentiment, and his meeting with members of the African Civilization Society appeared ever so pressing. But Buxton was not interested in sitting down with Gurley, and it took tremendous persistence for Gurley to attain a meeting with him at last.

Although it appeared likely that Buxton had read the negative press about the American Colonization Society, Gurley hoped he could change this perspective. Nearly two weeks after he arrived in Britain, he traveled to Upton to meet Buxton as a guest of Samuel Gurney, a banker and Quaker who was an associate of Hodgkin. When Gurley finally met Buxton during a dinner party, he was "in the company of Dr. Hodgkin, Capt. Trotter and several other gentlemen." As the men sat about, Gurley fielded questions in regards to the condition of Liberia. Yet, as Gurley recalled, "much of the time was occupied in conversation relating to the purposes and plans of the African Civilization Society." Although Buxton "read my letter from Mr. Clay, apparently with deep interest," the conversation began with Buxton stating "at the outset [that] he was an Abolitionist, and had regarded the society as operating injuriously in the United States." However, Gurley pushed Buxton to read the actual statements and publications of the ACS. This, Gurley thought, would change Buxton's views, which "had obviously been derived from the statements of its enemies." When the evening came to a close, Gurley was able to secure a specific time to meet with Buxton alone the next day to discuss the ACS further, as well as the future of the African Civilization Society.[59]

When Gurley met for a second time with Buxton, he attempted "earnestly to correct his errors, and remove his prejudices" to win Buxton over to the colonizationist cause. Gurley questioned Buxton about the goals of the African Civilization Society as well as the degree to which the British government had stood behind the organization. Buxton seemed adamant that "the Government should guard the benevolent industry and enterprise of such association as might apply their exertions to the suppression of the slave trade," yet he had not ascertained exactly how that should take place. Furthermore, Buxton argued that "public opinion of this country would demand such an expenditure and such efforts" if the African Civilization Society presented its plan candidly, in association with the spread of Christianity and the end of the foul practice of "trading in men."

Gurley was most certainly impressed, and he remarked that "the friends of African colonization in the United States regarded the main features of his plan, as exhibited in his work, as identical with the scheme and uniform policy . . . [of] the American Colonization Society." He explained to Buxton the various ways in which both societies could work harmoniously to accomplish the settlement of African Americans on the coast of Africa in order to spread Christianity and work toward demolishing the slave trade. While Buxton claimed that he was not able to speak in behalf of the African Civilization Society or the British government, he offered Gurley the "opportunity of presenting the subject to their consideration."[60]

By the end of August, the African Civilization Society still had not made any firm commitment to work in tandem with the ACS. As Gurley explained, "their Chairman was authorized to seek an early opportunity for further conference, and especially to impart whatever knowledge he might possess of the views and policy of the English Civilization Society," but the organization would not come out in favor of the ACS.[61] Gurley persisted, and finally, on December 3, he was granted an interview with the general committee of the African Civilization Society. Buxton chaired the meeting, and he was joined by a Dr. Lushington, Sir Robert Ingis, William Allen, Dr. Hodgkin, and "others of honorable fame in the cause of humanity." When the meeting began, Gurley recalled, "I stated, concisely, the object of my visit to London; spoke of the attachment felt by thousands in the United States to the scheme of their association; of the interest awakened by the able work on the slave trade, and its remedy; of the origins, principles and success of the American Colonization Society . . . and, finally, submitted a definite proposition for the extension, prospectively, of the Liberian territory as far south and east as the river Assinee, or even to Axim."

The men listened respectfully to Gurley, yet he later admitted that their attentiveness seemed like a matter of courtesy rather than a sign of any sincere interest in the ACS program. Gurley struggled to bring the majority of the members around and achieve the goal he came to England to accomplish. Yet he maintained his optimism, writing to the directors of the ACS: "I am convinced that a gradual but great change is taking place among the members of the Civilization Society in our favor." However, American abolitionists' negative opinions clearly held sway over the majority of members, causing them to shy away from Gurley's proposition in order "to retain the confidence and support of the Abolitionists." At the conclusion of the meeting, the African Civilization Society committee passed a resolution stating, according to Gurley, "that they trusted cordial feelings of regard would be cherished between the friends of Africa in both countries."[62]

Regardless of how African Civilization Society leaders may have felt about the ACS, Gurley knew Buxton was the key to uniting the two organizations. Thus, Gurley continued pushing Buxton in several letters that he mailed to him in a final attempt to win him over. As Gurley recalled, "Before I left London, I had addressed a letter to Sir T.F. Buxton, yet, until some weeks after my return, late in September, received no reply."

In fact, Buxton did not write back to Gurley until October 9, 1840.[63] Buxton had read the literature of the American Colonization Society and pondered the benefits of associating with such a controversial American organization. After nearly two months, he finally wrote a letter to Gurley, which was published in the *London Patriot*. In it, Buxton explained, "It is with real reluctance that I address you upon the subject of those plans for the African race which you so ably and . . . so zealously advocate, but on which I find myself compelled to differ from you." He thanked Gurley for "the very friendly mention, which you have made of me personally," and acknowledged Gurley's sincere interest in his "desires of the good of Africa." However, Buxton reminded Gurley that "I joined with some of the most tried and experienced English Abolitionists in expressing my dissent" towards the American Colonization Society, and would not renounce his previous position. Also, he called the conflation of the British African Civilization Society with the American Colonization Society "a serious mistake," arguing that "our object is to civilize, not to colonize" West Africa as a means of teaching "natives their use and value." In addition, Buxton confirmed that "it is no part of my plan to extend the British Empire, or to encourage emigration to Africa," and thus, "our professed objects, therefore, though akin, are not the same."[64]

Buxton's biggest point of disagreement came when he challenged Gurley and those who supported gradual emancipation and colonization to look at the West Indies for an example of the potential for civil rule and order after emancipation. Buxton sought to illustrate that the ACS's call for colonization after emancipation remained entirely unrealistic because the United States was no closer to ending slavery than when the ACS first started its operation. Buxton argued:

> You have repeatedly acknowledged that you are adverse to immediate abolition, only because you fear it would be a source of anarchy, and would entail misery on the negro himself, not because it might, for a time, involve a pecuniary loss to the master. Let me then entreat you to look at the actual condition of our West India Islands; there you will find the utmost social order and political tranquility, and a peasantry as peaceable, and, probably, as moral as any in the world.[65]

Buxton's opinion about immediate abolition and his devotion to "civilize, not to colonize," won the approval of African American leaders like Charles Ray, the editor of the *Colored American*. Ray printed Buxton's letter in his newspaper to warn black Americans of the vitality of the ACS in Europe, claiming that "the colonizationists of this country have claimed Mr. Buxton as favoring, yea more, as having fallen in with their ill-adapted and wicked scheme." Yet, in Ray's estimation, "It has been in vain" because Buxton's letter explained that he still maintained the views he held since signing the well-known "Protest" issued by leading British abolitionists back in the early 1830s.[66]

Although Ralph Gurley had arrived in London just after the World Anti-Slavery Convention concluded, many notable American abolitionists, such as Charles Lenox Remond, remained in Europe. Upon Gurley's arrival, both the Tappan and Garrison factions united to oppose him and those who supported colonization.[67] In this sense, colonization benefited the American abolitionist movement by providing an issue that abolitionists in both camps could agree on. Regardless of where they stood in relation to "the woman question," political agitation, or black Americans' role within the movement, the American and Foreign Anti-Slavery Society and the American Anti-Slavery Society were one in finding colonization to be antithetical to their quest for immediate abolition and universal emancipation without compensation to slaveholders.[68]

Ralph Gurley's troubles in England seemed only to get worse. While he struggled to gain support from the African Civilization Society, the ACS Executive Committee decided to shift gears, and refused to continue to fund his trip. In the fall of 1840, they drew up a resolution asserting that "the Executive Committee do not feel authorized, or deem it expedient, to enter into any of the arrangements with the British African Civilization Society." Furthermore, the executive committee claimed that its members did "not feel themselves authorized to extend the term of his absence furnished by the Board of Directors." However, the Board did suggest, with an air of doubt, that if his mission was going so well, Gurley should have no problem raising money for his stay through the connections he made while on tour.[69]

Although the resolution passed unanimously, "a personal friend" of Gurley's, who also served on this committee, slipped a letter in with the resolution mailed to Gurley, which he hoped could soften the blow. "We do not doubt that you have already done much to help us," he reminded Gurley, but "you also know how much some of them were opposed to your mission." It appears that those members who had frowned on Gurley's trip had secured broad enough support among the committee to put an end to his mission. According to Gurley's friend, this group of antagonists balked at "the suggestion, in one of your late letters, of an extension of your visit to London," and they spread general resentment about Gurley's propositions to the British African Civilization Society. Moreover, as his friend explained, "Several of those propositions were deemed very inexpedient," and some directors had actually believed Gurley sought to defect to the African Civilization Society. Gurley's friend confided, "They seem to have no confidence in your success there, nor, indeed, in your negotiations either, for they apprehend mischief if you do any thing. . . . [I]t is alleged that you are seeking for yourself an appointment under Mr. Buxton; and it is assumed, which I cannot believe without evidence, that after a life devoted to our service, you are about to identify yourself with the British interest, and sacrifice us and our noble enterprise in America!!!"[70]

Gurley was devastated, yet he maintained his composure when he responded to the executive committee's directive, writing that he had "the honor to acknowledge the receipt of your recent resolution . . . [and] I can feel no desire that they should assume responsibilities, except when they judge it expedient for the interests of the institution." Then he set about the task of persuading the committee that he was engaged in "no enviable task" trying to overturn the misrepresentations and slanders that had maligned the ACS in the British public mind. Gurley claimed, "I should immediately return to the United States, did I not feel bound by regard to the interests of the cause of African colonization, to remain for a few weeks longer."

In four clear, concise sentences, he outlined his reasons for remaining in Europe. First, he argued that he had not yet been able "to secure an interview with the general committee of the African Civilization Society." Gurley explained to them that Buxton had recently replied to his letter in a manner that called for a public response. Furthermore, at a meeting of "learned and scientific men at Glasgow," he had successfully changed the minds of individuals who had previously viewed the ACS with contempt. This victory encouraged Gurley that, through his influence, more could be converted to colonization. Finally, Gurley explained to the committee that he had not yet reorganized the British Colonization Society to continue promoting the cause once he had gone. Nevertheless, as the weeks passed Gurley received no reply from the committee.

Gurley's presence in England continued to disturb abolitionists, even if he had little support back in the states. Black abolitionist Charles Lenox Remond claimed that he had been "put not a little upon nettles" by Gurley's effort to rebuild the British Colonization Society. Remond had been the single African American selected as one of four American Anti-Slavery Society delegates to attend the World Anti-Slavery Convention in 1840.[71] A well-known black American leader, Remond had distinguished himself through his oratorical skill, which earned him a position as a lecturer for the Massachusetts Anti-Slavery Society in the late 1830s. According to Lois and James Horton, "[Remond] was so popular as an antislavery speaker that when a group of whites in Lynn, Massachusetts, refused to allow him to address the Lyceum, "a majority united in the formation of another institution . . . in order that they might hear his speech."[72] Remond joined William Lloyd Garrison's protest over the World Anti-Slavery Convention's decision to refuse to seat their female colleague, Lucretia Mott, and he remained active in England after the convention ended, speaking against slavery and colonization.[73] Unaware of the tension between Gurley and the executive committee, Remond followed Gurley's trail through Britain to undermine him and destroy his influence among British philanthropists and abolitionists.

In a letter to Garrison, Remond explained that he planned on "exerting to the best of [his] abilities to counteracting such influence as the accredited Secretary of the American negro-haters' scheme of cruelty and extirpation may exert in its favor."[74] He also described Gurley's attempt to win support in Glasgow as a "total failure." Aware of Nathaniel Paul's success nearly six years earlier, Remond believed that the very sight of an African American rejecting colonization, and speaking in behalf of the vast majority of free black Americans in the North, would be effective at undermining Gurley's efforts. He asserted that "there is little doubt of success in thwarting him," and Remond seemed confident that the ACS's "high-handed injustice done to the colored population" would soon be known in Britain.[75]

At home, Garrison alerted readers of the *Liberator* that "this arch enemy of the colored race," Ralph R. Gurley, had landed in Europe on the "very day that we left England." It appeared to Garrison, however, that Gurley had failed to make inroads among reformers outside of London; Garrison had learned that "Mr. Gurley seems to meet with a cold reception in Scotland, and we are quite sure that he will succeed no better in England." Garrison felt confident about Remond's abilities, commenting to his readers, "We leave Mr. G in the hands of our friends [George] Thompson and Remond."[76]

In January 1841, Remond jumped at the chance to confront Gurley in front of a crowd of London's most respected reformers, and "hope[d] to be there" to drive him back "to the land of slavery and prejudice."[77] After only thirty minutes, Remond explained to the audience that he "wished to be in London" to confront Gurley, and rushed out of the chapel and into a "horse and gig" to make it to the train depot by 8:00 pm. After traveling day and night, Remond arrived at the station in London only to learn that "Gurley had left town that day for the Isle of Wight." Having lectured for twenty-three evenings out of thirty, Remond returned to Newcastle-on-Tyne to regroup, frustrated and exhausted.[78]

While Garrison kept his readers privy to the events unfolding in Europe concerning Remond and Gurley, Charles Ray's newspaper the *Colored American* published Remond's description of the racial prejudice he endured as he sailed from the United States to Britain. Apparently, a white friend had purchased Remond's ticket for passage to Europe without informing the agent of Remond's race. When Remond stepped on the ship, the crew was shocked to discover that Remond held a ticket permitting him to travel on par with white passengers. They found this unacceptable and rushed to prepare sleeping quarters belowdecks, near the gangway, compelling Remond to endure whatever weather conditions befell the ship. This account reinforced to black readers the reality of racial prejudice in America, with all its "professions of religion and republicanism." When Remond and his traveling companion, Nathaniel P. Rogers, spoke before British audiences, they cited such experiences to highlight the inhumane way whites treated blacks in the United States. Rogers remarked sarcastically:

> Look at him now. There he is on a platform at Exeter Hall, cheered by 5,000 people. What gentleman is that who takes him by the hand? That is Sir Thomas Fowell Buxton: Look at him in conversation with the lady up in yonder gallery. That lady is the widow of Lord Byron. What will Americans say to that? . . . We all dined with her, at the table of a great lady there, with several other ladies, and when they went from thence to the meeting of that evening, Remond was invited to go in the carriage with them, and we had to follow after on foot.[79]

In the eyes of pro-colonizationists, Rogers had alluded to a level of intimacy that most white Americans found unacceptable. Indeed, some colonizationists believed this was the exact reason free blacks threatened the "social order" and "well-being," and therefore ought to be deported to Liberia. Thus, anticolonizationists like Rogers and Remond played on these notions when challenging American social norms by placing them in contrast to those of British reformers "sympathetic to the cause of racial equality."[80]

When Remond finally left Europe, he must have been satisfied by what he had accomplished. Gurley had failed to win the support of Thomas F.

Buxton; most British reformers remained opposed to the American Colonization Society; and Remond had made important allies, such as John Scoble, secretary of the British and Foreign Anti-Slavery Society. Like Elliott Cresson in the early 1830s, Gurley could not overcome opposition from abolitionists, especially African Americans such as Nathaniel Paul and Charles Lenox Remond. Furthermore, Cresson and Gurley had lost support from the national office and, faced with the activities of British and American abolitionists, they failed to defend the ACS from critics charging them with proslavery sympathies and a lack of black support. As Richard Blackett notes, "Paul and Remond were instrumental in this victory over colonization," a "victory" that took place as the ACS struggled for its existence amidst the great structural and ideological changes it endured in no small part due to the work of black and white abolitionists. By the beginning of the 1840s, "Black Americans took great pride in their contributions to the international effort against colonization."[81]

This pride would wane as colonizationists returned to Britain nearly ten years later to pick up where Gurley had left off. After two unsuccessful campaigns to win British support for the ACS, one might expect that the Colonization Society would relent, but in the spring of 1849, Alexander Crummell, a renowned black abolitionist, alerted black American leaders that yet another American Colonization Society agent had been working covertly to further its interests in England. The Rev. John Miller had evidently been sent to England to revive the interest in colonization by highlighting to British reformers the new relationship between the ACS and the independent nation of Liberia. Aware of Miller's work, Crummell made a point throughout his tour of denouncing, from pulpit to parlor, the American Colonization Society and its agent.

In the United States, African American leaders applauded Crummell's effort to discredit the ACS. Frederick Douglass, speaking to an audience at an anticolonization meeting in New York, remarked: "I am equally thankful that one Alexander Crummell, whom you all know, is on the ground at this moment doing battle against the equally subtle foe." Douglass reminded his audience of the alliance between British reformers and black American abolitionists, who had throughout the years repelled the ideology of the American Colonization Society. But just as the previous decade's anticolonization agitation faded from the minds of the British public, the Colonization Society began a new campaign to garner support from a younger generation of British social reformers. As Douglass explained:

Scarcely have the graves of the philanthropic Wilberforce and illustrious O'Connell become green, ere this same saucy, impudent
Colonization Society appears again on the shores of old England
to deceive the public and mislead them . . . [but] it cannot succeed.
Crummell is there. The spirit that warmed the bosom of Clarkson
and Wilberforce and O'Connell is there. Thompson and Surge are
there. They will meet this man, disrobe him of his mask, and send
him home. . . .[82]

The next day Douglass published an editorial restating his admiration
for Crummell's effort to discredit Miller, who, according to Douglass,
had been "misrepresenting the views and feelings of the colored people
in this country" while meeting with various individuals in England to
"organise societies in that country auxiliary to the American Colonization Society." Douglass claimed that after Liberian president Joseph Jenkins Roberts received support in Britain, the ACS dispatched Miller to
ride on his coattails. When Miller arrived, he began in earnest to recruit
sympathizers, and he seemed to have "made a decided impression" on
British philanthropists by propagating the notion that "colored people in
[America] are generally turning their attention to Liberia as their future
home." This, Douglass assured his readers, may have succeeded had it
not been for Alexander Crummell, "to whom the colored citizens of New
York are indebted" for being such an "able and faithful" representative.
However, by 1851, Douglass had become impatient with Crummell's
extended stay in England. In an editorial on July 31 entitled "Colored
Americans, Come Home!" Douglass cried out, "We have felt in common,
with every other well-wisher of the colored people of this country, highly
gratified with accounts of the cordial reception and welcome everywhere
extended to our distinguished co-workers who are now abroad. . . . But
we begin to want them home. . . . We need them to inspire hope and
save our afflicted people from desperation. . . . Come home and stand
between our people and the hateful scheme of Colonization."[83]

The ACS agent, however, was not totally stifled by Crummell's campaign to discredit him. Miller had gained enough recognition to earn a
hearing in early 1850 before a parliamentary select committee investigat-
ing the slave trade. In February the *Liberator* published the questions
and answers from the parliamentary session for African Americans at
home to learn of the "perfidious" ways of Miller, as well as his moderate
success. The committee questioned Miller's motives for traveling in England, wondering if he had "been sent to England by Mr. Clay, or by the

American Colonization Society?" To this question, Miller responded, "I have not a very formal official connection with the Society." Yet, as a "traveler" who was sympathetic to their cause, he agreed to do what he could to further the Colonization Society's agenda. "I promised, on leaving America," Miller explained, "that I would give information, whenever I thought it valuable," about Liberia and the ACS. With the confidence of "Mr. Clay," Miller was granted "informal authority from the Colonization Society," and he claimed to have a letter "in my pocket" to attest to Clay's endorsement.[84]

Garrison was livid. In an editorial, he snapped, "The answer of this Miller is as wary and tortuous as the scheme which he presents is hypocritical and unchristian." Never one to mince words, Garrison railed against Miller's apparent deception, charging him with "absurd, contradictory, and blasphemous sentiments" that required little effort to refute; one need merely read the annual reports of the ACS to uncover the true intent: "a desire to give greater security to the slave system, by the removal of the entire free colored population across the Atlantic." Rather than spread benevolence and Christianity in Africa, Garrison explained to his readers, the ACS's "scheme of expatriation" was in his view "only a pretence 'to sugar o'er the devil'" and could never lead to "the improvement of that population, or the civilization of Africa."[85]

Garrison presented several of the questions that the committee had asked Miller, such as, "Is the prejudice against the colonization decreasing among free blacks?" Miller affirmed: "Decidedly(!)—they have sent over, in many instances . . . agents to examine Liberia, who have returned with favorable reports, which have led to a number of free colored people paying their own passage over." Again, Garrison refuted Miller's response, writing, "The real truth is, that our free colored population were never more hostile to the colonization scheme than they are at the present time."[86]

Unfortunately for Garrison and African American anticolonizationists, though, white Americans seemed as supportive of colonization as ever. Not only had annual revenues of the ACS increased between 1849 and 1851, but with the passage of the Fugitive Slave Law, blacks who had fled north from slavery were now contemplating emigration to Liberia, due to their fear of being captured by slave catchers unleashed in the North. Furthermore, western states such as Indiana asserted the benefits of colonization as a means to promote abolition, destroy the slave trade, and maintain racial purity. According to a joint resolution in the Indiana legislature signed by George Carr, Speaker of the House of

Representatives, and James H. Lane, president of the Senate, "in the name of the state of Indiana . . . [we] call for a change of national policy on the subject of 'the African Slave Trade,' and that they required a settlement of the Coast of Africa with colored men from the United States."[87]

By the end of August, the Committee of the Navy in the House of Representatives recommended "a line of mail steamships to the Western Coast of Africa, having as its principal object the removal of free persons of color from this country, and their colonization in Africa, and the more effectual suppression of the slave trade." The committee submitted letters from various governors as supporting documentation, including one from Governor Joseph A. Wright of Indiana, and "the opinions of Chief Justice Marshal, Thomas Jefferson, and other great jurists, upon the constitutionality of the General Government undertaking the measure."[88] Further, in January 1851 Senator Henry Clay, president of the American Colonization Society, stood before the Senate to present a petition calling for the government to endorse colonization as a means to prevent the slave trade. This move on Clay's part illustrated the vigor of the ACS as the 1850s began.[89]

While African Americans convinced many influential reformers and philanthropists in Britain that the American Colonization Society worked neither in their interest nor in the interest of spreading Christianity in Africa, the ACS continued to push their agenda abroad. Although free black spokesmen in the North continued to attack colonizationists in writing, the rise of a black-led emigration movement in the 1850s created much confusion. Black leaders began to rethink their positions on West African emigration and on the creation of a black state in Latin America, the Caribbean, or Canada. Indeed, the 1850s was a decade of rivalry, fragmentation, and frustration among free black leaders in the North, with new challenges, such as the U.S. Supreme Court's Dred Scott decision, that compelled some of them to reconsider their allegiance to the United States.

Anticolonizationist agitation in Britain during the 1830s and 1840s had three important consequences. First, it demonstrated the marked role played by black abolitionists in the movement to end slavery in the United States. While itinerant abolitionist lecturers faced significant hazards in the Northeast and Midwest, the warm reception they received in Britain offered them tremendous hope as they struggled against colonization and for racial equality in America. The British campaign against slavery also demonstrated that black Americans were perhaps best suited to taking the message of abolition and anticolonization to

an international public. That was certainly the case with their anticolonization campaign. Despite ACS agents' best efforts to convince British
reformers of their noble intentions, black American anticolonization
activism completely undermined these attempts.

Moreover, the behavior and public performance of free black Americans reinforced the humanistic notion that underpinned emancipation
in the British Caribbean during the 1830s. Now these free black activists
found that their own efforts fit within a comprehensive humanist vision
that challenged American racist ideology. The assumption that black
people were best suited for slavery had been overturned in England by
the end of the 1840s. Emancipation had worked quite well, according to
British reformers, and colonizationists needed to spend less time con-
cocting ways to drive free blacks to Liberia and more time focusing on
the campaign to end slavery. For it was the emancipation of millions of
African Americans enslaved in the South that deserved their resources
and energy rather than grand plans of settling hundreds of thousands of
free blacks in Africa, which seemed more and more preposterous.

Finally, African Americans who traveled to Britain were afforded a
respite from the dangerous work of agitation in America, and they had a
much greater opportunity for raising funds with which they could continue the work of ending slavery and destroying colonization domesti-
cally. One such individual, Henry Highland Garnet, spoke in glowing
terms about traveling on the abolition lecture circuit in Britain, where
he was free of the types of racial insults that he had to endure while
advocating for the cause in the United States. With financial resources
and a sense of support beyond what white American allies offered them,
black Americans returning from Britain felt that they were in a stronger
position to confront slavery and colonization in the North.

Despite these achievements, though, the struggle against colonization
would not be won abroad. In fact, the American Colonization Society
had engaged in a battle on two fronts. Rather than wait around for funding and support from a British public that seemed all too interested in
applauding the efforts of a few black and white radicals, beginning in the
early 1840s ACS agents worked all the harder to spread their message
into the territories of the Midwest and West. ACS agents took up the task
of convincing residents of midwestern states such as Ohio, Indiana, Illinois, and Michigan to consider the tremendous consequences of southern emancipation on their own communities. Would white residents of
Indiana, for example, want newly emancipated slaves to flood their communities, essentially allowing southern slaveholders to pass the burden

of taking care of freedmen and freedwomen onto them? Playing on white fears and anxieties over a potential black presence in the wake of emancipation, the American Colonization Society proved that it still had some fight in it. Thus, an organization that had withstood constant attack from abolitionists during the 1830s now set its sights on the western frontier in an effort to rekindle the colonizationist fire in the breasts of whites who simply could not imagine black citizenship in the United States.

4 / Resurrecting the "Iniquitous Scheme": The Rebirth of the Colonization Movement in America, 1840–1854

In May 1847, the Reverend Heman Humphrey, a former president of Amherst College, traveled to a meeting of the Massachusetts Colonization Society in Boston to reignite the colonization cause in the Bay State. After members listened to a report discussing a "most interesting and encouraging picture of Liberia," Humphrey took the floor, explaining that, since the founding of Liberia, "the slave trade had been abolished over 400 miles of coast; and all the neighboring tribes had been greatly benefited."[1] His closing comment that "no benevolent Society had done so much in the same time: and with the same means, as had the Colonization Society," likely provoked the Garrisonians in the audience.[2]

Nearly a month later Humphrey was still making his rounds in Massachusetts, speaking for the cause of colonization at churches and various social engagements. This pro-colonization advocacy prompted free blacks to meet at the Belknap Street Church in Boston to discuss Humphrey's presence and the progress of the American Colonization Society. According to the resolutions drafted during that meeting, the American Colonization Society remained "an apologist for slavery . . . the enemy of immediate emancipation . . . [and] in direct opposition to our best hopes, prospects, and rights, and at variance with the dictates of Christianity and Republicanism." Those gathered acknowledged an "apparent resurrection of this iniquitous scheme, called African Colonization," and vowed to continue to protest against it whenever and wherever it attempted to convince blacks to leave America for Liberia. "We are

Americans by birth," the group declared, and "we do now, *as we have done ever since its origin*, protest against the operations of the American Colonization Society, and its various auxiliaries."[3]

African Americans' protest notwithstanding, white Bay Staters listened to Dr. Humphrey "with interest and good feelings," becoming increasingly confident that the cause of colonization would redeem "an oppressed race," many of whom, they surmised, would soon leave for Liberia if given the opportunity. According to members of the Massachusetts Colonization Society, "It appears that the wills of masters who liberate their slaves, are often contested by heirs at law," and this interfered with the Society's ability to fulfill its mission.[4] Yet even with "some discouragements which the cause had been compelled to suffer," events earlier that year, such as Liberian independence, left members optimistic that "the cause of colonization [was] advancing."[5]

Humphrey's successes compelled William Lloyd Garrison to go down to the Old South Church and listen to Humphrey speak. After the gathering, Garrison raced home to pen a letter to "the Rev. Heman Humphrey, D. D., Agent of the Colonization Society," admonishing Humphrey that "I give you all your clerical, divine, and official titles, though I have no respect for them whatever; and, what I regret to be compelled to add, none for you personally." Garrison went on to explain that "you are too late to be formidable," and "within the last fifteen years, one of the revolutions which never go backward has taken place—a revolution in public sentiment at the North, which has almost obliterated from the memory of the people, even the existence of the American Colonization Society."[6]

In the letter Garrison recounted the numerous reasons he believed colonization would never succeed, reminding Humphrey of his *Thoughts on African Colonization*, which, according to Garrison, "almost immediately arrested the popularity of the scheme" when it was published in 1832. But Garrison did point out that Humphrey's mission to Massachusetts did have one benefit: "it shows who are the real friends of the colored population . . . and who are the persecutors and despisers of that population." Any friend of the ACS was an enemy of blacks, Garrison argued, regardless if such men had benevolent intentions, because colonization "vilifies and persecutes the free people of color, and prevents as far as possible their moral and social elevation in the United States." For this reason Garrison concluded, "I feel no personal respect for you."[7]

If Garrison had as much power to change public opinion as he had at demolishing opponents through rhetoric, then the Colonization Society would have had much to fear. But the ACS increased in popularity during the late 1840s, having overcome financial ruin and black rebuke. By the early 1850s the ACS had risen to an apogee unprecedented in the organization's history. In 1849, the question of colonization would be discussed in Congress, in churches, and among state governors throughout the nation at political gatherings—Democrat, Free Soil, and Republican. When Frederick Douglass's *North Star* announced that "over forty churches in this vicinity have pledged themselves to take collections for the Colonization Society," anticolonizationists, led by Douglass, had to accept that the heightening anxiety over slavery, national destiny, and "free soil" ideology had truly exhumed colonization from its grave, and its spirit had gained strength.[8] And, as the war with Mexico for the West came to a close, Americans pondered the circumstances by which new states would join the nation. Immediately, whites in Indiana, Illinois, and California began legislating to preserve these new states for whites only. State officials attempted to ensure racial stratification in hamlets, towns, and cities where blacks had tremendous potential for self-determination and advancement. Ultimately, westward expansion under the banner of "Manifest Destiny" breathed new life into the Colonization Society.

News of the growing pro-colonization tide in the Old Northwest made its way back to New York. Blacks led by abolitionist Jermain Wesley Loguen helped organize a mass meeting to discuss the so-called Black Laws geared toward "the expulsion of colored citizens from Delaware, Indiana, and Iowa, and more recently from Illinois," which they attributed to colonizationist ideology. Several resolutions were passed, expressing "that we regard the revival of colonization societies in various sections of the Union [with] . . . the most intense hatred of the colored race." One of the main reasons for their fervent opposition to colonization came from the impression that it was "clad in the garb of pretended philanthropy." Furthermore, the "formation of a colonization society" in Onondaga County had caused some African American leaders to remind those in attendance "that, even in view of this sad event, we have reason to congratulate ourselves on the fact, that the great majority of its members are of a character so generally and definitely known as to raise doubts with reference to the real benevolence of an association thus considered."[9]

Between Liberian Independence in 1847 and the first National Emigration Convention in 1854, Frederick Douglass and other black abolitionists were compelled to admit that colonization was most certainly not a "nullity."[10] The evidence was irrefutable. For starters, by 1851 the ACS claimed nearly $100,000 as the annual receipts for the year, which surpassed any amount ever raised over the course of a year in the organization's history.[11] Second, the number of blacks who left for Liberia increased after 1847. While the organization only sent 51 African Americans from the United States to the independent Republic of Liberia in that year, which amounted to the second-lowest total in the organization's history, in 1848 it sent 441 blacks to Liberia. And the number of emigrants would climb over the next decade. Specifically, between 1848 and 1854 the American Colonization Society sent 4,010 African Americans to Liberia after having sent a total of 5,829 during its first thirty years of existence.[12] For an organization that William Lloyd Garrison had called a "dead horse," the American Colonization Society apparently was neither dead nor lacking in vitality by the 1850s.

As Liberian political leaders prepared their Declaration of Independence in November 1847, the ACS issued an "Urgent Appeal" to its auxiliaries, stating, "To meet these and other foreseen demands, the society urgently needs to receive about twelve thousand dollars by the end of this year."[13] While on the surface such an appeal would appear to indicate dwindling interest in the organization, in reality this "urgent" need for more revenue was due to an upsurge in African American interest in leaving for Liberia. Two months later, at the annual meeting in Washington, D.C., in January 1848, the Society proclaimed that it had raised nearly $50,000 for the coming year, which was nearly $11,000 more than the year before. However, more interest in leaving among free blacks meant greater costs, and even with the $10,000 increase, the Colonization Society had to borrow from creditors to meet this financial strain, even while struggling to maintain its legitimacy in the eyes of those waiting for passage to Liberia.[14]

A year later, in November 1848, a second appeal went out by the ACS, due to what its leaders called the "peculiar condition in which we find ourselves now placed." According to one article, the ACS was $9,500 in debt as a result of sending nearly 443 African Americans to Liberia when they had only budgeted for 310. In addition, 95 eager blacks in Baltimore, and 472 more in New Orleans, still waited for passage to Liberia. After ten months, the ACS had only raised just over $30,000, which meant they were in need of $20,000 of the $50,500 it would cost to send blacks from Baltimore and New Orleans to their "motherland." "Here is a field of the exercise of benevolence and philanthropy upon the largest scale," the article explained, especially since 415 of those in need of passage were slaves who would be emancipated under the condition that the Colonization Society would send them to Liberia.[15]

This revived interest in Liberia and colonization was an encouraging sign for members of the American Colonization Society, even if some abolitionists—black and white alike—denied the organization's progress. Not all abolitionists remained silent about the growing interest in ACS, however. Some, such as British-born abolitionists, and George Thompson, an old foe of colonization, warned those attendees at an antislavery convention in Rochester that "the scheme of colonization had been recently revived, and is designed to be carried out by State law."[16] Henry Clay's speech during the ACS's thirty-fourth annual meeting affirmed this upsurge in support, and Thompson argued that Clay's views reflected the "opinions of the mass of [white] people" in the nation. Support for colonization was not merely rhetorical, Thompson explained, citing the "one million of dollars [that] had been lately bequeathed to the society by a rich planter in Louisiana," and the "large steamers" that were "being built" to cart off free blacks to Liberia.[17] Although the ACS Annual Report for 1851 did not note this one-million-dollar donation, what Thompson connoted in his message was far more important than his accurate accounting. The reality for free blacks—North, South, East, and West—was that they needed to take seriously the reemergence of colonizationism that was sweeping across the nation, converting poor and working-class whites into colonizationists eager for a peaceful and painless way to purge the land of blacks who competed with them for jobs and choice land.

As the 1850s approached, colonization gathered strength among ministers as well as state and federal politicians. Whites united across class lines in support of colonization, and soon colonizationism became a moderate position in a nation divided over slavery. For this reason, whites in Ohio, Indiana, Illinois, Wisconsin, and Michigan provided the ACS and state auxiliaries with a large pool of potential recruits into the cause and gave the organization a second life.

Various religious denominations promoted colonization, but few embraced it with as much ardor as the Illinois Methodist Episcopal Church. When ministers and church officials met at their annual conference in August 1847, they expressed their "sympathies" for African Americans as "children of bondage, the subjects of political oppression, the victims of caste in society," and trapped in "intellectual darkness." This "unfortunate race," they argued, was pitiful wherever they lived— be it the United States, Africa, or Europe. In their view, free blacks in the North were in some ways worse off than the "negro slave" because they lived in limbo, neither accepted socially nor accorded full rights as citizens. These realities led members of the Methodist Episcopal Church of Illinois to ponder: "How shall we be able to give a proper expression to our sympathy for the colored man?" The answer, they believed, was in colonization. For only the American Colonization Society and its state auxiliaries could provide "satisfactory answers" to this and other vexing questions on the minds of Church leaders, who felt tremendous "pity and commiseration" for blacks in the state and nation.[18]

This pity moved church officials to resolve "that the members and preachers of this conference be . . . respectfully requested to co-operate with the agents of the American, and the Illinois Colonization Societies . . . in the prosecution of the work of their agency." Not only did official church resolutions illustrate the rise of colonization, but they also showed one means by which colonization agents gained an audience in order to raise funds and make converts. The "specter of colonization" was not only alive but was progressing rapidly. For this reason, members of the Methodist Episcopal Church claimed that "the increasing interest which exists in the public mind in regard to the enterprise of African Colonization" represented a future that was "full of promise."[19]

Anticolonizationists in Chicago appeared eager to counter this pro-colonization upsurge, and they arranged a public debate against B.T. Kavanaugh. Originally, Rev. Dr. Blanchard, president of Knox College, had agreed to make the anticolonization case, but he declined shortly before the scheduled debate. Instead, a man by the name of St. Clair stood in, and he attacked the colonizationists' position aggressively from the start, barely allowing the colonizationists to respond before jumping to another point. When the debate began, there was "discouragement on the part of Colonizationists" because they couldn't find "ten men who would come out boldly and stand by [them] as friends." Yet, given this paucity of support, the colonizationists were determined to hold their ground, "not withstanding this great odds against [them]."[20]

According to B.T. Kavanaugh, the board of moderators overruled "almost everything we claimed as a right," thus compelling him and his few allies to "run the gauntlet alone" and try to win sympathy from an audience that most certainly supported the abolitionist stance. Still, Kavanaugh was excited to learn, as the debate came to an end, that he had "found a host of friends among strangers, who waived all ceremony and approached us in the streets and everywhere with the warmest greetings and most decided support—support not only in the full and favorable expression of their opinions and feelings, but unasked and unexpectedly, they put hand in pocket and launched out for our cause." Such an upsurge of interest in the colonization position compelled these new friends to invite Kavanaugh and his partners to a meeting they had called for "the following evening to express to him their sense of high claims of the cause of African colonization." As Kavanaugh recounted, this meeting, held in the courthouse, was filled with supporters of the cause, and by the end of the meeting a series of resolutions were passed showing great support for the Colonization Society.[21]

B.T. Kavanaugh's success appears to have taken place after some of the same supporters in the Chicago community had been turned off by previous colonizationist recruiting tactics. Apparently, back in the spring of 1847, the Rev. R.S. Finley, secretary of the Missouri State Colonization Society and national agent for the ACS, had traveled throughout Illinois denouncing abolitionists and promoting the colonization cause in a manner some found disrespectful.[22] Furious about the "harsh and denunciatory measures of Abolitionists," Finley let loose a tirade, accusing abolitionists of being "liars, traitors, and rebels" who defiled "the name of God" as they preached "falsehood, treason, and rebellion." This type of vituperation against the abolitionist cause unnerved one man who had previously considered himself a colonizationist, prompting him to accuse Finley of uttering "more slanderous, downright abuse against them, in one discourse" than he had heard "from all Abolitionists in the State against his Society." While the author of this letter published in *The National Era* "bewail[ed] [abolitionist] fanaticism and folly," he had "profound respect for the Abolitionists 'as men.'" Thus, Finley's disparaging remarks unsettled him and caused him to announce that he was "done with all Colonization" as long as the ACS "sanctions and circulates such agents among the people."[23]

While most of the 250 African Americans who resided in Chicago rejected colonization, in late 1847 and early 1848 some had been persuaded to take seriously the prospects of colonization in Liberia. By February 1848, on the heels of the establishment of a colonization society in the city, African Americans met to debate the merits of African colonization.[24] Colonizationists took notice of this, and they were most certainly quite pleased that blacks in Illinois were willing to give them a chance. According to a May 1848 article in the *African Repository*, colonization had attracted the "attention of large numbers of the more respectable, industrious, and intelligent among the free colored people of Illinois." And by the end of the meeting, they agreed to send the Reverend Edward Samuel S. Ball to Liberia on a fact-finding mission.[25]

A year later, an article in Douglass's *North Star* announced Ball's return, claiming "that all the arguments used to induce us to go to that country are undeserving of our confidence."[26] Upon returning from his trip, Ball had a pamphlet published entitled "Liberia—The Condition and Prospects of That Republic" to share with the public his impressions. In some respects the pamphlet was relatively positive. Ball declared that "[w]ith respect to the propriety of our removal to Liberia, I give it as my deliberate opinion, that, as to men of intelligence and means, there is no better country to my knowledge than Liberia." However, Ball cautioned the man "without means" that Liberia was "one of the worst countries he can go to," due to the rampant poverty and unhealthy conditions. As he observed during this trip, those blacks who had traveled to Liberia without proper resources were compelled to stay in the "emigrant house," with meager rations, and eventually they were forced out with no promise of employment, no means to procure land, or any way to make a living.[27] Still, this was far from a whole-hearted denunciation of Liberia, and other black communities in the Old Northwest sent their own delegates to investigate Liberia. Time and time again, though, these investigators declared that colonization impeded racial progress in America because the American Colonization Society worked to undermine black attempts at citizenship or social equality.

A year after blacks in Illinois protested against colonization, ACS agent B.T. Kavanaugh traveled to Shawnee Prairie, in Founty County, Indiana, to spread the word about the rise of the Colonization Society across the West. Colonization supporters gathered at Bethel Meetinghouse to discuss establishing a colonization society, and Kavanuagh "addressed the meeting with a forcible speech" linking colonization in the Hoosier State to the rise and progress of colonization throughout the nation. By the end of the meeting a committee had prepared a constitution for the "Shawnee Prairie Colonization Society," and nearly fifty people signed their names to the document.[28]

The colonization campaign was nothing new in Indiana. As early as January 1820, members of the Indiana General Assembly organized a meeting in the state Senate chambers for the purpose of establishing a colonization society. Hoosier colonizationists in the 1820s regarded slavery as "wholly unrecognized with the free constitution of the American government, and the feelings of human nature," and they pledged "to aid and assist the American Colonization Society . . . in its laudable and humane intentions." Membership dues were two dollars annually, and Governor Jonathan Jennings became the Indiana

Colonization Society's first president.[29] This move was in step with the congressional act authorizing President James Monroe to allocate resources "to send beyond the limits of the United States all captured negroes, and to appoint agents, residing on the coast of Africa, to receive them."[30]

Like colonizationists all across the nation, those in Indiana claimed that white racial animosity amounted to an insurmountable barrier for free blacks. African colonization, white colonizationists argued, was the only humane way to spare free black Americans the pain of racial prejudice in Indiana and the rest of the nation. By the late 1840s, colonizationists in Indiana were using their mouthpiece, *The Colonizationist*, to proclaim that their mission was indeed benevolent. P.D. Gurley, the newsletter's editor, argued that the organization's goals were pure and were rooted in a concept he identified as "speaking truth in love." While he believed abolitionists had sincere intentions, he criticized them for having no practical plan for emancipation. Furthermore, Gurley claimed that abolitionists had for decades obscured the benevolent intentions of his organization, "but now," he explained, colonization "is shining again with augmented luster."[31]

Blacks in Indianapolis disagreed. Ever since a state convention was called for the winter of 1841–1842, free blacks in Indiana had been publicizing their disapproval of colonization, calling all colonizationists the enemies of the black race. In January 1842, Bethel African Methodist Episcopal Church in Indianapolis hosted a meeting at which local blacks could affirm their support for the state convention's statements against colonization and offer their own views. While some of those present approved of emigration to Oregon, African colonization was dismissed. When the meeting concluded, a committee had been formed to unite blacks across the state in opposition to African colonization.[32]

Perhaps it was African American resistance to colonization in Indianapolis that provoked colonizationists there to reorganize the Indiana Colonization Society. Intent on learning from previous mistakes, the Society met in November 1845 with the goal of recruiting a member of the black community to travel to Liberia and see firsthand the benefits of colonization. The Reverend Willis Revels, an African Methodist Episcopal minister from Terre Haute, was appointed by the society for this task. But when blacks flooded Revels with letters protesting his association with the state colonization society, he resigned.[33]

Yet white colonizationists remained certain that colonization had a bright future in Indiana. According to a July 1847 article in the

Colonizationist, a "spirit of inquiry has been awakened," and such a spirit was leading colonizationists to "rejoice that the Colonization enterprise has received a new and a strong impulse in this state within the last eighteen months." African Americans were finally being provided with "correct information" about Liberia and the potential for elevating free people of color to a level on par with whites. As far as they were concerned, colonization was "the greatest benevolent enterprise of the age," and Indiana should be honored to participate in such an important social movement. "Let Colonization societies be formed, at least, in every county, uplifting of a long-degraded race," Hoosier colonizationists proclaimed.[34]

In August 1849 African Americans in Fort Wayne, Indiana, gathered together to consider the colonizationist William W. Findlay's claim that they could "enjoy social, civil, and political privileges" in Liberia. After deliberating, the group answered the appeal by reshaping words from the Declaration of Independence to fit their sentiment: "That the enjoyment of life, liberty, and the pursuit of happiness belongs to us as an inalienable right from our Creator, in common with all mankind," they would not leave this land where their "forefathers fought, bled, and died to secure for us and to us these things, in common with other citizen soldiers, in the Revolutionary War." Hope was not lost in the struggle for equal rights in Indiana, even though they were "denied some things." Colonization represented a "destructive scheme for the annihilation of the Free Colored People of this land," they argued, adding that they felt "insulted when asked to emigrate to Liberia." Consequently, African Americans in Fort Wayne declared that those who did leave for Liberia were in direct conflict with blacks who remained in the United States. With indignation the delegates proclaimed, "every one that leaves this country for that American Golgotha, weakens our hands and throws obstacles in our way that are hard to be overcome."[35]

While some free blacks in Ohio agreed with those in Indiana, others found the racial climate in the Old Northwest too much to bear. In fact, in the early 1840s a "race war" in Cincinnati signaled to blacks the extent to which whites, regardless of regional, class, or ethnic differences, would go to purge their city of African Americans. According to reports, a fistfight between Irish and black workers in August 1841 escalated into a full-fledged riot. The militia, sent in to "keep the peace," instead invaded the black sections of the city, arresting blacks and preventing others from leaving their neighborhoods. John Mercer Langston called this moment in Ohio history "the blackest and most detestable" moment in Cinncinatti's history.[36]

Even within the context of this sort of lawlessness and blatant racial animus, some African Americans in Ohio still rejected colonization. This became quite apparent when, between 1844 and 1847, colonization agent John B. Pinney traveled through Ohio to recruit blacks to emigrate to Liberia. According to one account, Pinney gave a speech in which he argued that "the negro did not have ambition enough to raise to eminence in this country, and tried to show why they could not or did not."[37] Pinney claimed that even when blacks were given the same rights as whites, they were unable to succeed in America. This did not go over well with some free blacks in the audience, who told Pinney that they could not understand why they should leave their enslaved relatives. Why not "give to us, our slave mothers, farthers [sic], brothers, sisters, husbands, wife, children and relatives" some land in the West where "the climate is more salubrious and congenial to our health."[38] Other critics of colonization also pointed out the impractical nature of colonization, given the nearly 400,000 free blacks in the nation, to say nothing of over 2 million slaves. How could the Colonization Society raise the vast funds that would be needed for the removal of all blacks from the United States?

African American resistance notwithstanding, whites in Ohio regarded colonization as an expedient that was in the best interest of the Buckeye state. The *Ohio Statesmen* announced Pinney's call for a colonization meeting at a church in Columbus in 1846, where, according to the article, "there will no doubt be a full attendance. Mr. P. is able-eloquent."[39] Eloquent, perhaps, but according to reports in Douglass's *North Star*, "thoroughly insane." As Douglass recounted, Rev. Pinney was "guilty of fabricating the grossest falsehoods respecting the colony." This "insane" behavior, the *North Star* reported, "had been given occasion for a rumor" when Pinney visited the colonizationist Dr. Leonard Bacon in New Haven, Connecticut. According to Douglass's statements in the *North Star*: "J.B. Pinney had been detected in giving out, as one who had been an intelligent eye-witness, and therefore to be relied upon, statements respecting Liberia, which were utterly false and without foundation; and secondly, that he has at different periods of his life, shown himself to be insane."[40] While Douglass never hid his disdain for the American Colonization Society and its ideology, his calling Pinney "insane" was certainly libelous if false. In any case, such accusations did not stop Pinney, and having toured Ohio, he returned to New York two years later to attend a "Great Colonization Meeting." Even in a city where abolitionists and anticolonizationists met frequently to denounce colonization, a man they deemed "insane" was still able to attract sizable audiences when he preached his pro-colonization message.[41]

While African Americans continued to denounce colonization throughout the nation, by the end of the 1840s a cadre of blacks in Ohio began to embrace a pro-emigration stance. In January 1849, African Americans meeting for a state convention in Columbus listened to a group of delegates who spoke openly about the benefits of emigration. But the anticolonizationists in the room immediately rejected this position because they believed such comments only aided the colonization cause. The first day of the state convention passed with no discussion of colonization or emigration, but by the second day, a motion casting emigration in a disparaging light was opposed by one delegate who claimed, "there was a great change going on in the minds of the people" in regards to emigration. When another delegate rose to correct the man, arguing that there was a misunderstanding, the pro-emigration delegate argued that blacks would never amount to anything as a people in the United States. As tension mounted, J.L. Watson, a delegate from Cuyahoga, cried out: "Go to Liberia . . . become President, Senator, Judge, or what not. Come to this country and see how the founders of this scheme will treat you." But this comment did not quell emigration supporters, one of whom stood and claimed that he had grown weary of "looking up to the white man for everything." As Paul Cuffe had done in the 1810s, Watson argued: "We must have [a] nationality. I am for going any where, so we can be an independent people."[42]

As tensions rose, John Mercer Langston stood to address his peers and announced that he regretted "exceedingly that this question has been forced upon the Convention." Yet Langston explained that, "trusting as we do, in the omnipotence of truth," he must stand behind those who supported emigration. "I love my native land," Langston declared, but "the prejudices . . . were strong in this country, against the colored man," and thus "the very fact of our remaining in this country, is humiliating, virtually acknowledging our inferiority to the white man." Interestingly, that year, 1849, marked one of the most important moments in African American history in Ohio. The Free Soil Party used the animosity between the Whig and Democratic parties to push for the state legislature to repeal the Black Laws and to allocate funds for the establishment of a school system for blacks. Nevertheless, John Mercer Langston, who would go on to become an officer in the Union army during the Civil War, expressed a spirit of emigrationism that is more commonly associated with Martin Delany's work in the early 1850s.[43]

Friday's session did not end with a unified position on emigration, however. The majority report, which John Mercer Langston presented, stated: "That in the event of universal emancipation ... prompted by the spirit of '76 ... we are willing, it being optional, to draw out from the American government, and form a separate and independent one, enacting our own laws and regulations. ..." Rather than have their views left out, those who opposed this statement presented a minority report which included the resolution: "That we will never submit to the system of colonization to any part of the world, in or out of the United States; and we say, once for all, to those soliciting us, that all their appeals to us are in vain. Our minds are made up to remain in the United States, and contend for our rights at all hazards."[44] Furthermore, it seems clear that, as early as 1849, the pro-emigration constituency among free black leaders was prepared to stand by their position, regardless of whether their pro-emigration statement empowered the colonizationists, as the anticolonizationists claimed it would. Although this debate over emigration would lead to a much wider debate in the mid-1850s, the argument over emigration during the Ohio state convention of 1849 illustrates that such a debate had begun earlier than is often acknowledged.[45]

As African Americans debated emigration, ACS agent David Christy traveled to Ohio and met with state legislators. Intent on using scare tactics, Christy claimed "that the Ohio Valley is now the focus towards which nearly the entire free colored emigration of the country is concentrating." After placing before the legislature a series of "facts" suggesting that Ohio was one of the most popular destinations for newly emancipated slaves, Christy then attempted to prove that colonization was the only way to curb the inevitable statewide increase of blacks, whom, he pointed out, "The framers of the constitution under which you act, never designed" to be equal. Given white racial hatred, black efforts at citizenship were a waste of time, Christy explained, and it would be "unwise, therefore, for any one to urge them to a prolonged and fruitless warfare for citizenship in Ohio." This being the case, Christy explained that he was appealing to whites throughout the nation for the finances to purchase "additional territory on the coast of Africa, to form a new State for colored emigrants from the Ohio valley." According to Christy, "a gentleman of ample means" had agreed to purchase 200 square miles of land just outside the borders of Liberia, which the American Colonization Society was prepared to call "Ohio in Africa."[46]

David Christy's appeal to the Ohio state legislature was the culmination of nearly two years of recruiting for the Colonization Society. After researching the "statistical facts" of Ohio, Christy presented his colonizationist peers with a report about the condition of the colonization movement in Ohio, a statement that must have been intended to arouse his white constituency to "do something" about the increased number of black migrants into the state. Between 1830 and 1840, he explained, the number of free blacks in northern states, except for Pennsylvania, had decreased, yet Ohio's free black population had increased nearly 82 percent. "Supposing the emigration into Ohio since 1840, to have been no greater than before that period," Christy concluded, "her present colored population will be 30,000."[47]

As Christy concluded his report, his dual purpose became apparent. First, he sought state aid in spreading the word about the benefits of African colonization, since some blacks in the state abhorred the Colonization Society, distrusted white agents, and held prejudices against the colonization mission. And since blacks "still distrust[ed] white men, and wish[ed] to send out colored delegates to investigate the claims of Liberia," the state legislature needed to fund the travels of an African American community leader to gather favorable information and bring it back to black communities in Ohio. Christy had just the man: "The Rev. Moses Walker, a colored man of Portland, Jefferson County, Ohio," could do this task and help the Society to "dispel the illusion that African colonization is a scheme of the slaveholder." If this worked, he explained, the "large number of colored men who express a willingness to emigrate to Liberia" would leave the state "as soon as they can be convinced of the truthfulness of the reports in relation to the present prosperity of the Republic of Liberia."

Christy's final appeal was financial. The American Colonization Society was enduring a financial crisis and needed state or federal funds to make its enterprise succeed. Christy, describing this situation as an "emergency," asked the Ohio legislature to "make a suitable appropriation to aid the American Colonization Society for a few years to come, in carrying out its designs in relation to the colored people of Ohio, and in promoting the spirit of emigration to Liberia."[48]

By December, Christy boasted to the *Cincinnati Gazette* that he had raised nearly $2,000 toward his "Ohio in Liberia" project. He had done this by procuring funds from a "benevolent gentleman" eager to aid the "Colored People of the Western free States" in forming their own colony in Africa on the condition that two hundred could take "immediate possession of the territory." This area of land, between Sierra Leone and Liberia, represented "one of the darkest dens of the slave trade," and such a purchase would go a long way to "not only drive the trafficers [sic] in human flesh from the coast, but at once emancipate many tens of thousands of slaves at present held in bondage by the kinds and head men of that region." With Christy uncertain about his prospects of winning over such a larger number of blacks in Ohio, he extended an invitation to "friends of the cause in Indiana" to aid in "accomplishing great good to the world."[49]

While African Americans could not agree on emigration, they did agree that the American Colonization Society and its state auxiliary in Ohio posed a serious threat. African American delegates at the January 1849 state convention denounced Christy's colonization efforts in Ohio over the previous year. Having read the "Memorial" that Christy presented to the state legislature, a committee composed of distinguished black leaders, including William Howard Day and Charles Henry Langston, wrote a statement entitled "To the Citizens of Ohio" that condemned Christy's work and challenged him, if he could, to "show to candid minds . . . that the increase of the colored people in this state, is an evil." As far as recruiting black leaders to help in promoting the "Ohio in Africa" scheme, the committee asserted that "we independently but humbly beg leave to differ with Mr. Christy and the Colonization Society, and say . . . we mean, in the spirit of our resolution, here to remain amid the broken columns of our temple of liberty."[50]

Nearly two weeks after the state convention, blacks in Columbus, Ohio, called a meeting to discuss Christy's "Memorial" and the impending threat of mass deportation as a result of Christy's urging. Blacks at the meeting adopted resolutions reflecting the belief that colonization went hand-in-glove with racial discrimination. This discrimination was most frequently expressed through laws designed to deny black people political, economic, or social equality. Thus, colonization was not merely a foolhardy attempt to persuade free blacks to leave. It represented, after reenslavement, the second-most disturbing movement in the nation. While African American abolitionists demanded an end to slavery, they realized that colonization coming in the wake of emancipation would be a terrible fate to befall a people who had struggled so hard to share in the fruits of citizenship after "toiling under the lash" for generations. Blacks who gathered at the meeting claimed that the "primary objective" of Christy's memorial was to repeal the recent legislative move that ended the Black Laws. Thus, they declared Christy to be their "inveterate enemy, a poor, contemptible servile of the slave power—a 'lick spittle' for slaveholders and their smiles and money, dripping with human blood."

His words, petitions, and memorials did not deserve even the slightest acknowledgment from "the legislature of an intelligent and free people."[51]

Such a bold anticolonization declaration may have discouraged others, but not Christy. Ten months later, he wrote to his superiors in Washington, "I am justified, from assurances given, in believing that the old custom of collections in behalf of the Colonization Society, can be revived in our churches." Overcoming the trend among ecclesiastical bodies to prevent discussion of abolition or colonization in churches was indeed a major accomplishment. And over the course of 1849, Christy spoke on several occasions with white ministers about the benefits of colonization, the progress of Liberia as an independent republic, and Liberia's role as a beachhead for spreading Christ's gospel in Africa and curbing the slave trade. In Dayton, for example, Christy claimed to have convinced all but two members present at the Ohio Methodist Conference to sign a petition in support of the Colonization Society. "During that same week," Christy wrote, "I visited the Synod of Cincinnati, Old School Presbyterian holding its session in Springfield." After speaking of the glories of colonization and the rise of Liberia, Christy claimed "unanimous" approval, and this was especially sweet since "all those ministers of this Synod . . . have heretofore been so ardent in the anti-slavery cause." Christy moved on to collect signatures from the members of the Synod of Cincinnati, New School Presbyterian, Ohio Baptist Annual Convention, Synod of Ohio, and the Old School Presbyterian. After addressing his Lecture on Colonization to each group, Christy passed out his "Memorial" to the state legislature, and he felt confident that it had been "put in circulation in most of the counties of the state."[52] When whites read it in Mercer County, Ohio, they declared, "we will not live among negroes; as we have settled here first, we have fully determined that we will resist the settlement of blacks and mulattoes in this county to the full extent of our means, *the bayonet not excepted.*"[53]

While Christy gathered support among whites in Ohio, down in slave-state Kentucky the Colonization Society's agent Rev. Alexander M. Cowan worked to recruit free blacks to leave the state and start anew in Liberia during the summer of 1847. Like their Ohio brethren, Kentucky colonizationists concluded that "if we wish to benefit the free negro, we must remove him to a country where none of these adverse influences are operating on him."[54] After "several prominent gentlemen of the State" had urged the Kentucky Colonization Society to recruit African American delegates from Lexington, Maysville, Danville, and Richmond to travel to Liberia "for a full examination of its condition and prospects, (remaining there twelve months for that purpose,) and return and make a report to their constituents," blacks in Louisville "approved of this plan," resolving to elect suitable people for such an adventure.[55]

Colonization sentiments had also infiltrated Kentucky's political debate. In February 1847 the state colonization society sent a memorial to the legislature requesting funds "to enable them to remove such of the eight thousand free people of color in this state, as are willing to go to the Colony of Liberia." One newspaper article stated that this memorial was one of many such petitions being "circulated in every county in the state, and numerously signed by the friends of the scheme," reflecting a trend towards colonization that must have terrified free blacks in the state. Soon Senator Joseph R. Underwood of Kentucky became one of several congressmen who regarded colonization as the only means to the eradication of slavery in the nation.

When a discussion over "the great Territorial Bill" was debated in the Senate in November 1848, Underwood declared: "I am no advocate for the institution of negro slavery . . . if I had the power to colonize and remove every slave within the borders of my own State I would most cheerfully do it." This removal, according to Underwood, was necessary because emancipation without colonization "would be a calamity which would induce every sane man who could escape, to fly from a society so constituted." Thus, Senator Underwood outlined a gradual emancipation plan that harkened back to the 1820s, calling for the government to set an age when children once "weaned" could be gradually freed. He went on to speculate that "one-half the expenses of the Mexican war invested in a six per cent stock would, by a proper system of African colonization, in less than fifty years extirpate slavery in the United States." Underwood offered to pilot this program in Kentucky, and, if it succeeded as he expected it would, have his gradual emancipation and colonization program become federal policy.[56]

This would not be the last time Senator Underwood would pursue his colonization plan. In early 1849, he once again proposed that the U.S. Senate consider appropriating "money for the purpose of removing free people of color to Liberia, or elsewhere, from the United States, and also to make an appropriation for the purpose of colonizing such slaves as may be hereafter manumitted for that purpose." In this instance, Senator Underwood wove his colonization petition together with westward expansion, because, as he argued, slavery continued to cause general "sensitivities" among whites in these communities. Even though southerners were intent on avoiding any discussion of slavery, Underwood brushed their objections aside, arguing that slavery was the most pressing issue of the day. With new states requesting admission into the nation, the question of slavery would continue to arise. Some slaveholders in the South, he explained, were willing to emancipate their slaves "if they know they will not be allowed here." Therefore, why should the Senate ignore his colonization plan for free and newly emancipated blacks since some southern slaveholders supported it? Although Underwood did not get very far with his plan, his erstwhile attempt to procure funds for colonization illustrated the growing interest within the national government in a federal colonization plan.[57]

Perhaps Senator Underwood had consulted with fellow Kentuckian Henry Clay, who remained adamant about the potential for colonization. As one of the founders of the Colonization Society, by 1848 Clay had retired to his Kentucky plantation after a lifetime of public service. But Kentuckians coaxed him out of retirement and elected him to the U.S. Senate in 1849 at a time of crisis that called for the skills of the "Great Compromiser." With the nation torn over the question of slavery in the territories acquired after the war against Mexico, the federal government needed to determine which territories would enter the Union as slave states, and which ones as free states. Having resolved such a conflict between the free states in the North and slave states in the South in 1820, Clay had made a name for himself as the one who could bring proslavery men and those who opposed slavery's expansion in the West to the same table. This time Clay collaborated with Stephen Douglass and Daniel Webster to fashion the Compromise of 1850, which brought California into the United States as a free state, while New Mexico and Utah were permitted, independent of federal legislative intervention, to determine whether or not slavery would be legal. Texas was compensated with $10 million for land lost to New Mexico, slavery was abolished in Washington, D.C., and a stricter law that would require the return of fugitive slaves was passed. Of course, this "Fugitive Slave Law," as it would be known, caused tremendous anxiety for free blacks in the North and Midwest, many of whom were fugitives, or the relatives and friends of fugitives.

When President Millard Fillmore signed into law a provision of the Compromise of 1850 identified as the Fugitive Slave Act, anticolonizationists like Martin Delany were stunned. This Act, coupled with the rising militancy of abolitionists, culminated in a surge of interest in emigration among many of those who once took a hard line against leaving the United States. Although the Act had been designed to offer a sort of olive branch to southerners who had for years bemoaned what they believed to be a total disregard for the Fugitive Slave Act of 1793, it only irritated sectional tensions. The Fugitive Slave Act allowed a slave-holder or an agent acting in his behalf to merely present an affidavit that described a runaway slave, for federal authorities to apprehend a black person for enslavement in the South. The accused runaway slave was unable to speak in his or her defense, nor was a trial by jury used to determine the accuracy of the accusation. Such blatant violation of constitutional principles even compelled President Mildred Fillmore to ponder whether or not the Act would hold up to Supreme Court scrutiny. Nevertheless, the Fugitive Slave Act sent a clear message to free blacks in the North and Midwest that the hand of slavery did, indeed, stretch beyond southern boundaries.[58]

Martin Delany came to regard the Fugitive Slave Act as the most disgraceful act of legislation ever passed by the U.S. government. It was one thing for southern states to enact strict slave codes and laws that reinforced racial hierarchy. But the Fugitive Slave Act, signed by a north-ern-born president, had disregarded the entire notion of "due process," which remained the bedrock of the American legal system. This Act, more so than anything else, pushed Delany toward emigration from the United States. In his classic pro-emigration text, *The Condition, Eleva-tion, Emigration, and Destiny of Colored People*, he reprinted the entire Act, devoting considerable space to demonstrating its pernicious intent.

Of course Delany was not alone. Alexander Crummell had ceased his attack on the ACS after the passage of the Act, deciding to settle in Liberia when he finished at Oxford. Before he left, Crummell shared the stage with Henry Highland Garnet and other black Americans vis-iting Britain, and he blasted the Act. Crummell claimed that the Act remained conjoined with a "general rising of the surges of slavery and oppression throughout the world, presaging wrath and destruction to the cherished liberties of mankind."[59] Edward Blyden, the progenitor of Pan-Africanism, had just arrived in the United States to study theology when he learned of the Act. Having been denied admittance in several colleges because of his race, and in the wake of the Fugitive Slave Act, Blyden decided to set sail for Liberia, where he would become one of the most influential African intellectuals of the second half of the nineteenth century.[60]

With such a great sense of dissolution among black Americans, the ACS moved in to capitalize on this discontent and recruit a new generation of leaders for Liberia. With Blyden and Crummell on board, the ACS sought after the others, hoping to persuade them that despite their agitation against slavery, whites had continued to prove themselves more interested in national unity than black equality or even the most important tenets of American constitutional law. This realization shook the most ardent anticolonizationists and antiemigrationists, like Frederick Douglass, to consider leaving. Yet Douglass held strong, while Delany initiated an emigration movement that he hoped could rival the ACS colonization program.

Given the great conflict over slavery that roiled the nation, Clay saw a fresh chance to advocate within the federal government on behalf of the Colonization Society, as he had been doing for over thirty years with limited success. Clay now saw this moment as being ripe for a mass colonization plan in association with gradual emancipation. For years colonizationists had attributed the lack of federal support for colonization to the position held by the vast majority of southern slaveholders, who dismissed any plan that even suggested emancipation would benefit the nation. While the ACS only tepidly accepted emancipation, some within the organization spoke frequently about the long-term vision of using colonization as a means to ending slavery in the United States. Northern colonizationists most frequently came into the organization because they supported emancipation. Southerners, on the other hand, rejected any plan to end legal slavery. By 1847, however, the national crisis over slavery's expansion westward ignited pro-colonization sentiments among whites—North and South—who regarded colonization as a compromise between proslavery interests and the rejection of slavery's expansion into the West.

At a speech in Lexington, Kentucky, Clay pointed out that "every state has a supreme, uncontrolled, and exclusive power to decide whether slavery shall cease or continue within its limits, without any exterior intervention from any quarter."[61] However, Clay himself did not support slavery, claiming that he would "rejoice if not a single slave breathed the air or was within the limits of our country." Instead, he hoped that whites in Kentucky and the nation would embrace his "system of gradual emancipation," which included colonization. It was the abolitionists, Clay determined, who had done "incalculable mischief even to the very cause which they espoused" by undermining the ACS's efforts at emancipation and colonization. If the abolitionists hadn't stirred up southerners, Clay surmised, slaveholders would not have acted so ardently against gradual emancipation and colonization.

Frederick Douglass published this speech, perhaps to taunt his fellow abolitionists a bit by reminding them that Clay still refused to abandon his colonization scheme even in the last years of his life.[62] Douglass, however, waited until January 1848 before publishing his critique of Clay and colonization. "On examining this speech," Douglass commented, "we scarcely know what part of it most to condemn. It is diabolical, from beginning to end; abounding in willfully blind and false assumptions respecting our character, and condition as a people." Douglass thought about leaving "it to speak for itself," but feared his silence may be misunderstood as his "inability to reply." After commenting sarcastically that Clay's speech had been "the most successful we ever heard or read on the subject of colonization," Douglass explained that Clay refused to "give offence, to anyone," and instead used the language of paternalism and peace. Rather than allow the "poor, despised, injured, and maltreated blacks" to remain in the United States and continue to suffer under inhuman racial prejudice and slavery, Clay called out to his white friends of Christianity to help deport them to a place where they could truly live as a free people. Clay's tone was ripe with "arrogance and impudence," and Douglass reminded his readers: "The great central falsehood of Mr. Clay's speech is the same that has been set forth in colonization journals, and proclaimed by its lecturers, for the last twenty years—the assumption that white and colored people cannot live together on terms of equality. On this hangs, not only Mr. Clay's speech, but the whole structure of colonization." For Douglass and other anticolonizationists, this notion of irreconcilable differences between the races was pure fiction, and even in the South this assertion was unfounded. "Now we wish to inform Mr. Clay," Douglass concluded, "that the condition of the free colored people has been steadily improving."[63]

Like Douglass, William Lloyd Garrison downplayed the ACS's advances in the late 1840s, attributing the large audience at the ACS meeting in 1848 to Clay's fame. Even though the *Boston Recorder* noted that "When Mr. Clay entered the Hall, he was saluted with by a universal shout, and with nine cheers," nevertheless, Garrison argued, the great crowd that gathered in Representatives' Hall had not the "slightest interest" in the ACS or its colonization plan.[64]

In March 1849, both Douglass and Garrison responded to a letter Clay had written to Richard Pindall on slavery and emancipation by first summarizing Clay's views on the subject and then offering detailed criticism. Garrison's critique reflected his enduring frustration with the way in which colonizationists bashed abolitionists and free blacks to further their own ends. Garrison spoke to the general apathy among most whites regarding slavery. "You say that the 'vast majority of the people of the United States deplore the necessity of the continuance of slavery in any state,'" Garrison explained, but "this assertion is not true." In his opinion, "a vast majority of people really care nothing about it: they are agreed in nothing so well as in despising and proscribing the colored race, whether bond or free."[65] "How dare Henry Clay or any one else undertake to decide where an equal brother man shall live?" Douglass cried out, arguing that neither Clay nor any white American could compel black people to leave their native land.[66]

When Douglass joined notable black abolitionists and leaders such James McCune Smith and George T. Downing at a meeting in April 1849 at Shiloh Presbyterian church in New York, he called the ACS "one of the most impudent Societies in the world." Yet his speech began in jest: "I shall return to this resolution after I shall have said a few things in favour of Colonization and against ourselves." Once he had dealt specifically with a resolution that had been brought to the floor, Douglass lambasted the ACS, mocking the notion that those convened were "so unthankful that we meet here to denounce this very class of men who are going to shower upon us those offices of honour and profit!" The audience erupted in laughter at Douglass's masterful rhetoric.

But although Douglass spoke humorously, the smiles and applause from the audience may have actually masked the uneasiness that he and others felt about the rising support for colonization among whites throughout the nation. Douglass knew how dangerous this was to the anticolonization cause, and in his conclusion he remarked, "I want to feel that this is no effervescent thing—that the feeling got up against Colonization, and in behalf of freedom, is not to disappear and die out the next week, but that the fire kindled here is to continue to burn until slave prejudice, and last, though not least, Colonization, with all its deceptive acts, shall be utterly consumed."[67] As Douglass had argued for over a decade, any and all efforts among blacks to emigrate, regardless of motive or location, merely supplied colonizationists with fuel for what he considered to be a scheme for ridding the nation of free blacks and making slavery more secure in the South.[6]

While Garrison and Douglass dismissed Henry Clay's colonization dream, whites in Illinois, Indiana, Ohio, and Wisconsin pushed for new state constitutions that included a provision to ban free blacks from entering their states, and in the case of Indiana and Ohio, to deport those living in the state to Liberia. In February 1848, for example, a newspaper called the *Harbinger* (an appropriate name, given the context) announced: "On the first Monday of March the people (whites) of Illinois will be called upon to accept or reject the new Constitution offered to them by their Convention," a referendum that included a proposition relative to "the exclusion of the colored population."[69] By March, voters in Illinois had accepted a state constitution that included Article XIV, which prohibited free blacks from migrating there and prevented slaveholders from entering the state to set their slaves free. These so-called Black Laws, as the *National Era* called them, reinforced the trend towards antiblack legislation in the West. This particular piece of legislation stated that "any negro or mulatto, who shall come into the State, and remain ten days, with the evident intention of residing therein, shall be arrested, and fined fifty dollars."

Antislavery sympathizers were outraged. The *National Era* called the law "inhuman and devilish" and an affront against "the declaration of rights in the Constitution of the State." Furthermore, such an act, the *National Era* editor surmised, must have been passed without the consent of the actual people of the state, since no one could be so blind as not to see the contradictions of such a law.[70] Abolitionists in Illinois agreed with the *National Era* statement, calling a meeting to denounce the measure and to remind "antislavery friends" in the state "that the guilt attached to those laws past rest, not merely upon those who have labored to enact and execute them, but also upon those who have not labored for their total repeal."[71]

Unfortunately for blacks in other western states and territories, this trend toward restricting African Americans' entrance continued. The revised state constitution of Indiana included an article excluding blacks, which was put to a popular vote among the whites of the state. It read: "No Negro or mulatto shall come into or settle in this State, after the adoption of this Constitution."[72] Even more troubling was a portion of the article that fined white individuals up to $500 for conducting business with blacks. This aspect of the constitution was rooted in the notion that such business encouraged African Americans to stay in the state. The *National Era* called this act a work of the "devil," claiming, "Whenever the Devil intends to do a particularly mean thing, he sets some of his imps to work to harass and torment the unfortunate free people of color."[73] By the end of 1853, the General Assembly of the State of Indiana enacted legislation that provided for a Board to be created and funded to aid the colonization cause.[74]

Wisconsin was no safer for free blacks seeking refuge from slavery and white racial hostility in the South and East. As historian Michael J. McManus argues, although colonization never found a serious following among Republicans in Wisconsin, the very fact that Wisconsin senator Doolittle became a major player in the resurgence of colonization shows that colonization ideology may have found fertile soil in the Badger state. However, it is important to note that leading politicians often endorsed colonization even when the majority of their constituency did not. According to McManus, colonization "seems to have inspired little popular enthusiasm in the North and Wisconsin," even if it remained popular among government leaders.[75]

Northern and southern state leaders also expressed their support for colonization by allocating funds to support the colonization of free blacks throughout the 1850s. For example, in 1850 state legislators in Virginia offered up to $30,000 a year for five years to fund black colonization. In Maryland, state officials, having years earlier stopped giving money to the ACS for colonization, offered $10,000 annually over the period from 1852 through 1858 to fund African colonization. In the "free states" of New Jersey and Pennsylvania, members of the state governments appropriated $5,000 and $2,000, respectively.[76]

Douglass printed various examples of antiblack legislation and pro-colonization measures in his paper. He even reprinted an article from the *Presbyterian Herald* that rejected the pro-colonization tide in the nation. According to this article, the migration of blacks into western states only led to antiblack legislation when there was a sense that too many blacks were coming in; only those states that felt "secure against any considerable influx" of free blacks seemed to pass laws recognizing the civil and political rights of African Americans. "[B]ut just let any large number of that class make their appearance among them," the article explained, "and assert their rights and exercise them, and those statutes will soon disappear." This "increasing favor now shown to this scheme" was ironic, the editor of the *Presbyterian Herald* claimed, because these same state officials applauded Germans and Irish "pouring into this land."[77] European immigrants, especially Germans, were encouraged to populate the West and provide the nation with much-needed laborers. "Emigration fever" had gained strength in Germany, and there was talk in Darmstadt of starting "a national society for the assistance of German emigration and colonization" to Illinois, Indiana, and Iowa—three states where politicians embraced the colonization of blacks to Liberia.[78]

The editors of the *National Era* also pointed out this contradiction, arguing in an editorial that "No restraint is imposed on the locomotion of white men" into the nation, yet free blacks were pushed to leave for Liberia. State and federal legislatures encouraged immigration of "every grade and character of foreigners," yet they "shut out Americans whom God has colored a little too deeply for their exquisite taste." Therefore they asserted: "On this ground we stand when we denounce all restrictions on the locomotion of colored people—all State legislation aiming, directly or indirectly, to exclude or eject them from certain States or sections, or to banish them from the country."[79]

Nearly a decade later, Wisconsin's Senator James R. Doolittle would tell an audience gathered at the New England Society that the question "What is to be done with the free Negro?" was more important than the "slavery question." In his estimation, the rejection of African Americans in the West highlighted the troubling circumstances blacks confronted and would continue to confront, even if the nation finally ended slavery. Doolittle went so far as to suggest that "the free states will not receive the emancipated negroes," explaining to his audience that many free states had gone so far as to "prevent them from coming among them."[80]

Free blacks in New York were following this trend closely. In 1851, for example, New York black leaders met in Albany to address "two great questions" that had presented "themselves for adjustment, the first of which is the recent edict enacted and sent forth by Congress, called the 'Fugitive Slave Law'; and the second in character, is the coercive and barbarous Colonization Scheme."[81] A committee led by C. Edward Seth, Benjamin F. Cutler, and William Gardener discussed "the bold move of our adversaries" and conducted an extensive investigation into the state of the colonization movement in 1851. By charting the origins of the ACS and the "result of the operation of the society, from its earliest state down to the year of 1850," the committee determined that "we find at this state of the society's existence, of more than a quarter of a century, a resuscitation of life, still vigorous; still growing; strengthening in its strength; accumulating in numbers; gaining in resources; and with a spirit of determination to effect the desire of its purposes, if possible, in the end."

While the committee believed that the ACS's most recent attempt to secure financial support for a federally sponsored mass-deportation project seemed unrealistic, they noted the great threat of such "bold moves," and their sense of pleasure "at the failure of the Colonization Society of this state to obtain, at the recent legislature, an appropriation of ten thousand dollars a year, for two years."[82] Such "failure" did not discourage colonizationists from attempting to recruit blacks in New York City, and this compelled the delegation to warn: "Fellow-citizens, let no fascinating inducements—no eloquent rhetoric—no eulogistic encomiums of Liberia draw you into the snares of your *dear, philanthropic, expatriating friends*." Instead, the members of the convention called on all free blacks to "battle against this subtle scheme and corruption, at all times, and under all circumstances."

Regardless of how ardently free blacks agitated against colonization in the Empire State, New York Colonization Society members were not particularly concerned. For example, the twentieth annual meeting of the New York State Colonization Society at Metropolitan Hall in 1852, with a Reverend Gardiner Spring presiding, produced an impressive spike in donations, which, according to an article in the *New York Daily Times*, "considerably exceed those reported at the last anniversary." When J.H.B. Latrobe, an agent of the American Colonization Society, took the stage, he addressed the audience for a "considerable length, reviewing the origins and progress of the Liberia enterprise," while taking a few moments to chastise abolitionists for their "interference in the affairs of the negroes."[83] Like colonizationists in the Old Northwest, members of the New York State Colonization Society eagerly cited the pro-colonization trend in the nation when presenting colonization to New Yorkers who showed an interest in relieving themselves of this "excess population." Regardless of how stridently Frederick Douglass challenged the efforts of New York colonizationists, he was unable to thwart the surge of colonization sentiment in his own home state.

Interest in colonization became an even far greater concern for African Americans in New York when Governor Hunt called "the attention of the Legislature of this State, to the condition of the colored people; and strongly commend[ed] the plan of Colonization."[84] The New York legislature allocated $5,000 annually for two years to "aid colored persons to emigrate to Liberia, under the direction of the Colonization Society." Led by Governor Hunt, newspapers, such as the *New York Evangelist*, commended the governor's move, deeming it "a humane purpose."[85]

The ACS's national organ, the *African Repository and Colonial Journal*, quickly made notice of Governor Hunt's initiative, declaring that "surely, every true philanthropist must agree with Governor Hunt, that the enterprise of African colonization is justly entitled to encouragement and support." Likewise, the editor of the newspaper *German Reformed Messenger* stated: "We are glad to see that the subject of African colonization is attracting serious attention throughout the country as a thing worthy of more than being talked about merely." The editorial placed Governor Hunt's move within the context of what he called a pro-colonization upsurge that had gripped the nation. "Every day tends to enhance the importance of African Colonization as a policy—national, if you will," the paper claimed.[86] This pro-colonization optimism may have been fed by a New York petition discussed in the Senate, which encouraged the creation of a system of "steamers between the United States and Africa" that would "develop the resources of Liberian Republic, and facilitate emigration by short voyages and low rates of fare."[87] Such a plan was not to be dismissed, and one article in the *Christian Watchman and Reflector* announced: "The measure has powerful friends, and the establishment of the Ebony line is barely an improbable thing."[88]

Blacks in New York were, as one would imagine, outraged at Governor Hunt's pro-colonization declaration, and the actions of the New York State legislature. Throughout the state, African Americans met to declare their disapproval of these measures and to condemn the Colonization Society.[89] Not only did African Americans denounce the appropriation of funds for colonization, they called this move "unconstitutional" for violating the "10th section of the 7th article," which states that "the credit of the State shall not in any manner be given or loaned to, or in aid of any individual association or incorporation." They also called the American Colonization Society a "giant fraud," pointing out: "Should it ever occur that we should be called upon to leave our native State, having means of our own, we shall not burden the public fund in our departure any more than we do while remaining at home."[90]

In May, a cadre of some of the best-known black leaders in the North convened in New York City to discuss Governor Hunt's virtual declaration of war against the black community.[91] Charles Reason, John T. Raymond, J.W C. Pennington, James McCune Smith, Samuel Cornish, and others comprised a "Committee of Thirteen" who sought, as Garrison put it, to "rebuke" the Colonization Society and its supporters for their "hypocritical philanthropy which demands the expatriation of the entire class of the free colored people on the alleged ground that they can never rise in this country."[92]

Disappointed that the *New York Evangelist* would actually endorse Governor Hunt's support for colonization, the black minister and community leader J.W.C. Pennington wrote a letter to the editor expressing the sense of betrayal in the black community at state support for a "scheme" that the community had rejected for years. "I deeply regret that reasoners [sic] on your side of this question should constantly allege the cruelty and depravity of your own race, as a conclusive argument in favor of the removal of the colored people from this country," he explained.[93] Pennington found the newspaper's support for colonization odd, given their lack of interest in aiding young black men to become pastors at Presbyterian churches. On the one hand, Presbyterians seemed sympathetic to blacks facing a lack of opportunities in the United States; on the other, this sympathy did not move them to help provide blacks with education and training for ecclesial service in their own communities. "Without the slightest intention of bringing a railing accusation against any," Pennington argued, "I beg to have it distinctly remembered that no evangelical denomination in this country has undertaken to supply the colored population with efficient ministers of color—[an] agency that is indispensable and loudly called for."[94] Here Pennington was addressing one of the major concerns some blacks had about colonization: resources spent on colonization could be better used for supporting, educating, and assisting blacks in the United States.

White abolitionist Gerrit Smith condemned Governor Hunt's endorsement of colonization, explaining to the governor: "You have suddenly fallen in love with the American Colonization Society. You are deceived by it as I was deceived by it." Like other white abolitionists, Smith had abandoned colonization after meeting black leaders, such as Frederick Douglass. This had forced Smith to shift from being a pro- to an anti-colonizationist in the late 1830s.[95] His open letter to Governor Hunt was one of his numerous attempts to show the hypocrisy behind the American Colonization Society and those who supported colonization. Smith claimed that, unlike the governor, he himself had been induced to support colonization as a "young man." Thus, he was disappointed that the governor was "guilty of such a folly in . . . [his] . . . mature years." Smith also criticized the governor and state legislature for advocating the use of public funds to support such a scheme. "[I]f there are members of the Legislature who wish to give money to the Colonization Society, let them give it from their own pockets, and not presume to give it from the treasury of the State," he declared. In his view, for state legislators to fund colonization was tantamount to thrusting "their hands into my pockets and the pockets of tens of thousands who, in common with me, regard that Society as an unparalleled compound of hypocrisy and meanness and malignity, and as the shameless servant of the slaveholders."[96]

Certain not to let such a vicious attack go unanswered, colonizationists in New York called on a citizen of Liberia to challenge Smith's criticism of Governor Hunt. According to the editor of the *African Repository*, Smith's letter to Hunt "aroused the people of Liberia to reply," and a man going by the name of Edward B. wrote a letter to the newspaper in opposition to Smith. According to Edward B., Smith was like many abolitionists who consistently provided the reading public with "misrepresentations of Liberia and colonization." In his view, although Liberia was no paradise, it represented the work of many intelligent and thoughtful individuals—black and white—who only hoped to create a nation where black Americans could live peaceably, and share the blessings of western civilization with their African brethren. "Are not the above considerations, if calmly viewed, sufficient to restrain any human person, not to say Christians and philanthropists, as many abolitionists profess to be, from vilifying the Colonization Society and Liberia?" he wondered.

The ACS had since its inception argued that black colonizationists were the organization's most useful advocates. Now that Liberia had become independent, ACS members were eager to call upon Liberians to speak out against "all the objections raised against African colonization."[97] With black Liberian support, the Colonization Society's leaders continued to argue that "it is obviously the will of Heaven that the races shall be separated; and if the colored race ever become a people elevated and respected, it must be through colonization and Liberia." But Douglass and other blacks disagreed. Regardless of whether or not Liberia was an independent nation or a territory under the control of the ACS, free blacks in Rochester "strongly deprecated" and "vehemently opposed" the work of the ACS, affirming that "it is the right and duty of every colored man to remain in this country, and use every possible effort to the overthrow of slavery."[98]

Undaunted by African American anticolonization meetings, the New York Colonization Society continued to seek the support of New York City's business and political elite for African colonization. Mercer Street Church in New York City was the site for an "exceedingly interesting meeting" to discuss "the immediate departure of six emigrants who are going out to Africa under the auspices of the New York State Colonization Society." While blacks hoped that the numerous anticolonization meetings across the state would, at least on some level, quell interest in the movement, a "large and highly appreciative audience" listened to reports from Rev. Pinney and others about the progress of the colonization movement in the state. This discussion "continued till a late hour without abatement," and New York colonizationists were quite pleased with Pinney's report.[99]

Not only did Pinney and Rev. Spring, the vice president of the New York State Society, applaud the pro-colonization enthusiasm in the room, but they also expressed with delight the advancement of the colonization movement within the state and nation. "[W]hen I came to New York to enter upon Secretaryship of the Society," Pinney explained, "there was but little progress in emigration," but now, he declared, "there was a great change." One cannot help but notice his use of "emigration" instead of "colonization," and it seems that the conflation of these two distinct notions was a tactic used by colonizationists to connect black-led emigration advocacy with the ACS's African colonization movement. Pinney actually used black emigrationists' efforts in the early 1850s to show that "they were beginning to see the great benefits they would receive under the auspices of the Society." Pinney argued that free blacks had previously viewed Liberia as a "sand-desert" but now were beginning to agree that "the only way for them to obtain a national character" is to join the second black republic.[100]

This discourse of building "national character" was in step with the rhetoric of racial destiny that had become popular among both whites and blacks in this era. Of course, black Americans often spoke of "national character" with regards to independent nation building, and for many of them, such as Martin Delany, Mary Ann Shadd Cary, and Frederick Douglass, Liberia was far from representing a dignified nation that could show the world African potential. Yet this rebuttal did not discourage white colonizationists and their Liberian allies from continuing to preach the gospel of "national destiny" as a feature of Liberian independence. After Pinney sat down, the brother of Liberian president J.J. Roberts rose and spoke, even though he claimed that he had not prepared to give a long discourse on the subject. After twenty years in Liberia, he told the audience, he saw that the day was here when his new nation had "taken a high position among the nations of the earth." For this reason, he called out to his black American brethren to embrace Liberia as a place where "God is preparing the way for great results," and thus Liberia "was destined to be a great nation."[101]

Nearly a year later, blacks at an anticolonization meeting in Philadelphia acknowledged that "the spirit of colonization at the present time [was] unusually active in striving to increase the prejudices of the whites against free colored people, in using the utmost flattery to persuade colored people into the absurd notion that Africa alone [was] their 'Fatherland,' and the only place on earth where they can be free and elevated." Mary Ann Shadd Cary was first to address the audience. Having completed her pro-emigration book *Notes on Canada West*, Shadd discussed the "hypocrisy and inconsistency of its advocates," while warning the audience to be on guard about the "unfair course pursued by [Elliot] Cresson and [Rev. J.M.] Pease when discussing the subject of colonization in Westchester." Furthermore, Shadd took time to reiterate her opinion about the drawbacks of African colonization, which she had discussed in *Notes on Canada West*. First, Shadd argued, "The condition of Liberia, the geography, and climate of Africa" did not bode well for African Americans eager to build a new nation. Ultimately, she concluded, "Africa was entirely unfit as a place of colonization and elevation of oppressed Americans." When Shadd retired to her seat, Frances Ellen Watkins rose to offer the audience two poems, the first one entitled "Bible Defence of Slavery" and the second, "Eliza Harris Crossing the River on the Ice." These poems were well received by the audience, and demonstrated, according to one account, that Watkins "is well cultivated, and evidently has given much reflection and attention to the wrongs of those with whom she is identified."[102]

In step with African Americans in Philadelphia, black Bostonians met at Belknap Street Church in 1852 to protest against the American Colonization Society. Those who attended the meeting called the ACS "inhuman and barbarous" in its effort to drive "us from the land of our birth to one of sickness, devastation, and death." In their view, this coerced emigration was "at war with the Scripture injunction, 'Do unto others as ye would that others should do unto you,'" and had at its very core "cruel, subtle, iniquitous, and devilish" intentions. William Watkins commented ironically that "If we will go three thousand miles from them, they will love us with a vengeance; but if we resolve like men to maintain our rights in the land of our birth, —rights guarantied by the Declaration of Independence, —we call forth their intensified hate." When the meeting concluded, the president of the gathering emphasized the importance of publicizing these opinions among the black community, and also showing white Americans that the free people of color condemned the ACS and its African colonization program.[103]

When African American leaders met for a national convention in 1853, the recent moves of the colonizationists attracted interest and lively debate among delegates. "We have no sympathy with [colonization]," one resolution explained, "having long since determined to plant our trees on American soil, and repose beneath their shade." Citing William Lloyd Garrison's *Thoughts on African Colonization*, this resolution called on those delegates unfamiliar with the history of black anticolonization activism "to procure copies" and "reiterate the resolves and addresses contained in the first part of the work, on the head of the Free People of Color."[104]

A committee led by J.W.C. Pennington was formed to evaluate the present state of the colonization movement and present its findings to the general body. While in this report African Americans upheld their opposition to the American Colonization Society, what makes it interesting is that the committee included a lengthy analysis of the history of colonization with "the view to show that every system of Colonization has proved a curse to that unhappy country." Rather than focus its study exclusively on the ACS, the committee placed the Dutch colonization of southern Africa that began in 1652 within this tradition of "treachery," explaining: "These settlers at first entered Africa with the most friendly intentions . . . however, at no distant period, the Dutch not only began to seize upon the best lands in southern Africa; but furthermore reduced the natives to a most cruel state of slavery."[105]

After placing colonization in a historical context, the committee discussed the basis for the American Colonization Society's plan, which it claimed had been derived from the British colonization efforts of the late eighteenth century. In its estimation, the British deportation of the "surplus population" to Africa coincided with the rise in colonization sentiment in the United States. Ironically, the British and Americans were pursuing "two schemes of colonization . . . from entirely opposite motives." For Britain, colonization originated from the desire "to relieve herself from what she believed to be a over-grown population; America, to relieve herself from what she calls an obnoxious population." While the committee claimed that the Americo-Liberian ruling elite was "in a league with the worse enemies of Africa's dearest interests," they argued that "the British colonization upon South Africa, and the interior and western coast, has been a curse to Africa; the whites there have nearly exterminated several tribes to make room for themselves." Through this discussion of colonization in Africa, the committee determined that colonization would never have any positive benefit for Africa, and this was another key reason for opposition.[106]

Furthermore, the committee pointed out that ACS agents were "still lurking about the seats of governments, both general and State, seeking influence, &c." But it did not find the ACS or colonization society agents had "increased numerically," and thus they had not become a greater threat. In the committee's view, the colonization movement's ideology "has appeared to increase, but that is a part of its policy. There have been changes. Some who were against us, and then were for us, are again against us."[107]

What troubled them most was the way mainstream intellectuals and politicians were embracing colonization in the mid-1850s. Governor Hunt's acceptance of colonization reflected this trend, and even *New York Tribune* editor Horace Greeley regarded colonization as a wise policy, although he disagreed with forced expatriation. As George Frderickson notes: "In an 1853 editorial in the *New York Tribune*, Horace Greeley, who represented a militant wing of the burgeoning free-soil movement, defended colonization on the grounds that the Negro race must prove itself abroad before it could expect its claims for equality to be recognized in America."[108] Three years later, the Republican Party would endorse colonization ideology on the grounds that it represented a moderate position in the debate over slavery and provided Republicans with a response when Democrats charged them with supporting race mixture.

Although white and black abolitionists considered the ACS a "nullity" after the 1830s, the organization refashioned itself and gained new adherents during the 1840s. With the war against Mexico and the heightened sectional tension in its aftermath, colonization gained traction throughout the nation. In fact, northern state legislatures allocated public funds for colonizing free black residents in Africa. Such actions would have been unpopular during the 1830s, but by the 1850s they seemed reasonable, and white state officials from New York to Indiana debated using state funds in this manner. Meanwhile, as new states emerged in the Old Northwest, white residents there appeared quite willing to embrace colonization ideology, rejecting free blacks' claim of citizenship.

Unfortunately for African Americans, the colonization movement expanded during the 1840s, forcing free black newspaper editors, abolitionists, and community leaders to organize and agitate in opposition to the movement with renewed vigor. When colonization was placed within the context of the Compromise of 1850, which included a strengthened fugitive slave law, free blacks could hardly claim to be moving toward real inclusion in the nation. For those who had fought against slavery and colonization for over two decades, this particular moment was as dire as ever. Whites in the North and Midwest seemed increasingly uncomfortable with a free black presence, and southern slaveholders were intent on maintaining slavery no matter the consequences.

By 1854, some free blacks who had previously rejected colonization to Africa now gave serious consideration to the possible benefits of leaving the United States and establishing an African American homeland abroad. This pro-emigration ideology took hold in bold new ways after the publication of Mary Ann Shadd Cary's *A Plea for Emigration, or Notes of Canada West* (1852) and Martin Delany's *The Condition of the Colored People* (1852). Soon, Douglass and other anticolonizationists began to argue that emigrationism actually aided colonizationists because it gave white Americans the impression that the majority of blacks wanted to leave. This was not the 1820s, when the Haitian emigration movement had actually worked to undermine colonization to Liberia, and recent national events made any advocacy for leaving America a liability to free blacks who sought citizenship. This rancor over emigration and colonization caused a major rift between Frederick Douglass and Martin Delany over the issue of race representation. The next chapter addresses these debates over emigration within the context of anticolonization activism during the 1850s.

5 / "An Undue Illusion": Emigration, Colonization, and the Destiny of the Colored Races, 1850–1858

When a delegate at the National Black Convention of 1855 read a "communication" from white colonizationist Jacob Handy in regards to the benefits of African colonization, what transpired was nothing short of a spectacle. As William J. Wilson recalled in a letter to his cousin, "You are, I know, accustomed to the torrent, the tornado, and the storm, as they sweep through your native forests, but the storm raised by this announcement, and the presence of this document in the house, you can form no conception of."[1] According to Wilson, "members took fire in every direction," and soon, "the house was ablaze" with anticolonization sentiment. Delegates condemned the document, and "its aid[er] s and abettors," who in their view sought to push forth an agenda that African Americans had rejected time and time again throughout the antebellum era.[2]

One delegate by the name of Gray stood, firing insult after insult at the ACS, and when he sat down, "nearly one-half of the Convention sprang to their feet at once" in support of his "detestation of the system of African colonization." Charles Lenox Remond ridiculed the document, behaving "fiercer than any lion from his den." Then George Downing "moved that the document be not returned to the correspondent, as no delegate, he hoped, would pay the three cents postage." Instead, Downing called for "it to be *burned*." Someone asked if any of the delegates had matches, while another "came forward with tinder." Soon, "the deed was done," to the dismay of some such as Frederick Douglass, who simply sat looking "grave," as Phillip Bell "tried to snatch the burning fragments from the pile in vain." George Downing, William Watkins, and other delegates "rubbed their hands joyfully over the black and smoldering embers," as white colonizationist Benjamin Coates "looked like a dying man, the very object of pity and misdirection."[3]

By the early 1850s, anticolonization ideology became standard among black reformers and abolitionists. Even those who argued that emigration to Latin America or Canada were acceptable alternatives to remaining in America had come to regard the American Colonization Society and colonization to Liberia as fundamentally flawed and an impediment to race advancement in all aspects of black life. Yet a rift among black leaders over emigration would drive them into a major debate over the consequences of calling for emigration when the ACS's "deportation" project had gained support throughout the nation. In essence, black leaders such as Frederick Douglass came to link pro-emigration rhetoric with pro-colonization ideas, intentionally conflating these two discrete notions.

This was something new among black spokespersons. As we may recall, previously African American leaders such as Richard Allen had acknowledged the distinction between emigrating to Haiti and colonizing West Africa.[4] During the 1820s, black Americans who had endured the ravages of race riots and antiblack legislation were able to gain support within the black community for considering Canada, Haiti, or Trinidad as possible settlements without being called "colonizationists." These movements had not divided black leaders, who in the 1820s and 1830s had argued that emigration movements actually pulled black recruits away from the ACS's Liberian plan. Furthermore, anticolonization had for years provided African Americans, divided over many issues in regards to their elevation, with a point of unity. Yet this was the 1850s, and pro-colonization rhetoric seemed to catch fire in various white communities throughout the nation. Now, black Americans who championed emigration—especially those who considered settling in Africa—were finding themselves under attack for perpetuating a movement akin to colonization.[5] In the first half of the 1850s it seemed that Frederick Douglass and others had succeeded in their efforts to convince most African American abolitionists and reformers that the emigrationists were, in fact, mere colonizationists.

Throughout his career Douglass supported individual emigration as having a rationale when it came to one's personal safety, or as being a matter of choice. But he could not accept the idea that a widespread emigration movement, or the emigration of the most capable black leaders, would benefit the majority of black people. Douglass argued that the pro-emigration rhetoric espoused by men like Martin Delany encouraged colonizationists' view that black Americans desired to leave the United States rather than press for inclusion. Thus, even though Douglass was well aware that Delany and other pro-emigrationists despised the notion of Liberian colonization, Douglass intentionally conflated colonization and emigration as a political strategy in order to forward his anticolonization agenda. But one should not conclude that Douglass did not see the difference between the two ideologies. Rather, Douglass equated emigrationism with colonizationism to destroy the emigration movement, discredit Martin Delany and his supporters, and bolster his own position as the preeminent black leader of the age.[6]

Douglass's anti-emigrationism, and his "stay and fight" position generally, were situated within a style of advocacy that emphasized traditional masculine virtues such as physical confrontation and aggressiveness when agitating against slavery and racial prejudice.[7] As political theorist Dean Robinson explains: "The abolitionist Frederick Douglass—fiercely critical of almost all emigration schemes—favored group efforts that would combat the 'lazy, mean and cowardly spirit, that robs us of all manly self-reliance, and teaches us to depend upon others for the accomplishment of that which we should achieve with our own hands.'" Robinson's point is well taken, and it reinforces the fact that the great divide between the emigrationists and the anti-emigrationists was over resources, leadership, and constituency rather than simply ideology.[8]

Even while Douglass claimed that "Some of us have fought and bled for this country . . . we are lovers of this country . . . [and] I feel that the black man in this land has as much right to stay in this land as a white man," he was aware that, after 1850, the resurgence of pro-colonization opinion among white Americans had set the country on a path towards further exclusion of African Americans, and perhaps even mass deportation.[9] Furthermore, the contingent of notable diaspora Africans who had emigrated to Liberia, such as John Russwurm, Edward Blyden, and Alexander Crummel, challenged the anticolonizationists' positions of Douglass and Delany. Having lived in Liberia for decades, by the 1850s Russwurm was instrumental in the upsurge of interest in Liberia among those, like Crummell and Blyden, who were revered for their intellectual gifts. This of course offered Russwurm the opportunity to join forces with these pan-Africanist pioneers in building Liberia into a democratic nation.[10]

Those black leaders and intellectuals living in Liberia were often the new nation's most astute critics. Yet some, like Edward Blyden, were furious about black American characterizations of Liberia as a fantasy of slaveholders and a "dependency" of the ACS. Blyden, who arrived in Liberia in 1851 and took charge of the *Liberian Herald* in 1855, reminded Delany that Paul Cuffe was the father of colonization, and he called on Delany to join him in his effort to make Liberia into a great African nation. In addition, Blyden wondered why Delany insisted on promoting black Americans' emigration to Latin America when it was "not their fatherland."[11] Here Blyden offered a pan-African framework that Delany would soon adopt.

As Douglass lectured audiences against emigration of Delany's variety, others began to take Blyden's charge seriously. For example, Henry Highland Garnet abandoned his previous anticolonization position and accepted the idea of Liberia's immense potential for stopping the slave trade and fostering "honorable business" in Africa after Liberian indepence in 1847. Garnet still rejected the ACS, but he was ready to join other pan-African intellectuals who arrived in Liberia from the diaspora and created a democratic nation free of racial discrimination. Yet even with his new interest in Liberia, Garnet would still protest against being tagged a "colonizationist."[12]

Although the majority of African American leaders continued to dismiss colonization and the American Colonization Society, the prospects of emigrating from the United States and creating an African American republic attracted at least some support within the black community. Emigrationism, the idea that black Americans should create a homeland in opposition to the United States, emphasized black empowerment. Thus, emigrationism thrived during the 1850s because it gave African Americans a sense that, as a people, they had a destiny to fulfill. As Eddie Glaude observes, nineteenth-century black emigrationists fit their programs within a "nationalist" tradition that encompassed the belief that blacks were a "chosen people." It is clear that those who advocated emigration, such as Martin Delany, Mary Ann Shadd Cary, and James T. Holly, believed their emigrationist programs suggested that black Americans had a duty to uplift black people globally. Furthermore, these were not individuals seeking personal fortune like those European explorers who published travel narratives, describing Africa as a barbaric land filled with savages who were incapable of a life on par with that of white Europeans.[13] On the contrary, black emigrationists took the position that Africans were not inherently unequal, though some of them spoke of Africa in ways that demonstrated tremendous American cultural chauvinism.[14]

The most common explanation for black leaders embracing emigrationism is that it came as a consequence of personal slights or failures in America. No individual has been more often cited to make this case than Martin Delany. Delany's dismissal from Harvard University due to complaints from southern students is often used as conclusive evidence that this type of personal slight, rejection, and out-and-out racist attack shaped the way he viewed his ability to thrive in America. However, one must avoid reducing Delany's emigrationist position to one that stemmed solely from his own personal frustrations. Delany knew all about the tradition of nation building that stretched back to the 1810s, and his own emigrationist views fit within this tradition. In essence, Delany's beliefs were rooted in a sort of nationalism common at that time. Delany explained: "We are a nation within a nation; —as the Poles in Russia, the Hungarians in Austria, the Welsh, Irish, and Scotch in the British domain."[15]

Delany's ideas were shared by others, and three notable treatises that expressed his notion of emigrationism were published during the 1850s. These three works ushered in a new era that has come to be defined by its emphasis on leaving the United States as a bold, assertive step towards self-definition and racial pride. Specifically, Mary Ann Shadd Cary's *Notes on Canada West* (1852), Martin R. Delany's *The Condition, Elevation, and Destiny of the Colored People of the United States* (1852), and James Theodore Holly's *A Vindication of the Capacity of the Negro Race for Self-Government, and Civilized Progress* (1857) presented arguments for leaving the United States that had been around for decades. However, in this historic moment these publications compelled Frederick Douglass and other leaders who characterized themselves by a "stay where you are and fight" ideology to view emigrationism as a legitimate threat to their own position within the abolitionist movement as well as the movement for black equality across the nation.[16] By discrediting black-led emigration efforts with the claim that they were nothing short of colonization schemes in disguise, Douglass and his allies cast Shadd Cary, Delany, and James T. Holly in a disparaging light.[17]

Meanwhile, the ACS was not beyond attempting to blur the distinction between emigrationism and colonizationism either. In fact, since the early 1820s, the ACS sought to convince white and black antislavery leaders that black-initiated emigration projects, whether to Haiti or Canada, shared the basic tenets of colonization ideology. But during each and every black-led emigration movement, African American leaders made certain to show that their initiative differed from ACS colonization to

Liberia. Nevertheless, nearly three decades later, white colonizationists framed the National Emigration Convention of 1854 in a way that made it seem like these black emigrationists shared their vision.[18]

Although Delany and other emigrationists held firm to their belief that colonizationists perpetuated the idea that black people were fundamentally inferior because of immutable racial differences, not all colonizationists believed this. In fact, some colonizationists agreed that the creation of a strong black nation in Africa would redeem the race and thus help eradicate slavery in America, albeit gradually. For instance, Robert J. Breckinridge, a politician and long-time member of the ACS, gave a speech before the Kentucky Colonization Society in Frankfort, the state capital, asserting that the Anglo-American and African American were both members of one human family with unique propensities and destinies to fulfill. Furthermore, he stated that although African Americans had not yet demonstrated their worth in the United States, this was no reason to suspect that they were not, in God's eyes, of the same human family. "There is not one page on which one fact is written—which favors the historical idea of diversity of nature of origin—while the whole scope of human story involves, assumes, and proclaims, as the first and grandest historic truth, the absolute unity of the race," he declared. The reality of the oppression of black people in the United States should be, according to Breckinridge, "attributed to the diverse circumstances" that led to whites in one position, and blacks in another. But in Africa, Breckinridge surmised, African Americans would not only partake in their own elevation, but help forge "a powerful nation" that would lead to "the ultimate redemption of the black race in Africa" and place the race "on a footing as secure as that on which the prosperity of any existing state rests!"[19]

When, in 1847, the Independent Republic of Liberia became the second black republic in the world, its newly elected president, J.J. Roberts, embraced black American emigrationists, calling on them to join him and other inhabitants of Liberia in making it a great nation.[20] Using his inaugural address to set up a race redemption platform that he hoped would unite blacks in the United States with their expatriate comrades in Liberia, Roberts claimed that American blacks were not the only ones pondering racial destiny. Calling out to black Americans, Roberts argued that "the free people of color in the United States, wearied with beating the air to advance themselves to equal immunities with the whites in that country, and tired of the oppression which weighs them down *there*, are seriously turning their attention to Liberia as the only asylum they can flee to and be happy."[21]

However, Roberts's message had barely circulated in the press before Frederick Douglass, William Lloyd Garrison, and others dismissed the new nation as a house built upon a faulty foundation. Although Douglass acknowledged the "determination of the colonists to occupy a highly commendable position among the nations of the earth," he looked scornfully upon the motives for establishing such a nation. Colonization, he explained, had only brought misery to free blacks in America by encouraging the federal and state governments to pursue a policy of deportation—a clear violation of black Americans' civil rights. "The bitter fruit of their yielding to the infernal spirit of expatriation," he argued, "is now in full bloom with us." Free blacks in Virginia, Douglass pointed out, had recently been threatened with mass expulsion "by the bayonets of these same American Christians" who called themselves colonizationists. What Roberts didn't understand, Douglass explained, was that black Americans had to convince whites that the United States was the home of the African American, and, "if we fail in this," he pleaded, "our case is hopeless."[22]

Douglass remained optimistic that black Americans would never embrace colonization, calling the entire colonization movement "an undue illusion." "The fact is colonization is now, just what it was twenty years ago," Douglass explained, and "those engaged in it, are our enemies." These "enemies" Douglass argued, could not claim Liberia's independence as an example of race progress as long as the state remained dependent on people who were "either slaveholders or are pro-slavery in sentiment and their uniform practice."[23]

While Douglass used editorials in the North Star to warn black Americans away from supporting President Roberts and Liberia, the American Colonization Society's newspaper, the African Repository, cited each and every occasion in which black people stood in support of the new republic in order to discredit Douglass. After a group of blacks disrupted President Roberts's meeting with black New Yorkers interested in learning of the progress of Liberia, a second meeting was called at Zion's Church. Liberian delegates fielded over forty questions about the Republic, about matters from the soil to the government, and "the utmost harmony and good feeling pervaded the meeting to its close." According to this ACS report, the meeting generated enough interest to entice some to think "seriously of emigrating to Liberia."[24]

President Roberts's mission to America challenged those like Douglass who denied Liberia's significance. As Roberts explained to white audiences across the country, African Americans had much to be proud of in Liberia, and with the help of free blacks in America, this new West African nation could help foster a greater race redemption mission throughout the world. Indeed, redeeming Africa became a key theme of President Roberts's speeches as he toured Europe and America in search of recognition and support for the republic. Writing to the president of the New York State Colonization Society, Roberts considered his success in New York within the context of his similar efforts in England and France. The French and English had pledged to support Liberia's efforts to end the slave trade on the coast, and had acknowledged Liberia as a legitimate nation. Roberts also bragged that "the Prussian minister in London, informed me that his government had been notified of the change which had been effected in the political relations of Liberia, and that he was authorized to say that the Prussian government would follow the example of England and France, and recognize the independence of the republic." The European trip, Roberts noted, had truly historic significance. "I have every reason to believe," Roberts declared, "that my visit to Europe will result in great good to Africa in general, and Liberia in particular."[25]

Could Liberia "redeem the race" and aid in fulfilling "the destiny of the race," given its relationship with the American Colonization Society? While Douglass argued that "Liberia is as much a dependent as she ever was," members of the American Colonization Society affirmed Roberts's sentiments regarding colonization and African destiny, stating that the organization extended "to the people of Liberia our hearty congratulations on the auspicious result of their recent convention in the establishment of their independent government."[26] The creation of a "nation, which promises untold blessings to Africa," one state auxiliary claimed, would benefit " the African race who will avail themselves of its advantages."[27]

Like Douglass, Martin R. Delany questioned the notion that Liberia could, on any level, become a beacon from which African people would draw inspiration and guidance. Calling Roberts's letter to the New York Colonization Society an act of "degradation to himself" and his people, Delany railed against Roberts for acting "like a slave, cap in hand, obedient to the commands of the dons who employ them, bidden on an errand of his master." Rather than behaving in a "manly, dignified, statesman-like" manner, Roberts's "acts and conduct" would not only cast reproach and indignity onto Liberians, but also upon "the whole colored race in America, since having descended from the American colored race, whatever marks the course of progress in his present position, will be seized hold of by the slaveholders and their abettors, as true evidence of the American colored man's character and susceptibility."[28]

According to the Association of Congregational Ministers of Massachusetts, Delany's analysis of Liberia was misguided. While gathered for its annual meeting, a committee established to investigate "the rise and progress of slavery" came to the conclusion that colonization and the establishment of Liberia "demonstrates the capacity of the Africans for all that constitutes a Christian civilization." The future of Liberia and the possible redemption of the race seemed very likely, they argued, and they went so far as to assert that "there is more hope for the permanence of the Republic of Liberia, than that of France." While such a statement speaks more to the enthusiasm of those gathered than the reality of Liberian independence, Liberia's acceptance by European powers must have given legitimacy to the argument made at the convention that, "as if to afford to all nations a signal exemplification of the capacity of that race, and put the question forever at rest, divine Providence has planted the colony of Liberia."[29]

Likewise, members of the Massachusetts Colonization Society viewed Liberia as a crucial beachhead in the struggle to lift "six hundred millions of the heathen world" out of the darkness and into the light of Jesus Christ. Comparing Liberia's population to that of "Papal Europe," the Massachusetts Colonization Society declared that in Africa there "is about one-fourth of all the heathenism on earth, and in its most malignant form." No organization, the Society argued, had done as much towards making "more rapid and effectual inroads upon its dark domain, than ours." Since without the necessary aid and emigrants, Liberia would not reach its full potential, members of the Massachusetts Colonization Society were called upon to work hard to raise enough money and gather numbers of emigrants sufficient to build upon this extraordinary foundation. "And we confidently hope that the necessary funds will not be withheld. The appeal to all the friends of Africa, and the descendants of Africans, is such as cannot easily be resisted."[30]

Even with these supportive declarations regarding Liberia's potential, black Americans continued to denounce the new republic, while still celebrating Haiti as a more adequate representation of a nation with the potential for race redemption. Frustrated by black Americans' eagerness to celebrate Haitian independence while ignoring Liberian independence, colonizationists took the first black republic to task for its "savagery" and political turmoil. An article in the *African Repository and Colonial Journal* spoke directly to African American fawning over

Haitian independence, complaining that "nothing is said of the African Republic, the Christian Republic of Liberia." These "intelligent colored people" offered only "scoffs and sneers" rather than "some *general*, if not *public* manifestation of their joy at the birth of this new, independent Republic." Colonizationists could not "see any reason why they should not feel and give public demonstration of joy and gratification at an event that must have so favorable an effect upon their own destiny."[31] Indeed, Haiti remained fractured by regionalism, yet Haiti's Faustin I followed in the tradition of his predecessors by publishing advertisements in American papers promoting Haiti as ideal for free blacks eager to abandon the United States for a nation where they could enjoy full civil and human rights. And indeed, African Americans continued to celebrate Haitian independence, while cursing Liberia.[32]

In Europe, those who supported American colonizationists recognized this contradiction. An editorial in *Chambers's Edinburgh Journal* claimed that Liberia had much more potential to demonstrate the capacity of the race than Haiti. "Hayti commenced its career in blood and violence"; Liberia, though, had been founded upon "Christian love," while in Haiti, despite being founded beneath "French polish," there was "neither intellectual culture nor moral or religious restraints." Also the article reminded its readers that Liberia's "civilization" was "essentially Anglo-Saxon, and with the English tongue and the English Bible, not to speak of the spirit of English industry," the new nation was bound to become much more than "the imperfect nationality of Hayti."[33]

This colonizationist message had gained traction among free blacks in Maryland in the early 1850s, pushing some delegates of a black state convention to consider the Maryland Colonization Society's argument for Liberian colonization. With bleak prospects for equal political and civil rights after the Fugitve Slave Act, some free African Americans in Maryland had come to regard colonization to Liberia as an attractive alternative. Perhaps these black leaders had learned that the Maryland Colonization Society had embraced emancipation, having rejected the parent organization's opposition to this position in the early 1830s.[34]

During the 1852 Maryland Free Colored People's Convention, the debate over accepting the Maryland Colonization Society's colonization plan began when a resolution was presented on the floor that called on Maryland blacks to consider emigration to Liberia over Canada. The resolution sparked mayhem among delegates, but pro-emigrationist, pro-colonizationist delegates held their ground, claiming that "in comparing the relative advantages of Canada, the West Indies, and Liberia . . . we are

led to examine the claims of Liberia." And although "it is not our purpose to counsel emigration as either necessary or proper in every case,"
in their opinion "sooner or later removal must take place."[35] James A.
Handy of Baltimore presented the pro-Liberian colonization resolution,
calling on blacks to return to their "native land" as a feature of a redemptive project. In his estimation, God had given African Americans the
benefits of Western civilization, but now they were being called by "the
voice of heaven" to "arise and depart" to Africa. Handy argued for a van-
guard of African American leaders and their families to redeem Africa
vis-à-vis Liberia, thereby providing a "star of hope to the benighted millions of Africa."[36]

After Handy spoke, James A. Jackson called on black American delegates to look toward Haiti instead of Liberia. Jackson claimed that Haiti
held more promise for influencing the Western hemisphere, and in turn
the future of enslaved African Americans. "Hayti," he argued, stood as
"high above the West India islands as the United States does above the
republic of Mexico, in the point of commercial importance." Thus, he
believed that Haiti was a better site than Africa to begin the process of
redeeming the race.[37]

In answer, Nicholas Penn, a delegate from Dorchester, claimed that
black Americans did not "want an island," and more often than not
favored Liberia over Haiti. Penn had actually spent eleven months in
Liberia traveling throughout the country to examine its potential for
settlement, and he claimed that "all these statements about Africa were
theoretical—gained thro' geography." What the delegation needed to do
was to determine if they actually believed in the efficacy of emigration,
and then, after research into these various locales, determine "whether
they should remain here, or to seek a home in Liberia, or elsewhere."[38]

As the members of the convention argued back and forth, "John A.
Walker, after some difficulty, got the floor and offered a substitute" resolution for dealing with the issue of colonization and emigration. His new
resolution emphasized the need for the convention to send out representatives from various communities throughout the state to gather "information in relation to the condition of the colored emigrants in Canada,
West Indies, Guiana, and Liberia, as can be obtained." With this information, representatives would meet monthly to discuss the information
and determine if blacks would benefit from emigration, and if so, where
the best location would be for settlement.[39] Walker's compromise seemed
acceptable to some, but those who opposed the original resolution were
not persuaded by his alternative.[40] While little had been accomplished by

the end of the debates, the delegates did demonstrate the broad range of opinions about emigration and colonization—just a sample of the texture of the national conversation over race advancement in light of the progress of the American Colonization Society and the rise of federal and state legislation adverse to African American improvement.

The same year that black Americans in Maryland debated colonization and emigration, Martin Delany completed his work *The Condition, Elevation, Emigration, and Destiny of the Coloured People of the United States, Politically Considered*. It offered a critique of the "stay and fight" position expressed by Frederick Douglass and other abolitionists—black and white—who came to regard the recent upsurge in pro-emigration ideology as ominous. Like David Walker, Martin Delany called on African American leaders to move beyond what he considered to be white handouts and to act independently by creating black-led organizations independent of white philanthropy. Delany also linked the creation of an independent African American nation with a broader pan-African effort throughout the world in opposition to the doctrine of Manifest Destiny, which justified not only Anglo-American expansion westward, but Anglo-Saxon and Anglo-American world dominance. It is important to note that Delany's brand of racialism must be understood in its historical context. For Delany, racial destiny was an ideology of self-empowerment, not racial exclusionism. Later in his life, he would boldly proclaim that his mission had remained humanistic and universal, and therefore did not privilege one race over the other. For those who considered leaving the United States, Delany's racial rhetoric articulated their desire to build an independent black-led nation to demonstrate their equality.[41]

While Delany declared that his sense of racial loyalty underpinned this commitment to emigration, he also found it necessary to justify himself to those black leaders who held a "stay and fight" position. Since Frederick Douglass and other "stay and fight" advocates criticized emigrationists for abandoning their "enslaved brethren," Delany argued that emigrationism was a way of defending the race against the argument used by whites to justify slavery and racism. By creating a black republic independent of whites, black Americans would prove their equality. Racism in the United States had robbed the black race of its "manhood," according to Delany, and this made them impotent against slavery and racial prejudice. Consequently, black men were unable to raise themselves to a level of respectability on a par with whites, and they were unable to challenge white men engaged in a process of racial emasculation on a global scale.[42] Using the abolitionists' claim that sexual assault against black women demonstrated one of the slaveholders' greatest abuses, Delany cast race redemption in gendered terms.[43]

Delany's *Conditions* also provided readers with a specific way to frame emigrationism within the context of racial destiny. As he explained, "A child born under oppression, has all the elements of servility in its constitution; who when born under favorable circumstances, has to the contrary, all the elements of freedom and independence of feeling."[44] For black Americans, freedom would only truly be achieved when African Americans were no longer living in an oppressive nation. Thus, Delany pondered, "the question will then be, Where shall we go? This we conceive to be all important—of paramount consideration, and shall endeavor to show the most advantageous locality."[45] For Delany, Central America, Mexico, and the West Indies were ideal locations for an African American nation. While "our oppressors, when urging us to go to Africa, tell us that we are better adapted to the climate than they," Delany argued against Africa at this point because he believed it to be less suitable than a location in the Western hemisphere near the United States. Regardless of where African Americans chose to create their own nation, what mattered most to Delany was the question: "Shall we fly, or shall we resist?"[46]

Douglass apparently ignored *Conditions* when it was published, prompting Delany to write Douglass in July 1852 to ask why he failed to review it in his newspaper, or at least write back to him with his impressions. Delany questioned Douglass's "cold and deathly silence," since, as Delany explained, "you could have given it a circulating notice, by saying such a book had been written by me." Delany further criticized Douglass's apparent fawning over white authors for support and patronage at the cost of black writers who needed all the publicity they could get. Barely concealing his contempt for Douglass's support of Harriet Beecher Stowe's novel *Uncle Tom's Cabin*, Delany complained: "This is not the course you pursue towards any issue, good or bad, sent you by white persons." Rather than come off desperate for Douglass's support, Delany concluded, "I desire not to make an undue allusion, but simply to be treated as justly as you treat them."[47]

Douglass's strategy of ignoring Delany's work may have been personal as well as political. Having toured with Douglass and worked as a correspondent for the *North Star*, Delany had come to know Douglass personally as well as professionally. It seems clear that by 1849, Delany and Douglass had begun to move in different directions, and this may be attributed to the fact that two men with such great intelligence, oratorical skill, and charisma would find working together challenging.

Nevertheless, Delany and Douglass, in 1849, had shared a common disdain for both colonization and emigration. Writing about Liberia's new independence, Delany exclaimed that it was necessary for the black community in America to "protest against [President Roberts's] whole course in regard to his agency and intercourse, either directly or indirectly, with the Colonizationists."[48]

Even in 1851, Delany remained committed to Douglass's "stay and fight" ideology. That year, he signed a petition at the North American Convention in Toronto, which protested a resolution that passed encouraging Canadian emigration. According to Delany and three others, "whereas, the convention, in adopting the first resolution, inviting the colored people to leave the northern part of the United States, has done so contrary to the desires and wishes of those of us, from the States, who believe it to be impolitic and contrary to our professed policy in opposing the infamous fugitive slave laws, and schemes of the American colonization."[49] But what had once united them would divide them in bold new ways by 1852, and the tension that had built between the two for nearly four years would turn into a public confrontation of seismic proportions. While it is difficult to pin down the exact reason the two major black activists and intellectuals came to blows, the conflict between the two men exploded into the public sphere, causing black leaders from Boston to Chicago to choose sides.

This public debate between Douglass and Delany began after Harriet Beecher Stowe completed *Uncle Tom's Cabin*.[50] Abolitionists in the 1850s acknowledged the novel as one of the most influential works in the American literary tradition for unveiling the horrors of slavery, igniting a storm of controversy in the South, and pushing African American abolitionists to debate the way in which Stowe captured the essence of her black characters. Some blacks embraced the novel as a realistic portrayal of the horrors of slavery, while others dismissed the work as a tool of colonizationists. One particular irritant for some black readers was the characterization of African Americans as "docile, timid, and effeminate."[51]

If Stowe's problematic depiction of African American characters didn't attract enough scorn from some black leaders, the book's view that colonization in West Africa was the only means by which African Americans could rise to greatness as a people led some to call her a colonizationist. Historian George Fredrickson actually refers to her as a "neocolonizationist," arguing that "in the conclusion to *Uncle Tom's Cabin*, Mrs. Stowe made her colonizationist sentiments very clear, not only by suggesting that the romantic racialist vision of the Negro future could be attained only in Africa but also by explicitly describing how Negroes would be prepared for the transatlantic refuge that God had provided for them." While Fredrickson succeeds in proving that Stowe had imbibed the "romantic racialism" of her day, the character George Harris's monologue about leaving America for Africa resembles an "emigrationist" position more than it does a "colonizationist" one.[52] In fact, even if Stowe may have sympathized with the colonizationist ideology of the day, the language she uses to describe George Harris's desire to leave America sounds more like a Martin Delany speech than one of pro-colonizationists like Henry Clay. Soon after completing the novel, Stowe was dismayed by those who called her a colonizationist, claiming that if there was one aspect that she would change it would be George Harris's endorsement of emigration to Africa. What is interesting about Delany's condemnation of Stowe's work is the way Delany intentionally conflated colonization and emigration, which was the same tactic Douglass used against him.

This conflation between colonization and emigration has continued among scholars of Stowe's work. One such author writes: "Next to Tom's excessive meekness, the most controversial aspect of Stowe's rhetoric of race . . . is her apparent endorsement of emigration." This scholar goes on to argue that "George embraces colonization and rejects social equality as his goal," and that "Stowe appropriates the ideas and language of the colonization movement to talk about the desirability of expatriation for free blacks. . . . We may ask what is her purpose in having George . . . declare he does not want social equality with whites in America?" George's call for black emigration resembles Delany's affirmation of the futility of fighting for equal rights in America, rather than the idea that black people lacked the capacity for achieving equality in the United States. Virtually all emigrationists rejected colonization and the ACS, while calling for blacks to create their own nation to *oppose* America and prove they were the equal of any white person.[53] In fact, not only did Stowe claim she was no colonizationist, meaning that she did not support mass deportation of African Americans; her character, George Harris, explicitly differentiates between colonization and emigration.[54]

When George Harris describes his feelings about Liberia "in a letter to one of his friends," he explains that "it is with the oppressed, enslaved African race that I cast in my lot; and, if I wished anything, I would wish myself two shades darker, rather than one lighter."[55] Here, Harris expresses the classic claim that Delany would make about the importance of skin color in representing the race. In fact, Delany often spoke of his "darker hue" as a way to legitimize his self-proclaimed status as a true representative figure of black Americans.[56] Harris goes on to proclaim that "the desire and yearning of my soul is for an African *nationality*. I want a people that shall have a tangible, separate existence of its own. . . ." Like Delany, the character emphasizes the notion that through the creation of an "African nationality," black Americans could demonstrate their unique gift to the world and prove their "manhood" and worth against "Anglo-Saxonism."

George Harris's imagined "African nationality" is an important feature of Stowe's conclusion, and this statement sets it apart from much of the pro-colonizationist literature. Stowe's character offers his own explanation about how he came to view his emigrationism as opposed to colonization when he refers to this same debate between "abolitionists and colonizationists," about whom Harris claims to have "received some impressions, as a distant spectator, which could never have occurred to me as a participant." These "impressions" have led Harris to conclude that, while the colonization scheme may have been created to the detriment of free blacks, the idea of forming an African republic must not be dismissed because "Liberia may have subserved all sorts of purposes, by being played off, in the hands of our oppressors, against us." But Harris asks, "Is there not a God above all man's schemes? May he not have overruled their designs, and founded for us a nation by them?"[57] As for the claim that anti-emigration, anticolonizationists made about their unwillingness to leave their African kin in the South, Harris posits: "Do you say I am deserting my enslaved brethren? I think not." He explains that individual blacks were powerless against the South. But, as a representative of a great African nation, his chances of pressuring America into universal emancipation were much better. Harris concludes: "A nation has a right to argue, remonstrate, implore, and present the cause of its race, —which an individual has not."[58]

Stowe's character George Harris expresses the basic tenets of emigrationism in a manner that shows that she understands the difference between colonization and emigration. And, as literary critic Samuel Otter argues, "While these opinions technically belong to George, they certainly are Stowe's too."[59] Stowe's emigrationist position is not void of some of the assumptions implicit in colonizationist ideology, however. Her view, for example, that free African Americans would never be able to achieve equal rights in the United States is one of the platforms that colonizationists used to defend their project. While Stowe agrees with

this notion, her reason for advocating the creation of a black nationality, like Delany's, rests on the principle that this black republic could
actually challenge the United States over the legitimacy of slavery, and
could undermine America's dependence on enslaved laborers. Here is
the essential difference between the colonizationist doctrine and the
emigrationist agenda. Most colonizationists believed Africans were
naturally inferior and could never reach the level of Anglo-Saxons, and
Stowe seems to suggest that this is untrue. In this regard, George Harris
claims, "I think that the African race has peculiarities, yet to be unfolded
in the light of civilization and Christianity, which, if not the same with
those of the Anglo-Saxon, may prove to be, morally, of even a higher
type."[60] This is not to suggest that Stowe was not a victim of what George
Fredrickson has called "romantic racialism" or "internalized racism."
Like William Lloyd Garrison, Gerrit Smith, and many white abolitionists, Stowe was a product of her times, and in that regard she accepted
a popular wisdom about blacks that was often condescending, paternalistic, and racist. Yet these flaws in Stowe's thinking should not be a
reason to dismiss her as a "colonizationist." Instead, her argument for a
black nationality through repatriation as a means for achieving "racial
destiny" resembles more closely the "emigrationist" ideology of the day
than the racially exclusionary vision expressed by most—although not
all—"colonizationists."[61]

Nevertheless, this distinction did not matter much to those like Martin Delany and Mary Ann Shadd Cary who continued to call her and
her novel a tool of the colonizationists.[62] At the American and Foreign
Anti-Slavery Society meeting, black members introduced a resolution
that remonstrated against the novel for its colonizationist message. Even
though Stowe sent a letter claiming she was not a colonizationist, and
one person told those gathered that Stowe confessed that had she rewrit-
ten the novel she would have taken out the part in question, many still
viewed the work in such a light.[63]

Ironically, given his disdain for emigration and colonization, Douglass defended the novel against the claim that Stowe's work perpetuated
the views of the American Colonization Society. From his perspective
the work was one of the best means available to change the "hearts
and minds" of slaveholders specifically, and whites in general. As Robert Levine observes, "Convinced that Stowe's novel had the power and
vision to do just that, Douglass over the next two years set aside numerous columns in *Frederick Douglass' Paper* to publicize, promote, and
shape the reception of Stowe's novel."[64] In fact, Douglass went so far as

to dismiss those who charged her with colonization sympathies by conflating Delany's emigration with that of colonizationists as a means to defend Stowe. Writing in response to Delany's effort to discredit Stowe, Douglass claimed, "He says she is a colonizationist; and we ask, what if she is? . . . A little while ago, brother Delany was a colonizationist."[65]

Douglass's actions, statements, and editorials conflating emigration and colonization reflect his increasing concern over the leadership potential of Delany and the growing momentum that emigrationists had gathered in the black community. As David Blight notes: "Although Douglass rarely gave in to emigrationist arguments, he wrote to Gerrit Smith of his "fear that some whose presence in this country is necessary to the elevation of the colored people will leave us." Douglass came to the conclusion that the more educated the black person, the more likely he or she embraced emigration. He lamented to a friend: "It would seem that education and emigration go together with us," citing the departure of John Russwurm and Alexander Crummell for Africa. This outgoing stream of intelligent and capable black leaders frustrated Douglass, yet he claimed that he did not "blame them" for leaving. However, he continued to struggle against emigrationist sentiments, hoping that he could purge African American leaders of any impulse to begin anew in Africa, or anywhere else.[66]

Nevertheless, in a speech that he delivered in May 1853, Douglass acknowledged that emigration somewhere within the western hemisphere was an option that far exceeded the colonization project for its practicability among free blacks and their enthusiasm for it.. As Douglass explained:

> The people of this Republic may commit the audacious and
> high-handed atrocity of driving us out of the limits of their bor-
> ders . . . but to compel us to go to Africa is quite another thing.
> Thank God, the alternative is not quite so desperate. . . . Other and
> more desirable lands are open to us. . . . We can hover about the
> Gulf of Mexico. . . . With the Gulf of Mexico on the South, and
> Canada on the North, we may still keep within hearing of the wails
> of our enslaved people in the United States.[67]

This passage does not suggest that Douglass should be considered an emigrationist; it does, however, show that on some level he understood the value of forming a black community outside of U.S. borders. Furthermore, this passage, written after he had dismissed Delany's *Conditions*, reveals that he understood the difference between pushing forth a platform that was colonizationist and one that was emigrationist. While Douglass remained committed to remaining in the United States, and thus near to his proverbial "brothers in chains," his conflation of colonization and emigration appears to have been a rhetorical strategy used to discredit Delany and the emigration movement.

Although Delany and Douglass are often positioned as two leaders at opposite ends of a spectrum in regards to emigration (and by extension black nationalism), a close examination of Douglass's speeches reveals similarities between the two men in regard to emigration and racial destiny. The destiny of the African Americans had been an important feature of Frederick Douglass's rhetoric on black advancement, and his ideas about the "elevation of the race" mirror those of Delany and other emigrationists more than he may have cared to admit. One particular speech Douglass made in May 1853 in New York, entitled "The Present Condition and Future Prospects of the Negro People," offers an instructive example of how he incorporated elements of emigrationist ideology in his effort to demonstrate that black Americans had the capability to create an independent nation if they chose to do so. When Douglass stated that "We are a nation within a nation" and compares African Americans' plight to that of European ethnic minorities under the domination of Great Britain, Austria, and Russia, he acknowledges the efficacy of black American emigration to a location in the Caribbean, Mexico, or Canada. Like Delany, who also used the title "A Nation within a Nation" for one of his own speeches, Douglass admitted that "the fundamental principles of the republic, to which the humblest white man, whether born here or elsewhere, may appeal with confidence in the hope of awakening a favorable response are held to be inapplicable to us." In Douglass's view, this tradition contradicted "the glorious doctrines" of both "the revolutionary fathers" and "the Son of God." Yet he still argued for free black Americans to continue to struggle for equal rights in the United States rather than leave to create a new nation elsewhere.[68]

Delany was not Douglass's only opponent. In 1852, the same year Delany published *Conditions*, Mary Ann Shadd Cary completed her pro-emigration work, *A Plea for Emigration, or Notes of Canada West*. This book attempts to show black Americans that Canada was the most realistic location for would-be emigrants. While Delany argued that "We are satisfied that the Canadas [sic] are no place of safety for the colored people of the United States; otherwise we should have no objection to them," Shadd Cary declared Canada to be a more suitable place for black American emigration than Africa, Haiti, or Latin America. Like Delany,

Shadd Cary held firm her anticolonizationist posture, writing that the American Colonization Society was operating "in the garb of Christianity and Philanthropy," when it really held blacks in contempt. Rather than leave for Liberia under the guidance of the ACS, she explained that "tropical Africa, the land of promise of the colonizationists, teeming as she is with the breath of pestilence, a burning sun and fearful maladies, bids them welcome."[69] While scholars frequently mention Shadd Cary as an important leader in the emigration movement, rarely do they analyze "A Plea for Emigration" in any depth. Part of the reason is that it lacks the type of rhetorical grandstanding so prevalent among leaders such as Delany. But one must remember that Shadd Cary wrote her pamphlet from Canada and was not merely speculating on emigration; she had actually left.[70] Ultimately, her effort to present an unbiased view of the British colony served to make her influential pamphlet a virtual travel brochure for Canadian emigration.

In "A Plea," Shadd Cary confronts the "question whether or not an extensive emigration by free colored people of the United States would affect the institution of slavery" in a straightforward way. She writes:

> What are the facts[?] More territory has been given up to slavery, the Fugitive Law has passed, and a concert of measures, seriously affecting their personal liberty, has been entered into by several of the Free states; so subtle, unseen and effective have been their movements, that, were it not that we remember there is a Great Britain, we would be overwhelmed, powerless, from the force of such successive shocks; and the end may not be yet, if we persist in remaining for targets, while they are strengthening themselves in the Northwest, and in the Gulf.[71]

The concept of Manifest Destiny, in her opinion, made black American emigration to Canada an urgent matter. White Americans, as far as she could see, intended on taking over all lands west and south, and thus, African Americans had no choice but to emigrate to Canada to live free from the seemingly unstoppable quest for American hegemony, which drove whites to occupy every inch of the nation "from sea to shining sea." This Anglo-American spirit was, in her view, intertwined with a "slave power" determined to control the future of the nation. African Americans needed only to look at the actions of the federal government with regards to slavery and expansion to see the trend toward expulsion of free blacks, or worse.

By weaving her rhetoric of race advancement around her effort to convince African Americans to emigrate to Canada, she took on the "stay and fight" advocates by arguing that their "miserable scampering from state to state, in a vain endeavor to gather the crumbs of freedom that a pro-slavery besom may sweep away at any moment," seemed futile. Racial pride meant independence and freedom from the dictates of a nation, which had consistently legislated to the detriment of black people. Personal pride, as well as racial pride, called on African Americans to "demand freedom to the slave," rather than appeal to the consciousness of those who lacked any sense of moral worth. African American emigration to Canada would demonstrate black Americans' ability to create strong communities, and offer black people an option infinitely better than "scampering" around the North for mere "crumbs," which she viewed as pathetic.

While Mary Ann Shadd Cary's work focused on the practical advantages of Canadian emigration, James T. Holly's emigration treatise, *A Vindication of the Capacity of the Negro Race for Self-Government and Civilized Progress*, portrayed Haiti's legacy of violence and political power in a way that sought to reinvigorate African Americans' sense of racial destiny and duty. In *A Vindication* Holly acknowledges that "everything is done by the enemies of the negro race to vilify and debase them," and that consequently this has led "many of the race themselves" to be "almost persuaded that they are a brood of inferior beings." His "vindication" challenged blacks to demonstrate the masculine virtues of the race through nation building, which would destroy the credibility of those who claimed that blacks were inherently inferior.[72]

Ultimately, Holly shared Delany's belief that the independent spirit of the Haitians was an important expression of the racial pride which black Americans needed to embrace. Of course, Holly's portrait of Haiti is romantic, and he avoids any serious critique of the various challenges the black republic endured, but his main objective was to "vindicate" black people whom whites deemed biologically inferior and unfit for participation in a civilized nation. Emigration would allow a select group of black Americans to join Haitians in the journey towards the creation of a "black nationality of the New World" that would become "the lever that must be exerted, to regenerate and disenthrall the oppression and ignorance of the race, throughout the world."[73]

Holly denied that Liberia could serve the same purpose as Haiti. Sharing both Delany's and Shadd's criticism of Liberia, Holly argued that the American Colonization Society's role in shaping the politics of the newly independent nation undermined its ability to act decisively for the good of the race. Liberia, according to Holly, remained a "utopian scheme" that had been "forced upon us" by whites "to send us across the ocean" in what he viewed as "fruitless" and "ill-directed efforts at the wrong end of human progress." Progress, in Holly's opinion, would come when African Americans carried the "arts, sciences, and genius of modern civilization" to the Haitians, and abandoned the path of his critics (such as Douglass) who "indolently remain here, asking for political rights, which, if granted" would be unable to change the "social proscription stronger than conventional legislation will ever render nugatory."[74]

While Holly, Delany, and Shadd Cary were expressing the ideological tenets of emigrationism during the 1850s, it seemed apparent to them that they needed to organize others who shared their conviction in order to transform their emigrationist assertions into an actual plan of action. In 1853 emigrationists issued a call to be published in the African American press for a national emigration convention to be held in Cleveland, Ohio, in 1854. Scholars have dismissed the Emigration Convention as an ineffectual movement initiated by a few disgruntled black leaders, frustrated by racism and naive about the realities of European colonialism and imperialism.[75] Perhaps the lack of consensus over a location for black Americans to establish a nation, as well as the successful conflation of emigration and colonization, caused many ordinary black Americans to view the Emigration Convention as suspect. The hesitancy within the black community is often cited as proof that the majority of black people were not interested in emigration, and thus Delany and others did not have a noticeable constituency. While Douglass led others to condemn the convention as separatist, unrealistic, and useless, it seems quite clear that emigrationism and the emigration conventions held during the 1850s had a tremendous impact on the ideology of race advancement, pushing Douglass and his constituency to develop a better plan. Furthermore, the statements and resolutions that came out of the convention clearly established an ideology for race progress centered around black nationalist and pan-Africanist concepts, which would outlast the 1850s and inspire black community leaders and spokespersons for the next century.[76]

Certainly organizing a movement to create an African American homeland with the symbolic value of Haiti and the practical goal of challenging slavery, the slave trade, and Anglo-American Manifest Destiny was no small feat. Nevertheless, some of the most intelligent and dedicated African American community leaders took to the task and organized in opposition to Douglass and those who sought acceptance on equal terms with whites in the United States.[77]

By August 1853, a call for a convention of African Americans interested in debating emigration from the United States ran in *Frederick Douglass' Paper*. Within this call, Delany and others denounced colonization and the ACS, acknowledging that an inaccurate association between colonization and emigration stood as one major roadblock. Thus, Delany and William Webb used their call to assert that "colonizationists are advised, that no favors will be shown to them or their expatriating scheme, as we have no sympathy with the enemies of our race."[78]

Soon the emigrationists' following grew, and Douglass ceased printing the call or, indeed, any pro-emigration ideas.[79] Black Bostonians were disturbed by the sentence in the call stating that "all persons coming to this Convention must give assurance to the Committee on credentials." As they saw it, this statement "is an insult to the understanding of the colored people; precludes investigation; suppresses honest convictions; is a pitiable imitation of slaveholding attempts in Congress . . . to pass gag laws."[80]

On the other hand, blacks in New Bedford, Massachusetts, looked beyond the wording and decided to meet to discuss the merits of emigration. The group met twice at a Baptist church to consider whether or not to send delegates to the convention. But the pro-emigrationists failed to persuade the majority, and a resolution was passed stating that emigration "is nothing less than the old spirit of American Colonizationism in another disguise."[81] They condemned Delany and the others for acting "selfishly" in their effort at a "mistaken attempt to better their condition" while blacks enslaved in the South suffered under the lash.

As was usual at these local gatherings, the African Americans who gathered at the State Council of Colored People of Massachusetts also discussed the Emigration Convention Meeting in January 1854, just six months before the National Emigration Convention in Cleveland. Some delegates dismissed the Emigration Convention, even though they "gladly note[d] the enterprising spirit of individual colored Americans, which prompts them to seek fortunes in California and Australia, or elsewhere." Through a resolution adopted by the majority of those present, they declared that "the prominence now given to a general emigration scheme" had been tainted by the reality that the "American Colonization Society will connect every such movement among us as tending to promote their nefarious plan of expatriation." For this reason, they stated: "[W]e therefore avail ourselves of this occasion to express our entire and decided disapproval of the plan and objects of the Emigration Convention, to be held in Cleveland, Ohio, in the month of August, 1854."[82]

These statements, some harsh, others diplomatic, may have functioned to assure Douglass that his old friends in the Bay State still remained loyal to his views on the subject. And these vituperations sought to undermine and derail the convention rather than merely express the local opinions and attitudes of blacks in New Bedford. Douglass knew what he was doing when he published these declarations in his newspaper, and Delany understood as well. This contention over the call to the convention was, ultimately, contention over race leadership, and the battle over strategies and tactics between Douglass and Delany would continue up until the Civil War.

Although Delany may have dealt silently with Douglass's failure to acknowledge his book, he would not sit quietly when *Frederick Douglass' Paper* charged him and other emigrationists with "the spirit and design of disunion" for planning an Emigration Convention. Delany had finally had enough. Soon after reading this he wrote a scathing letter to Douglass, which declared: "I can submit to any other wrong—as I have ever been doing all my life—from colored men, except that of charging me with a design of injury to my race; and this I never shall submit to with indifference." Regardless of whether or not Douglass or the delegates of the Illinois state convention, such as John Jones, agreed with emigration, Delany refused to allow them to give "false representation" of his "motives and designs."[83] He snapped at Douglass, reminding him that "I am neither a neophyte, an ephemera, nor a novice in the cause of our elevation," and recounting publicly through his letter his numerous efforts at gaining African American civil and political rights. Ultimately, Delany charged Douglass with attempting to destroy his reputation. This was inexcusable to Delany, and he was furious that the resolution had coupled his name "with the odious enemies of our race, Colonizationists."

Perhaps Douglass was shaken by Delany's aggressiveness. Needless to say, Douglass was not prepared to lose face in such a public way. Thus he wrote a letter to Delany that explained the circumstances by which the resolution from the Illinois state convention had appeared in his newspaper. Douglass claimed that he had been traveling when the statement was published, and that he did not intend to defame Delany in any way. Whether or not Douglass had personally placed the resolution in the paper, Delany believed that it "meant something" even if it had been cut-and-pasted into the paper while Douglass was away. Furthermore, Delany reminded Douglass that he could "misrepresent others as you think proper," but he demanded that *he* not "be misrepresented" in such a way.[84]

By March 1854, John Jones, the individual who had apparently made this statement condemning Delany at the Illinois state convention, wrote to Douglass claming that he sought "to put [him]self right with M R Delany." In a letter to Delany, Jones recounted the way Delany's name became associated with the anti-emigration proclamation made at the Illinois convention. He explained, "I am neither the father nor the introducer of those resolutions," and he claimed that a reporter for the *Chicago Tribune* had given him credit for the resolutions by mistake. That was how Jones "came to get the credit for those resolutions which he has fretted so much about." In what seems like an obvious attempt to clear Douglass's name, Jones wrote that the article from the *Chicago Tribune* "was copied while [Douglass] was yet in Illinois."[85] Although it isn't clear why Douglass and Jones would respond this way, the ideological divide between Douglass and his allies, on one side, and Delany and the new emigrationists, on the other, remained substantial.

Right before Martin R. Delany, Mary Ann Shadd Cary, and other black leaders participated in the National Emigration Convention in 1854, Douglass and other anti-emigrationists gathered at the New York State Convention that same year to debate the rising tide of emigrationism. By the end of the program, black delegates had rejected *any* program to leave the United States whether by the American Colonization Society or what they decided was a "more dangerous and equally detestable scheme" of emigration planned by Delany and other organizers of the Emigration Convention in Cleveland. Ultimately, the delegates at the New York State Convention condemned "every system of colonization of the people of color from these United States" in a resolution approved unanimously.[86]

Despite these attempts to disrupt Delany's recruitment efforts, the National Emigration Convention was held in Cleveland, Ohio, on August 24, 1854. Most of those who attended the convention were from the "West," and nearly a quarter of those participating in the Cleveland Convention were women. This number of female delegates far exceeded the participation of women at other national conventions. As African Americans gathered at a "Universalist Church on Prospect Street" in Cleveland, white residents may have been taken back by the presence of so many well-mannered and eloquent black men and women walking down the street conversing about complex political ideas such as racial elevation and racial destiny. As one reporter for the white-owned *Cleveland Leader* observed: "Few Conventions of whites behave themselves more orderly or courteously, or observe parliamentary rules more exactly, or discuss important topics with more ability and self-possession, than the

Colored Convention now in session in this city." Such a view contributed to the idea that well-mannered black people, behaving in "respectable" ways, could change the way whites viewed blacks as a race. Thus, he explained: "Physically and phrenologically, there may be seen some splendid specimens of manhood under a swarthy covering. Every shade of complexion, and form of feature has its representative, from the ebon to the brunette, and from the physiognomy of the full-blood African to the Anglo-Saxon features."[87]

Delany's keynote speech, entitled "Political Destiny of the Colored Races on the American Continent," is a clear expression of emigrationist, as well as black nationalist, ideology. "A people, to be free, must necessarily be their own rulers," Delany explained; "that is, each individual must, in himself, embody the essential ingredient—so to speak—of the sovereign principle which composes the true basis of his liberty." For Delany, as long as African Americans remained a minority within the nation, they would continue to suffer at the hands of their white oppressors. Furthermore, without power—political or physical—black leaders would always be forced to live under the thumb of whites, whether in the North, the South, the East, or the West.

Delany drew upon the history of the Roman republic, the story of Exodus in the Bible, and the more recent Hungarian revolution of 1848 to contextualize his argument. Then he pointed to the various locales in Central and South America, the Caribbean, and "Canada West, where being politically equal to whites, and physically united with each other by a concentration of strength," blacks could stand and fight against any aggressive attempt to re-enslave, or deport, them to Africa. Even though U.S. statesmen claimed that the nation had been founded upon democratic ideals and natural rights philosophy, in practice racial hatred and white supremacy perverted these ideals and impeded the United States' ability to become the nation it claimed to be. Furthermore, Delany noted with a hint of sarcasm, those who claim "Universal Brotherhood" had traversed the world "propagating the doctrine in favor of a *universal Anglo-Saxon predominance.*" This brought Delany to his main point: "The only successful remedy for the evils we endure, is to place ourselves in a position of potency, independently of our oppressors."[88]

Delany believed Douglass and others had failed to defend the integrity of the race, and thus they needed to be awakened to the present crisis, pushed from their thrones, and forced to take an independent stand for the "future of the race." It was time for African American leaders to acknowledge that black people "have inherent traits, attributes—so to speak—and native characteristics, peculiar to our race—whether pure or mixed blood—and all that is required of us is to cultivate these and develop them in their purity, to make them desirable and emulated by the rest of the world."[89]

Delany's statement recasts Anglo-Saxon, Anglo-American race theory in a manner that challenges the premise that black people were inherently unequal, and thus ought to be ruled by others. Some whites shared this vision, and Delany claimed that "the Anglo-Saxon has taken the lead in this work of universal subjugation," yet there were some "great and good people in America, England, France, and the rest of Europe, who desire a unity of interests among the whole human family, of whatever origin or race." Yet the good deeds of a few courageous individual whites could not make up for the gross acts of treachery, Delany believed, that the majority of whites had committed over the previous two thousand years. He explained: "We regret the necessity of stating the fact—but duty compels us to the task—that, for more than two thousand years, the determined aim of the whites has been to crush the colored races wherever found." In his view, this destructive path, initiated by Europeans, especially Anglo-Saxons, had only been surpassed by the heinous behavior of Anglo-Americans. Thus, he concludes, "the Anglo-American stands pre-eminent for the deeds of injustice and acts of oppression, unparalleled perhaps in the annals of modern history."[90]

Underlining this sense of racial destiny was the notion of lifting up black people to the level of "manhood" required of "mature races." In Delany's view, African Americans could only cultivate the masculine virtues, such as physical strength, intellectual merit, and independence, in a black nation. America remained, for Delany, a white man's land where Anglo-Saxon dominance denied blacks all the possible avenues for them to assert their manhood.[91] Thus, for black American leaders to attempt to "stay and fight" was futile and did not represent the ultimate display of "manhood."[92] Through the numerous statements and resolutions made at the National Emigration Convention in Cleveland, it is quite apparent that emigrationist ideology was also steeped in notions of "manhood" and "masculinity" that defied the claim that any black Americans who left their enslaved black countrymen behind were, indeed, weak.[93]

As noted previously, this discourse of a "masculine" virtue did not necessarily seek to perpetuate the notion that women were fundamentally inferior to men and were to remain in the domestic sphere, out of sight, and without a voice in public affairs. Delany appears to have regarded women such as Mary Ann Shadd Cary as the equal of his male counterparts.[94] In fact, neither Delany nor any other attendee at the convention questioned the numerous women in attendance, nor did they discourage women's full participation in all aspects of the emigration movement. And in fact, African American women were both quite plentiful and visible at the National Emigration Convention in Cleveland. Historian Victor Ullman notes that out of the 106 delegates at the Emigration Convention of 1854, 26 were women with full voting rights. He argues that this large attendance was quite radical given the historical context, and that the number of women at state and national conventions didn't even come close to those at the National Emigration Convention. Historian Shirley Ann Yee points out that state and national conventions were inconsistent about accepting women delegates, and the participation of women on equal terms with men in Cleveland suggests that black male leaders did not necessarily have to deny African American women an equal place in order to advance the race.[95]

The personal and ideological differences between emigrationists and anti-emigrationists spilled over into the National Black Convention of 1855, and led to the debate over whether or not to seat Mary Ann Shadd Cary as a delegate. The arguments for and against are not detailed in the minutes left from the convention, yet accounts of the convention claim that Frederick Douglass led the challenge against Shadd Cary being seated. However, Shadd Cary had established herself as an important spokesperson among black editors and leaders, and when Charles Lenox Remond moved that Mary Ann Shadd Cary be admitted, Douglass "then moved a reconsideration." The convention recessed while Douglass had a chance to rethink his position, and when the delegates reconvened for the evening session, Douglass had changed his mind, calling for those present to allow her a seat. This didn't quell some in the audience, and several men stood to challenge this change of protocol. A final vote on the matter illustrated that the delegates were by no means unified: 38 delegates supported Shadd Cary and 23 opposed her. During the remainder of the convention, no resolution was passed condemning emigration (or colonization), and it is unclear to what degree Shadd Cary's presence caused this noticeable silence on such a contentious topic. The near absence of any serious discussion of colonization or emigration is quite curious given the previous two years of debate. Only through vague comments about black Americans' desire for equal rights in America was the issue even acknowledged, and no major challenge to colonization or emigration was noted in the minutes.[96]

Douglass and other advocates of the "stay and fight" ideology would continue to assert their position that emigration from America would do nothing to change race relations. Douglass maintained that "it was in the New, not the Old World, that black Americans' destiny would be realized." The progress of the black man in America, he claimed, would benefit blacks all across the globe, and thus he called on all blacks to embrace his "stay and fight" position as one with global significance.[97] This line of reasoning suggests that Douglass's position on black Americans' destiny was closely associated with the Christian-based "chosen people" trope more often associated with black ministers such as Henry Highland Garnet. By inverting Delany's emigrationism, Douglass claimed that his "stay and fight" ideology had the potential to transform America into a truly democratic nation that would ultimately lead the world beyond slavery, oppression, and all the indignities that oppressed people had endured throughout history. Patrick Rael writes: "Increasingly, African-American spokespersons believed they were to play conspicuous and active roles in the impending Apocalyptic contest, thus shifting the locus of black protest from messianic deliverance to political revolution."

Douglass would take this idea of an American apocalypse even further during the Civil War.[98]

6 / "For God and Humanity":
Anticolonization in the Civil War Era

"Your scheme of emigration," James McCune Smith wrote to Henry Highland Garnet in early 1861, "have [sic] neither the charm of novelty nor the prestige of success." Even though Garnet's newly established African Civilization Society tried to repackage emigration to West Africa as a feature of a broader race redemption mission, Smith called the Civilization Society "a feeble attempt to do what the American Colonization Society has failed to do; witness Liberia." As Smith explained, the emigration debates over the course of the decade had done little to change his own opinion about the pernicious link between colonization and emigration.[1]

James McCune Smith's criticism of Garnet's support for emigration reflected the views of many anti-emigration anticolonizationists during the 1850s and early 1860s. Rather than dismiss emigration outright, or, as Douglass attempted to do in the early 1850s, diminish the bold claims of the emigrationists, McCune Smith attacked the logic of emigration head on. First, in his view, emigrationism reinforced the notion that blacks sought to leave the United States, and this in turn added credence to colonization ideology. Second, black American emigration to Liberia, or anyplace in West Africa, under the direction of Martin Delany and Robert Campbell, required African American émigrés to adhere to the institutions of the people in that region of West Africa. As McCune Smith explained in his letter, "One of those institutions ... is THE INSTITUTION OF SLAVERY," and he wondered how these black leaders could claim to despise slavery in the United States while negotiating with African leaders who participated in slave trading on the West African coast.[2]

Next McCune Smith challenged Haitian emigration, writing, "I do not see any reason to believe that the present experiment will be any more successful" than the one that took place during the 1820s. As he saw it, Holly, Garnet, and other black leaders had failed to challenge their constituencies to "aim higher," and had instead "direct[ed] them to sink lower." Emigration would solve none of the problems that confronted the masses of African American people in the United States. "No, my dear sir," McCune Smith charged, "the free blacks of the United States are wanted in the United States. . . . And our people want to stay, and will stay, at home; we are in for the fight, and will fight it out here." In a final note of fellowship, Smith called out for Garnet to "shake yourself free from these migrating phantasms, and join us with your might and main. You belong to us, and we want your whole soul. We have lost Crummell, and we have lost Ward, and Frederick Douglass's eyes appear dazzled with the mahogany splendor of the Boston 'bureau.' Do not, I beseech you, follow their example, and leave an earnest and devoted people without a leader."

James McCune Smith's letter established the continual struggle between black leaders over emigration and colonization in the early years of the Civil War. While the emigration movement stalled after 1855, individual programs for the creation of black settlements continued. Martin Delany traveled to Africa with several other emigrationists to secure a location for building an African American nation near the Niger River; Mary Ann Shadd Cary and other Canadian leaders supported Delany, contemplating a mass exodus from the Elgin settlement in Canada to Africa; James T. Holly continued to push for Haitian emigration; Henry Highland Garnet, who had returned to New York City from a two-year stint in Jamaica, embraced the African Civilization Society's plan for African colonization at first, and then shifted to support Holly in Haiti. After 1858, it became obvious that one unified and concerted emigration movement was unlikely, and black leaders pursued individual ventures that, they believed, would galvanize African Americans towards the creation of a black American republic.

The controversy over African emigration among black spokespersons after the National Emigration Convention of 1856, as well as the various proposals for free black colonization during the Civil War, took on tremendous significance as African Americans came to believe that the war offered them hope for an end to slavery and racial oppression in the nation. For decades, free black Americans recognized that racial prejudice in the North and slavery in the South were inextricably linked. With abolition, they hoped, race-based oppression would subside, and black Americans could demonstrate their worthiness for citizenship. This worthiness depended on transforming the dominant view among white Americans that, as a race, African Americans lacked the capacity to participate in the social, political, and economic life of the United States on par with whites.[3]

In what ways did events leading up to the Civil War challenge staunch anticolonization anti-emigrationists such as Frederick Douglass to consider leaving the United States? Why did President Lincoln ignore anticolonizationists and embrace colonization in tandem with an emancipationist plan after the outbreak of the Civil War?[4] While the overlapping histories of colonization and emigration during the Civil War era have been treated well in numerous histories, these works rarely clarify the ways in which the two ideologies both converged and diverged in this tumultuous decade.[5] The reason for this confusion is most easily observed by exploring Martin Delany and Henry Highland Garnet's association with members of the New York Colonization Society in their failed effort to fund their emigration plans. It is not enough to point to Delany's or Garnet's personal failings in order to explain their capitulation to the colonizationists. Instead, one must look more closely at the shifting circumstances that brought about this puzzling change of course at the end of the 1850s.

When African American leaders convened the National Emigration Convention in Chatham, Ontario, in August 1858 to discuss the state of the emigration movement, much had changed. Delany's leadership had been eclipsed, and many of the more outspoken delegates of the previous two conventions, such as H. Ford Douglass, William C. Monroe, and James Whitfield, did not even show. William Howard Day, a black editor, was elected to the "Presidency of the Board of Commissioners," and it seemed quite clear that more conservative, reluctant emigrationists had gained control of a movement once led by the charismatic Martin Delany. Even Delany's Niger Valley emigration project only received a half-hearted endorsement from this organization.[6] James T. Holly recognized that the new leadership had as little interest in supporting his movement to Haiti as they did in Delany's project, and soon the name of the convention changed from National Emigration Convention to the Association for the Promotion of the Interests of the Colored People of Canada and the United States.[7]

By the end of the 1850s, white colonizationists such as Benjamin Coates noticed this change in leadership and hoped that emigrationists like Delany, Mary Ann Shadd Cary, and Henry Highland Garnet would consider accepting assistance from the New York Colonization Society, even though all of them had previously rejected any such support out of hand. But white colonizationists never tired of trying to associate colonization with emigration, and they considered Delany, Shadd Cary, and Garnet as important potential ambassadors of their project. This viewpoint was even discussed in the mainstream press. For example, a reporter from the Washington-based newspaper *The National Era* called for "every true friend of the race" to endorse and encourage the partnership of African American emigrationists with white American colonizationists. "It is a promising sign," this reporter declared, "when the colored men of this country voluntarily commence the work of colonization in any part of the world."[8] Aware perhaps that colonization had become anathema to blacks, the reporter made certain to point out that such a venture must not be associated with "the hopeless idea of conveying from this country all its colored inhabitants, but simply for the sake of building up large States in foreign countries, and bettering the conditions of individuals."[9]

By 1857, some southerners recognized the rise in racial tensions in the North and the Midwest, arguing that those in the Midwest who criticized the South for slavery refused to allow black Americans to live in their own states. In fact, these southern critics pointed to the pro-colonization ideology outside the South as an illustration of the general disdain that whites in nonslaveholding states had for African Americans. One southerner wrote that the "Black Republicans" in the North and West were hypocrites, and "[w]ith all their reproaches against the South for not emancipating their slaves, and allowing them to remain as freemen, they (B.R.'s) will not permit them, in numbers, to come and dwell among themselves." In Iowa, a frustrated white resident buttressed this point, explaining: "We approve of the effort of the slaveholders to release themselves of the burden that is weighing them down and crushing out the material prosperity of the Old Dominion . . . [but] why permit them to be turned off upon us? . . . Let the people of that State either repeal their law prohibiting manumission and settlement at home; or if they don't want them there, let them send them to Liberia."[10] These two viewpoints suggest that whites in the South and in the Midwest regarded the presence of free blacks as a burden to their communities. Such attitudes reinforced the colonizationists' claim that whites in nonslaveholding states would not accept blacks as equals upon emancipation. Although anticolonizationists and abolitionists had argued for three decades that emancipated blacks deserved full rights of citizenship in the United States, it was clear that whites had not moved that much closer toward accepting blacks. With the passage of the Fugitive Slave Act in 1850 and Roger Brooke Taney's statements after the Dred Scott case, anticolonizationists were pushed to ponder what gains they had really made in convincing the majority of whites that blacks ought to live equally in America.

When the Supreme Court handed down its ruling in the *Dred Scott v. Sanford* case, free African Americans who had been alarmed by the passage of the Fugitive Slave Act in 1850 now became despondent. Speaking before white and black abolitionists at the American Anti-Slavery Society's annual meeting in May 1858, Charles Lenox Remond lamented, "At the end of a quarter of a century, I discover that all efforts, of whatever kind, or in whatever spirit manifested, have proved complete failures, so far as the progress of the cause of universal liberty is concerned in our country."[11] In Boston, African Americans called the *Dred Scott* decision "a palpably vain, arrogant assumption, unsustained by history, justice, reason, or common sense." Although the Supreme Court had inflicted a blow against their "natural rights as natives of the United States of America," they were determined "to remain in this country" since they believed that they had just as much a right to it "as that of any class of people." Their commitment to justice remained firm, and, foreshadowing the violence of John Brown, African Americans in Boston threatened, "were [they] equal in numbers," they would respond with retributive violence. Yet even with the odds against them, African Americans were willing to do what it took to make sure "no attempt would be made to enslave us, nor to deny us the respect due to our manhood."[12]

These black Bostonians were not the first to threaten the use of violence in response to slavery and racial oppression. While David Walker's *Appeal* set a standard for radicalism within the black protest tradition, few black leaders of this era used the rhetoric of violence to assert African American masculinity as fervently as Henry Highland Garnet. By the late 1850s, Garnet had become one of the most famous black abolitionists, and his reputation as a radical grew after his statements at the National Black Convention of 1843, in which he defended slave insurrection. Garnet's speech, "An Address to the Slaves of the United States," provoked black delegates to debate both Garnet's assertions and the consequences of making such incendiary statements publicly.[13] Born in slavery and reared in freedom, Garnet never shied away from controversy or confrontation. Like other notable black leaders who attended the African Free School in New York City at the end of the 1820s, Garnet emerged as an outspoken young radical, fervent in his devotion to black rights and determined to challenge the older, more established black leadership. Garnet's "Address to the Slaves of the United States of America" called on black Americans in the South to "Let your motto be resistance! resistance! resistance!" and he reminded them that "No oppressed people have ever secured their liberty without resistance."[14] Within this context, Garnet also argued vehemently against colonization, emigration, or any form of mass movement of free blacks. Instead he proclaimed, "Some people of color say that they have no home, no country.... America is my home, my country, and I have no other. I love whatever good there may be in her institutions. I hate her sins."[15]

While Garnet never advocated large-scale emigration of free blacks, or supported the American Colonization Society, he did share Delany's view that creating an African American nation with a select group of blacks could work toward race redemption. His ideological shift towards emigration during the 1850s also coincided with personal issues, and when he found himself in Jamaica on a two-year stint as a missionary, he seemed prepared to accept, on some level, the value of the work of Delany and other emigrationists. Thus, he came to embrace the idea of African regeneration and redemption through the spread of Western civilization and Christianity. And when Benjamin Coates recruited him for the U.S.-based African Civilization Society, his opinions about selective emigration for strategic purposes had already taken root.

Garnet's biographer Joel Schor interprets this shift as a linear process. In his view, Garnet developed his emigrationist ideology under the influence of Lewis Woodson. On the other hand, biographer Earl Ofari Hutchinson claims that Garnet's experience in Jamaica led him to realize "that the conditions of blacks there were in some ways similar to those of blacks in the United States. This being the case, perhaps, he thought, emphasis on struggle in America alone was too narrow." Historian Martin B. Pasternak argues that this shift was a consequence of his previous association with the Free Produce Movement. Garnet recognized that British textile interests were very eager to develop cotton growing in Africa. Furthermore, Garnet's missionary activity convinced him of the need to spread Christianity in Africa, especially in regions where the slave trade still flourished. Pasternak asserts that these two reasons led Garnet to accept Coates's offer to join his effort to form the African Civilization Society. However, Garnet shared Martin Delany's determination to dismiss any association with the American Colonization Society, and he still considered himself an anticolonizationist.[16]

Perhaps it was Benjamin Coates's pamphlet "Cotton Cultivation in Africa" that most influenced Garnet's shift toward embracing emigration to West Africa. This may have led Garnet to regard the African Civilization Society under Coates's direction as more than a fad. Open to the ideas in Coates's pamphlet, Garnet also began receiving letters from Coates calling for him to join his effort to make real the ideas he laid out in his pamphlet. In one letter, Coates told Garnet that his interest in the endeavor had spanned almost ten years, and with the publication of his pamphlet in 1858, he was ready to begin recruiting people to make his program a reality. Certainly Garnet must have been impressed by Coates's thorough and comprehensive examination of cotton cultivation in Africa; he even had documents from the Cotton Supply Association of Manchester, England, expressing interest in the African Civilization Society's program of cultivating high-grade cotton in the Yoruba lands of West Africa, and creating a new source of cotton for Manchester cotton textiles—thus undermining not only the American cotton industry but the entire institution of slavery in the United States.[17] What Garnet did not know, however, was that Coates had never fully renounced his colonizationist beliefs, and Coates remained in close contact with the New York Colonization Society's chief leader, Rev. John B. Pinney.

Nevertheless, Garnet, having for years rejected the American Colonization Society, saw in the African Civilization Society the potential to create an African American nationality, and spread Christian and Western civilization in Africa while destroying slavery in America. Although Garnet believed the African Civilization Society was an organization rooted in emigrationist notions of race redemption, convincing blacks that the Civilization Society's plan differed from the ACS colonization project would be no easy task. Of course Coates recognized this, and in a letter to Rev. Alexander Crummell, an African American abolitionist who had left America for Liberia as an Episcopal missionary in 1851, he explained: "Such was the deep-seated prejudice in the minds of nearly the entire colored population against the colonization enterprise, that they would not listen with patience to any arguments on the subject." Coates called on Garnet because he shared the ACS's belief that the presence of a respected black leader would add credibility to their mission.[18]

With Garnet on board, Coates moved on to recruit other prominent black leaders, including Frederick Douglass. Even though he knew how ardently Douglass opposed colonization and Liberia, Coates courted

Douglass through a series of letters. In one letter, Coates explained how an African American nation in Africa could siphon off a portion of the enormous wealth that slaveholders made from cotton, which would in turn undermine the southern economy. As he explained, cotton profits had "been the principal if not the only cause of the continuance of Slavery in the United States." Yet Douglass proved obdurate, holding to his position on emigration and colonization while remaining courteous. Douglass wrote to Coates: "I am no nearer to the African Civilization Society than several months ago.... My reasons wise or foolish have been repeatedly stated—and I am willing to let them stand."[19]

While Coates appeared unnerved by Douglass's disapprobation, Garnet was not cordial, expressing his opinions about Douglass's views of the Civilization Society. "Mr. Fred Douglass is our bitter unrelenting enemy," Garnet wrote to Coates, "and I fear will endeavour to injure our cause in England as he has [done] here at home. My dear friend Benjamin Coates is deceived in the man if he expects anything else from him."[20]

Although their efforts to recruit Douglass proved futile, Garnet and Coates did score a major victory when they received word from Mary Ann Shadd Cary that African Americans in Canada had begun to consider endorsing the African Civilization Society's cotton cultivation plan. Shadd Cary, however, cautioned Coates that "the matter cannot be too forcibly urged upon the attention of the colored people of Canada as well as the United States," who were suspicious, she said, due to "the old prejudice against the name 'Colonization.'" The new plan, she explained, would lead to "a measure calculated not only to promote the civilization of Africa and the destruction of slavery but to remove whatever feature of American Colonization was known to be objectionable to colored people." In fact, Shadd Cary argued that this was not the first time she and her father, abolitionist Abraham Shadd, had thought of approaching Coates for advice and support for an emigration plan.[21]

Coates must have been excited by the support of such influential African American leaders as Mary Ann Shadd Cary, and soon, Martin Delany as well. However, he knew that their allegiance was tenuous because he relied on the ACS for financial support. Since so many blacks despised the American Colonization Society's plan, Coates made clear that the African Civilization Society pledged total, unwavering opposition to slavery, racial oppression, and mass deportation. Once black leaders viewed the two organizations as completely distinct, he would then try to convince them that the American Colonization Society had rejected its original anti-emancipation tenets, and could now be trusted.

This, however, would take time, and Coates's first plan was to gain support for the Civilization Society. In a letter to Gurley, he explained that "it is very difficult for [blacks] to get over their old [and] deep prejudice against the 'Colonization Society' . . . but they are gradually getting over it." In his view, this would come about sooner if "the Society should take a true Christian ground against the *increase* [and] extension of slavery, either from Africa or elsewhere." By using Coates's initiative, the American Colonization Society would benefit enormously. In fact, Coates argued that the African Civilization Society's project "has already created more interest in Liberia as well as Yoruba [West Africa] than has ever been entertained before." But the old organization needed to remain in the background and simply provide the financial means necessary to carry out Coates's program. If they made themselves too visible, African American leaders would "consider the African Civilization Socy [*sic*] only African Colonization under another name."[22]

Soon, however, Douglass and other anticolonizationists would detect the connection and start to wage war against the Civilization Society as they had against the ACS and emigrationsim, ushering in a new series of debates and quarrels among black leaders. This began when Henry Highland Garnet called on Douglass to defend his position against the civilizing of Africa through African American emigration. Clearly intent on drawing Douglass out from his position of silent neutrality, Garnet wrote a letter to him, asking: "What objection have you to colored civilization and Christianization of Africa?"

In response, Douglass restated his traditional anticolonization antiemigrationist philosophy. What was particularly noteworthy about Douglass's response to Garnet was that he avoided attacking Garnet personally, or others involved in the new organization. He explained: "Hitherto we have allowed ourselves but little space for discussing the claims of this new scheme for the civilization of Africa . . . doing little more than indicating our dissent from the new movement, yet leaving our columns as free to its friends as to its opponents." Yet, as Douglass continued, "We have not, dear brother, the least possible objection either to the civilization or to the Christianization of Africa . . . but rejoice to know that through the instrumentality of commerce, and the labors of faithful missionaries, those very desirable blessings are already being realized in the land of my fathers, Africa." While, in Douglass's view, the African Civilization Society "says to us, go to Africa, raise cotton, civilize the natives, become planters, merchants, compete with the slave States in the Liverpool cotton market, and thus break down American slavery," he found this plan unrealistic. Nevertheless, Douglass encouraged Garnet to "go there," if he wished, but he himself would "stay here." Rather than engage Garnet in the type of personal battle that Douglass had waged against Delany in the early part of the decade, he simply tried to take the wind from Garnet's sails by reminding him that individuals needed to follow their muse. While he and the great majority of blacks in the United States would "remain in America" to battle it out with those who defended slavery and called for black deportation, Garnet and his supporters were free to do what they liked.[23]

Still, Douglass did confront Garnet with "seven considerations, which prevent our co-operation." First, Douglass reminded Garnet, "The life and soul of this abominable idea would have been thrashed out of it long ago, but for the jesuitical and persistent teaching of the American Colonization Society." Second, the African Civilization Society seemed to "plant its guns too far from the battlements of slavery for us." Third, Douglass rejected the notion pushed forth by friends of colonization, and the Civilization Society, that "white and black people can never live in the same land on terms of equality." This "lying assumption" was, and continued to be, the central premise of the Colonization Society. Fourth, Douglass argued that the African Civilization Society would have little effect in spreading "civilization and of christianity in Africa" as long as the African slave trade continued unabated. In his view, the best way to destroy the trade was to cripple the market in slaves; the United States, even though it had banned the trade in 1808, continued to provide a "demand for the slave trade." Douglass doubted the African Civilization Society's claim that it would "break up the slave trade," and he considered abolition in the United States just as effective in achieving that result. "We are, therefore, less inclined to go to Africa to work against the slave-trade, than to stay here to work against it," Douglass explained. As for racial destiny and Garnet's attempt to change the Anglo-Saxon, Anglo-American attitude about African racial inferiority, Douglass's' fifth point was that "there is no place on the globe where the colored man can speak to a larger audience, either by precept or by example, than in the United States."[24]

Although Benjamin Coates, Henry Highland Garnet, and others who joined the Civilization Society argued that an increase in the supply of cotton from Africa would undermine American slavery, Frederick Douglass explained that the notion that "slavery depended for its existence upon the cultivation of cotton" seemed to deny the fact that "[s]lave labor can be employed in raising anything," and thus did not depend solely on the economic viability of cotton in the world market. This was his sixth point. In fact, Douglass found the entire notion of undermining slavery in the United States by producing cotton in Africa absurd, claiming "King Cotton in America has nothing to fear from King Cotton in Africa." And even if it had, he still rejected "enrolling ourselves among the friends of that new Colonization scheme, because we believe that our people should be let alone, and given a fair chance to work out their own destiny where they are." Here, Douglass made his final point. "When in slavery," Douglass explained, "we were liable to perpetual sales, transfers and removals; and now that we are free, we are doomed to be constantly harassed with schemes to get us out of the country. We are quite tired of all this, and wish no more of it." Exhausted by the sort of personal battles he had endured with Delany and Shad Cary in the mid-1850s, Douglass tried to avoid a conflict with Garnet along these lines at the final year of the decade. It appears that Douglass may have found that such vituperations only reinforced the charge that he would not back any initiative that he himself did not lead.[25]

But Douglass did employ a tactic against Garnet and the Civilization Society that was similar to the one he had used to undermine the black-led emigration movement of the early 1850s. First, he conflated colonization and "civilization," so those reading his paper came to believe that the African Civilization Society and the American Colonization Society were simply two sides of the same coin. Then, he moved on to demonstrate the impracticality of the Civilization Society program, highlighting those elements that seemed the least practicable, particularly the idea of trying to abolish slavery and the slave trade through the cultivation of African cotton. Finally, he linked racial destiny with antislavery work in the United States, arguing for the implementation of a racial uplift program geared towards the four million slaves eager for emancipation, education, and land. In this sense, he was finally responding to his critics who had in the past accused him of lacking a viable program to improve the race. No longer would Douglass allow others to claim he lacked a philosophy and program for race advancement, or that he relied too heavily on the benevolence of whites. In this vein, he argued that "We are perpetually kept, with wondering eyes and open mouths, looking out for some mighty revolution in our affairs here, which is to remove us from this country. The consequence is, that we do not take a firm hold upon the advantages and opportunities about us." To remain in the United States and join together with others interested in the uplift and advancement of black Americans, many of whom were in great need of support, was the most important mission for black leaders. And Douglass refused to allow colonization or emigration to distract him from that goal. No matter how Garnet and other black leaders fashioned their emigration project, Douglass believed that it undermined his effort to counter the ACS claim that black people favored leaving the United States. And indeed, when Lincoln initiated a federally sponsored initiative to deport emancipated African Americans during the Civil War, Douglass's fears seemed like they would be realized.[26]

Although African American leaders followed Douglass and Garnet's argument in *Frederick Douglass' Paper*, many of them organized gatherings throughout the North and Midwest to continue discussing the merits and drawbacks of the African Civilization Society. In New England, delegates at a regional convention called the African Civilization Society a "newer black version" of the American Colonization Society. Leading the charge against the Civilization Society was William Wells Brown, a longtime anticolonizationist anti-emigrationist. Brown called on his fellow delegates to be aware that "[o]ur old enemy the Colonization Society has taken advantage of the present state of feeling among us, and is doing all in its power to persuade us to go to Africa." Such efforts, Brown claimed, distracted black people from the fact that "our right to live here is as good as the white man's," and he argued that "our fathers fought side by side with the white man for freedom," to reinforce his argument. Risking one's life for the love of their nation was the ultimate expression of patriotism and the greatest assertion of one's right to the privileges bestowed upon the citizens of a nation.

George Downing, the president of the convention, concurred with Brown, stating in his address that "we will not be driven off. . . . All the injustice and wrong that has, or may be heaped upon us—and it may come heavier—will not crush out that heaven-giving part of our nature, patriotism, love of home, of our native hills, of our verdant valleys." For Downing this "stay and fight" ideology countered Anglo-American race ideology by calling upon African Americans to demonstrate their equality by expressing certain masculine virtues previously assigned to whites. While Delany and others believed emigration and the creation of a black nation was the best way to accomplish this, Downing argued that black people needed to "fight it out" here in the United States, which would prove that, as a race, African Americans were as strong as whites. Downing declared that his "native land" provided the most opportune environment for cultivating blacks' "mind and manhood."[27] Downing believed his "stay and fight" ideology would demonstrate this sense of masculinity in a way that could redeem the race more surely than emigration.

Ultimately, the members of the business committee of the New England Colored Convention of 1859 provided one specific resolution aimed at discrediting the African Civilization Society: "The African Civilization Society at this time (when so many of the American people are being moved to grant us our rights) is a deplorable fact, because it tends to feed the American mind with the idea that we may be induced to go to Africa." Because of this, they argued, their "oppressors" were less likely "to grant us our rights here" so long as the Civilization Society, "by deceptive inducements," continued to unnerve African Americans who had become "naturally restive under oppression," and who had failed to realize that "there is every hope here, in their native land."

Yet some attendees disagreed with the assumption that all emigration projects were bad. The Reverend J. Stella Martin, a friend and associate of Garnet, defended the African Civilization Society, claiming it was "one of the best means to break a link that binds England to this country." In Martin's mind, the African Civilization Society's cotton-growing plan was "the only avenue open for the enterprise of the colored people." He said that "he felt confident that colored men could go out to Africa, and develop the culture of cotton."[28] George Downing scoffed at Martin's views, claiming that "the advocates of the civilization movement" had essentially conceded that "this country was no place for the colored man." As Downing recalled, "Garnet, President of the Society, had declared that "a place should be set apart for the colored people."

The Reverend John B. Smith of New Bedford took the floor and "denied that Mr. Garnet had ever made such an assertion."[29] Another person called out that he had also heard Garnet make that claim. According to one witness, Smith "appeared staggered at this accumulation of proof" but held firm behind his defense of Garnet. This movement, Downing continued, "was a money making movement," and while he had no proof, he insinuated that "Mr. Smith had a money-interest in the undertaking," and this was the reason he advocated in its behalf with such force. In a debate that reportedly lasted nearly four hours, pro-emigration and anti-emigration delegates exchanged bitter words over the African Civilization Society.[30]

By the end of the convention, John B. Smith complained that the convention had turned into a meeting "to denounce the African civilization proposition," which, he argued, was one of the best ways "for evangelizing as well as for civilizing Africa." Those who conflated the African

Civilization Society's mission with the American Colonization Society's scheme only hoped to discredit an organization that made a legitimate effort "to elevate Africa in the scale of civilization and evangelical knowledge" that would place "her in an honorable position among the nations of the earth."

The two groups made peace on the final day of the convention, and no resolution was passed in support of or in opposition to the Civilization Society or African emigration. It appears that the anti-emigrationists thought that even if the African Civilization Society succeeded in convincing some African Americans to support their efforts, in the end these attempts would prove fruitless, given the magnitude of such an undertaking as the cotton-growing scheme. In an effort to bring both parties together, Charles Lenox Remond took the floor and "expressed regret that any hard feeling should be indulged." He called on his fellow delegates to "deal with the question of African civilization fairly and honorably," arguing that they "should cooperate with others in carrying on the great work of improving the condition of the colored race in this country."[31]

Nevertheless, the debate regarding the African Civilization Society was far from over. One month later, Henry Highland Garnet arrived in Boston prepared to confront his critics and win the city over to the African Civilization Society's mission.[32] Boston had long been the home to some of the most committed anticolonization anti-emigrationists. Garnet's task would not be easy. Before he even set foot in the city, his critics sought to undermine him by using their influence to convince ministers to prevent Garnet from booking a venue in which to defend himself and his organization against his critics. J. Stella Martin, who finally organized a gathering, introduced Garnet by recalling that the "Twelfth (colored) Baptist Church of this city . . . [refused] for him to speak in, the reason assigned for the refusal to open it to him was that the citizens of Boston did not wish to hear him, because they were tired of the discussion of the African civilization question." Martin found such an attitude inexcusable and not representative of the majority of "colored people" in the city. He explained: "I know too much about the generosity of the colored people of this city to allow our *dear friend*, Mr. Garnet, to go away with the impression that you are enemies to free discussion." After accusing a certain Mr. Grimes of not only refusing his church but conspiring to close the doors of all churches and halls to Garnet, Martin went on to assert: "A man who would violate the courtesy which he owed to a brother minister, with so little compunction of conscience as to go to every colored church to get them to act as he had done in refusing his church . . . is at once too contemptible for condemnation and too hypocritical to secure confidence." The room exploded in "applause and laughter," and when it died down, Martin continued to extol the importance of open-mindedness among black people, and then he introduced Garnet.

When Garnet rose to speak, the room was filled with applause even though, according to one report, "a large majority" of blacks in attendance at the Joy Street Church "[had] no sympathy with the movement as understood by them, yet a full house was present to hear" him speak.[33] When the "prolonged applause" died down, Garnet informed the audience that he was "happy that one impression, unfavorable to the liberality of the sentiment of the people of Boston . . . has been altogether removed." He explained how he wished he could have attended the New England Convention, but was "engaged in the State of Pennsylvania" near the border of Maryland, "lifting up [his] feeble voice in behalf of [his] oppressed and down-trodden brethren." After providing the audience with a brief context for his mission in Africa, he moved on to comment on debates at the New England convention a month earlier, defending himself from the charges of being a colonizationist, and discussing his various reasons for assisting in the formation of the Civilization Society.[34]

According to Garnet, certain delegates at the convention conspired to discredit the African Civilization Society in a disingenuous manner. Although some in the audience stood in opposition to Garnet's characterization of the New England convention, denying that any members of the convention had acted in a "concerted, well arranged way," Garnet retorted, "if it was not a concerted plan then what mean the resolutions brought forward on that subject by the Business Committee?" Before anyone could respond, Garnet queried, "Were they not arranged in private before you came to the meeting?" and then he answered his own question: "Yes, perhaps weeks before." He went on to characterize Martin's trouble securing a venue for the meeting as an outgrowth of the New England convention's conspiracy. This prompted Garnet to admonish his peers that "We have got to learn to tolerate free discussion. That is the first thing we want as colored people." Then he stated that "the first matter" he would discuss would be the charge that he was "a Colonizationist." To this he declared: "I am not a Colonizationist, [and] any man that says I am behind my back is an assassin and a coward." Garnet reminded the audience that he had "hated the sentiments of the American Colonization Society" since his childhood. He claimed the

Colonization Society "says this is not the home of the colored man" and that "the colored man cannot be elevated in this country." Such beliefs were anathema to him, and he argued instead that "the sky is brightening" for black people in America, and that "the day is not distant when, from the Atlantic to the Pacific, from Maine to California, the shouts of redeemed millions shall be heard."[35]

Once Garnet clarified his disdain for colonization, seeking to undermine the efforts of Douglass, Downing, and other anticolonizationists to conflate the two programs, he described the importance of black people acting independently from their white abolitionist allies. "I tell you, my friends, that we have been too long depending upon other people," Garnet argued. Instead, he explained that "abolitionists have done their part and done it well. . . . The rest of the work we have to do ourselves." Independent action was the key to race redemption, and would lead African Americans to a place where they could command respect, undermine slavery, and create opportunities to improve the material well-being of the race. Through emigration to Africa, Garnet proposed, a select group of black people could join the "eight thousand white men engaged in commerce and trade" there to build up a nation led by black Americans. "You might pass resolutions until they were stacked up as high as mountains," Garnet explained, but those who decide to follow their destiny and leave for this great opportunity would look back at such resolutions and "laugh at them." As things stood now, Garnet imagined that black people would continue to cross their arms and shake their heads in opposition to his plan until "our more active, energetic Anglo-Saxon brethren have got rich by trade and commerce in Africa, then our people will be trotting there." With this he came to his conclusion: "*If there were a dozen ships sailing out of Boston harbor, keeping up a trade between these countries, that fact would do more for the overthrowing of slavery, in creating a respect for ourselves, and breaking down the walls of prejudice, than fifty thousand lectures of the most eloquent men of this land.*"[36]

When Garnet finished, the audience erupted in applause and shouts of approval. Garnet had stood his ground, and he must have felt greatly pleased with himself as he sat down. Next, Rev. J. Stella Martin took the floor, calling for several resolutions to be passed in support of Garnet's mission and the Civilization Society. One resolution in particular stated: "That we, as colored people have the utmost confidence in his integrity, feeling that his constant identity with us, and the sacrifices which he has made to the anti-slavery cause are worthy of our respect and entitled to our co-operation." Although a "very large majority" carried the resolutions, "Dr. Knox and five others" refused to assent to them because they believed the resolutions "involved an endorsement of the African Civilization Society."

Within a few days, the *Liberator* published an article from William C. Nell that began with a cool, detached examination of the events at Joy Street and then went into an invective against Garnet's plan. "Whatever good may result to the individuals prominent in this African civilization movement," Nell explained, "suffice it to say that the present aspect of the question is a most vexious [*sic*] and distracting one to the colored people," which he believed only diverted "their activities and means from what should be cardinal with them—the abolition of Slavery in the United States, and the elevation at home of Colored Americans." Garnet had defended his organization and mission successfully in a public forum, yet the anticolonizationist anti-emigrationists maintained stubborn opposition to any plan that called on black Americans to emigrate from the land of their birth. As for Garnet's "victory," Nell explained in a letter to the *Weekly Anglo-African*, "all I have to say is, they are welcome to all the laurels won under such circumstances," but "had it been, however, a distinctive test vote, endorsing the *present* position of Mr. Garnet as President of the African Civilization Society, everybody here knows that the negative would have been a most emphatic one."[37]

By March, African Americans who gathered at a public meeting in New Bedford reiterated Nell's position, thus confirming that Garnet's success in late August had been ephemeral. These African Americans had crowded into a local hall "to investigate the claims of the African Civilization Society." When the meeting came to an end, the Business Committee expressed their members' respect for and uneasiness about the Civilization Society. One resolution asserted that "we deeply sympathize with the Mission to Yoruba," yet the Committee reiterated their anti-emigrationist position, claiming that they "must emphatically decline to give our influence or means towards a movement which we believe is fraught with more injury to our race than years of labor can bestow upon us." If the "best citizens from the United States" were to repatriate to Africa, those who remained would be left without many capable leaders. Moreover, while the committee even asserted that they sympathized with Liberia's effort to forge an independent identity, they claimed that its association with the American Colonization Society, which they described as "the unrelenting foe of the colored people of this country," caused them to withhold their support. In what could be interpreted as a jab against the African Civilization Society, which Garnet tried to distinguish from the American Colonization Society, the committee expressed disapproval of "whatever may be the garb it assumes, or under whatever specious pretext it presents itself." Ultimately, they argued that colonizationist ideology had infected the African Civilization Society, seeking "the same malicious object in view, viz.: the expatriation of the free colored people, that the slave may be rendered more secure in his chains." Some in the audience disagreed with this depiction of the African Civilization Society, and after these resolutions were read, "an animated and protracted discussion" ensued. Nevertheless, the motion to pass the resolution succeeded, and the resolutions were adopted.[38]

In an effort to combat the notion that Garnet's leadership in the African Civilization Society meant that black Americans favored colonization in any way, George T. Downing wrote an article for the *Evening Post* called "The Fate of the Free Colored People," which linked planter ambition to rid the country of free blacks in order to secure slavery with the "class of philanthropists . . . who propose to colonize them." This second group, Downing explained, had looked to Central America and Haiti as possible locations. These efforts, however, most often had been received negatively by the free black population, even when, as was the case with the African Civilization Society, black leaders championed such movements. Downing appealed to his white readers to consider the "Irish and Germans" who, like free blacks, "are sensitive about any scheme proposed for their regulation by another race, and may perhaps be unduly suspicious of the philanthropy of the projectors."[39]

Despite George Downing's article, white leaders of the newly established Civilization Society must have been quite pleased with Garnet's support. Yet they realized they needed a full-time recruiter to build more support for their program within white and black communities. By May 1858, the Reverend Theodore Bourne had entered the picture as the recruiter and agent of the new Civilization Society. A minister in the Dutch Reformed Church, Rev. Bourne gathered information about this upsurge in emigration sentiment among blacks in New York City during the summer of 1858, and by fall he had become an official agent of the newly formed African Civilization Society. Son of the venerable abolitionist George Bourne, Theodore Bourne never became as influential as his father. His most notable efforts at social reform were his role in Elihu Burritt's National Compensated Emancipation Society.[40] But Bourne had made a reputation for himself as a colonizationist intellectual by writing pro-colonization articles in the *Christian Intelligencer*. By the time he was hired on full-time with the Civilization Society, Bourne had a public record of his pro-colonization views.[41]

Soon after accepting this position, Bourne launched himself into learning all he could about the black American interest in Yoruba emigration within the free black community of New York City. According to an article on August 11, 1858, "a meeting has recently been held in New York, of colored men, to consider the propriety of emigrating to some region where they can enjoy more privileges than are accorded to them in the United States." During this meeting, some blacks championed Haiti as a possible destination, while others attempted to persuade the audience of the value of Liberian emigration. And Bourne was intent on making his presence and enthusiasm known: "A letter, warmly approving of the project was read, from Rev. Theodore Bourne" stating that "an independent nationality of Anglo-Africans" would benefit "the general interests" of the black community, and "of humanity and civilization."[42]

By the end of the summer of 1858, Garnet and Bourne had organized an official meeting to establish a constitution for the revived African Civilization Society. In this document, Garnet, Bourne, and others proclaimed: "The object of this Society shall be the civilization and Christianization of Africa . . . and of the descendants of African ancestors in any portion of the earth, wherever dispersed." By placing the Civilization Society within a pan-African framework, Garnet and Bourne called for black people in the Caribbean and Latin America to unite in the redemption and uplift of Africa. Likewise, the constitution called for "the elevation of the condition of the colored population of our country, and of other lands," and in this way obviated the anti-emigrationist claim that the Society's goals failed to include black Americans for whom emigration was not an option.[43]

As Garnet continued to advocate for the Civilization Society in the United States, in the summer of 1859 Bourne left for England. His mission resembled Ralph Gurley's and Elliot Cresson's previous efforts to raise funds, but this time Bourne represented an American organization with British roots. Setting the stage for his arrival, Bourne wrote to the British press, defending the African Civilization Society against abolitionists in the United States who continued to assail the organization and any emigration project. When black abolitionist George T. Downing wrote a letter to the British newspaper *The Independent* criticizing Coates and the Civilization Society, Bourne wrote back that such letters do "much injustice to an excellent abolitionist, and warm friend of the colored race."[44] Since Bourne was the son of a known British-born crusader against slavery, he used his connections to gain entry into various gatherings of individuals whom he believed could provide the finances necessary for an expedition to Africa.[45] And upon arrival in England, he took to the task of gaining approval from the British and Foreign Antislavery Society "and was most cordially received by them."[46]

At the autumn meeting of the Congregational Union of England and Wales, for example, a meeting of "500 Nonconformist ministers and laymen from various parts of the country" offered Bourne the chance to speak about the American-based African Civilization Society. According to one account, Bourne explained to those gathered that "so long as the people of this country paid 25,000,000 a year to the slave States of America for cotton, so long would slavery be upheld there."[47] Two days later Bourne attended a meeting in "the Mayor's parlour, Townhall, Manchester," to spread his views on "an exposition of the origin and objects of a society which has sprung up in the United States, and is promoted by the abolitionists and coloured people, for civilizing Africa by planting colonies in the central and other portions of the continent." When Bourne sat down, according to one report, a man named J. Clegg rallied support around Bourne's proposal. By the end of the meeting, "some resolutions approving the movement and pledging support to it were adopted."[48]

Bourne's influence on British cotton manufacturers as well as the general success of the African Civilization Society in England must have impressed British abolitionists, many of whom had been ardent anticolonizationists for years. For example, George Thompson, the British abolitionist who joined Nathaniel Paul and other anticolonizationists during the 1830s and 1840s, apparently endorsed Bourne's African Civilization Society. Even some of the well-traveled black anticolonizationists such as J.W.C. Pennington began to agree with the Civilization Society's logic that through appealing to Manchester cotton manufacturers, the American South's cotton monopoly could be subverted. Pennington couldn't help admitting that "I am no colonizationist or partisan of African civilization, as it is now understood; but we think that if ANY PARTY IN AFRICA can come into the market of the world and share a part of the $100,000,000 which free Europe gives to the slaveholders of America for their slave-grown cotton, it will be a handsome thing, to say nothing of rice, sugar, and tobacco."[49]

While Bourne succeeded in gaining much support from the British elite, black abolitionist Sarah Parker Remond condemned Bourne's work while she was in England.[50] Like Garrison, Nathaniel Paul, and others,

Remond challenged the merit of the Civilization Society, pointing out its link to the Colonization Society. During one meeting in Manchester, she declared: "I must now introduce to your notice the subject of African colonization, which is at present being presented to the Manchester public by the Rev. T. Bourne of New York." As she explained, "When Mr. Bourne asserts that the free coloured population of the United States are generally desirous of emigrating to Africa, I must say that he misrepresents their feelings and intentions." Remond presented resolutions passed at various meetings of free blacks in the United States that expressed such views, concluding that "similar resolutions were also presented at one of the largest conventions of coloured persons from the several states in Boston, on August 1st, 1859." The fact was, as she attempted to convince the audience, that "the Colonisation Society, sustained as it is by slaveholders who hate the free coloured people, and would like to expatriate them all," worked through the deeds of Bourne and the Civilization Society. While some African Americans were interested in "the civilization of Africa," many more were "still more interested in the civilization of America, and they will not leave their country and their homes for any society."[51] As historian Richard Blackett observes, Sarah Remond considered Bourne's plan "as ludicrous . . . as thinking that the Pilgrims wished to return to England to civilize the natives."[52]

However, by the time Bourne returned to the United States in November 1859 he had endorsements from a number of wealthy men in England and even from the pro-Garrison London Emancipation Society. What Gurley and Cresson failed to accomplish in the 1830s and 1840s, Bourne had finally achieved. Perhaps the new organization, copying the name of the British-based organization established by Buxton, had greater appeal to British reformers than the Colonization Society. Bourne's greatest success, it would appear, was in distinguishing the African Civilization Society from the American Colonization Society. But on the other hand, British interest in the Civilization Society came from a new influential proslavery contingent in Britain, which had less sympathy for the plight of free blacks and hoped for a way to break American slaveholders' domination of cotton production.[53]

Although the aforementioned explanations may have caused British reformers to support the venture, the endorsements from Martin R. Delany and Robert Campbell may have provided Bourne with a sense of legitimacy that Cresson and Gurley had lacked in the previous decade. Delany and Campbell's influence in England, particularly in the spring of 1860, went far in convincing the British public that some influential free blacks supported the goals of the Civilization Society. And, even if Delany was a bit uneasy about British perceptions that white men such as Bourne ran the Civilization Society, he maintained his partnership with Bourne.[54]

Why, then, did Delany come out in support of the African Civilization Society when he realized that Bourne, Coates, and the well-known New York colonizationist Rev. Pinney sought to control the organization? There are several possible answers to this question. First, Delany realized that he had to compete with other projects, such as James T. Holly's Haitian emigration program, and he needed the money. Second, he was also aware that most New York, Boston, and Philadelphia black leaders—including African Americans with the financial means to support Delany—held firm to their anti-emigration posture, which inhibited his ability to raise funds in the black community. With few resources and little support, Delany turned to whites such as Coates for the necessary backing to support his trip in the spring of 1858. This list included some, such as Henry Ward Beecher, who, Delany knew, supported colonization. Third, when William Day became one of the most important leaders at the National Emigration Convention of 1858, Delany realized he no longer could rely on either funding from the national black emigration movement or support from the new leaders who had eclipsed his influence among black emigrationists.

With Garnet as the public face of the African Civilization Society, Delany saw another blow to his leadership and he capitulated, organizing an African Civilization Society of Canada in the summer of 1858. To make matters worse, Delany's partner, Robert Campbell, turned on him in October 1858, and Delany found himself scrambling for someone else to join him in his venture. Campbell's flight from the project was short-lived, however, and soon he returned to Delany's side. But Campbell further undermined Delany by soliciting funds for his passage to England from the Pennsylvania State Colonization Society. Before Delany left the United States to negotiate for land in Africa on board the *Mendi*, Campbell had raised £200 in England. When Delany met up with Campbell in Lagos he appeared quite pleased with Campbell's fundraising efforts, yet he criticized him for taking donations from whites so freely.[55] All of these backdoor dealings complicated the notion of an independent African American–led emigration movement that was distinctly different from the American Colonization Society's "colonization scheme."[56]

Delany, however, failed to distinguish his Niger Valley project from the Civilization Society's operation, and this ambiguous relationship hindered Campbell and Delany's fund-raising efforts in Britain.[57] In one instance, Theodore Bourne was compelled to explain this murky relationship to the Reverend Henry Venn, a member of the Church Missionary Society, which had influence in the region of Nigeria where Delany and Campbell hoped to scout around for a possible African American settlement. Rev. Venn was unimpressed by Bourne's explanation, and he deemed the Niger Valley expedition an unrealistic enterprise that was too close to colonization to ever work. This, however, did not deter Campbell, and he continued his fund-raising efforts.

As the evidence suggests, Delany struggled to create an autonomous black-led emigration initiative, and he ended up relying heavily on whites for financial backing. Regardless of his ideological problem with white participation in his emigration plans, Delany capitulated and soon found himself requesting donations from those whom he had deemed enemies of the race for many years. Even when Delany arrived in Liberia and stood before Edward Blyden, the Caribbean intellectual and professor who had become an ideological force in West Africa, he recanted his previous condemnation of colonization, causing Blyden to wonder: "Is Dr. Delany to be the Moses to lead the exodus of his people from the house of bondage to a land flowing with milk and honey?"[58]

Delany's turn towards colonization further complicates this question over the difference between emigration and colonization. While Delany and others tried desperately to distinguish the two movements, financial realities compelled the emigrationists to cross over and give at least tacit approval of the civilization project led by Garnet, even though they knew it had been infiltrated by colonizationists. While each and every major black pro-emigrationist had at one point or another condemned colonization as the enemy of the black race, by 1860 the former emigrationist leaders Shadd Cary and Delany were compelled to acknowledge colonizationists as potential allies. Ironically, Abraham Lincoln and the Committee on Emancipation and Colonization used Delany's "Address Issued by a National Emigration Convention of Colored People Held at Cleveland, Ohio, in 1854" as evidence that blacks supported colonization.[59] Regardless of how fervently Delany and other emigrationists had distanced their program from that of the ACS, the ACS's much-needed financial support and organizational backing tangled them into one indistinguishable entity.[6]

Although Abraham Lincoln was no card-carrying member of the American Colonization Society, he did embrace colonization ideology. In some ways Lincoln was the chief executive that the ACS had dreamt of for decades. However, Lincoln's enthusiasm for colonization did not lead him to commit himself to Liberia or other African colonization schemes. This must have disappointed members of the American Colonization Society who had hoped that one day a president would finance their mission with federal funds. Nevertheless, Lincoln shared ACS members' belief in the irreconcilable differences between the two races.[61]

With the publication of Lerone Bennett's book *Forced into Glory: Abraham Lincoln's White Dream* in 2000, the debate among scholars over the nature of Lincoln's colonization views was rekindled. Perhaps Lincoln's tag as the "Great Emancipator" and his advocacy of colonization led Bennett to challenge the notion that a person advocating colonization could never have been truly an ally of black people trapped by slavery in the South and by racial oppression in the North and West. It's quite possible, as Michael Lind has written, that "the popular conceptions of Lincoln as Savior of the Union, Great Commoner, and Great Emancipator, then, have been half-truths promoted to serve partisan purposes by different groups at different times."[62] Was Lincoln's support of colonization an indication that he was racist? Did he advocate for colonization for political reasons? Eric Foner has argued that Lincoln's colonization beliefs were consistent with his view that, while black Americans were considered men in terms established by those who signed the Declaration of Independence, he would not as president pursue a course of political and social equality of the races in America.[63] Lincoln's own personal views about black Americans, and for that matter on slavery as well, may be difficult to ascertain, but the reasons he supported colonization are quite clear, and they had particular meaning to people like Douglass who had fought for two decades against the ACS and colonization ideology.

Any attempt to explore Lincoln's position on colonization must begin with a broader study of the rise of pro-colonization views within the Republican Party. As a Republican, Lincoln shared the position on slavery inherited from the Free Soil Party advocating that the lands of the West be reserved for whites. According to Free Soilers, slavery undermined the labor market and for that reason, rather than slavery's inhumanity, it needed to be abolished.[64]

For whites within the Free Soil Party, colonization linked up with the rhetoric of Anglo-Saxon destiny and the growing anxiety over threats from southerners that they would "unleash" emancipated blacks from their states into the North and West.[65] Also, colonization sentiment coincided with the Wilmot Proviso, which embraced the notion that the West should not be sullied by slavery but instead should remain "free soil" for whites to exploit. Eric Foner notes: "During the fight for free soil in the 1840s, they had linked racism and anti-slavery in a way which was repeated in the pre-war decade. David Wilmot, for example, insisted that his Provision of 1846 was the 'White Man's Proviso,' and he told the House that by barring slavery from the Mexican Cession he intended to preserve the area for 'the sons of toil, of my own race and own color.'"[66]

While, on the one hand, the issue of the future of slavery and the nation's character occupied much of the attention of those dedicated to the Proviso, on the other hand, an important byline was the question over whether these areas would be dominated by whites or blacks.[67] George Fredrickson explains: "The political free-soil movement, which developed out of Northern anxieties about Southern expansionism and the extension of slavery, combined principled opposition to slavery as an institution with a considerable amount of antipathy to the presence of Negroes on any basis whatever."[68]

Although not all Free Soilers accepted this doctrine of black inferiority or the notion that blacks should be driven from the nation, the American Colonization Society gained mainstream political power by hitching colonization to the Free Soil Party's agenda, and this Free Soil ideology proved essential for an organization on the verge of collapse.[69] When Free Soilers recruited white Democrats and Whigs into the party, colonization became the remedy for the question many whites had about what to do with newly emancipated slaves and free blacks.

When the Republican Party was formed in 1856, the "impending crisis" over slavery and the Democrats' aggressive attempts to cast the new party as "nigger lovers" or "black Republicans" compelled Republicans to adopt a pro-colonization stance as a middle ground. Even though the nascent party opposed the expansion of slavery and many Republicans considered slaveholding immoral, they embraced emancipation only with colonization. While well-known Republicans such as Salmon P. Chase and Abraham Lincoln endorsed colonization, this does not mean that all members of the party closed ranks behind an antiblack/pro-colonization position. In fact, as Fredrickson points out, "[a]lthough Lincoln was advocating a separation of the races, he did so in this instance without suggesting that the races were inherently unequal. Blacks, he implied, have capabilities, perhaps as great as those of whites, but they could realize them only in Africa or at least outside the United States."[70] Furthermore, Republican legislatures in New Hampshire, New York, Ohio, and Vermont rejected the notion that blacks were not worthy of citizenship.[71]

By 1860 pro-colonizationists had gained prominent positions within the party, but some of them, such as Wisconsin senator Doolittle, seemed less interested in promoting black colonization to Africa than in colonizing black people in Latin America. Perhaps Doolittle had heard one too many times that African colonization was impractical. Nevertheless, the American Colonization Society could not have been too thrilled with coming so close to federal endorsement and national policy only to see it vanish due to what some considered "practical considerations." As for African Americans such as George Downing, it didn't necessarily matter *where* white advocates of colonization sought to send blacks. For him and other black leaders, any state or federal mandate that required them to leave America would be considered an affront to principles of natural rights philosophy and the democratic and republican ideals on which the nation had been founded.

As antislavery politics evolved from the Liberty Party to the Free Soil Party to the Republican Party, colonization moved from the periphery of party policy to center stage. In fact, Lincoln became the first chief executive to allocate federal dollars for building a black American colony just off the shores of Haiti. Although he did not mandate that blacks leave, as anticolonizationists feared he might, his colonization initiative during the Civil War represented the apogee of federal action. Even though Lincoln did not provide funding for ACS colonization in Liberia, his pro-colonization position shows that colonization ideology continued to be strong among politicians in the early 1860s. [72]

African Americans denounced Lincoln and the Republican Party for embracing colonization, and by 1860, black spokesmen such as H. Ford Douglass would go so far as to equate Lincoln with Henry Clay. Ford Douglass proclaimed, "I want to know if any man can tell me the difference between the anti-slavery of Abraham Lincoln, and the anti-slavery of Henry Clay? . . . Abraham Lincoln is simply a Henry Clay Whig." As for the future of racial progress, Ford Douglass saw little hope in the election of Lincoln or any candidate then running for president, claiming, "So far as the principles of freedom and the hopes of the black man are concerned, all these parties are barren and unfruitful; neither of them seeks to lift the negro out of his fetters, and rescue this day from odium and disgrace." [73] This not only demonstrates the colonization lineage linking the two venerated statesmen, but it also expresses African Americans' greatest fear: that Lincoln would use his powers as president to make real the grand scheme of colonization that Clay dreamed of but could never accomplish, having failed to win the office five times.

As the presidential election of 1860 approached, the colonization movement had claimed the governors of Iowa, Wisconsin, Illinois, and Ohio as allies. In Congress, several notable Republicans supported colonization, including Ben Wade, Lyman Trumbull, and James Harlan. The prospect of colonization becoming a part of the Republican Party's national platform seemed likely, but for several reasons this didn't take place. First, pro-colonizationists looked forward to creating an African American colony in Central America to spread U.S. influence in that region. This position clearly differed from that of Republicans who supported the program of the American Colonization Society and Liberia. Second, the Republicans were divided over volunteer emigration and compulsory colonization if it was deemed necessary. All in all, colonization proved to be a divisive topic among members of the Republican Party, yet it remained an important ideology for Lincoln.[74]

As it has been argued throughout this study, colonizationists often had diverse motives, and some of them did believe that their plan was the only realistic way to end slavery and provide newly emancipated blacks with an opportunity for a better life. This group of colonizationists struggled amongst peers who detested blacks almost as much as they detested slavery. With a national crisis falling on the doorstep of the White House soon after Lincoln took office, he and other colonizationists, and their sympathizers, found themselves compelled by circumstances that had troubled the nation since Thomas Jefferson and the early Founding Fathers first outlined their colonization plans. By the time South Carolina seceded, colonization could not be viewed as an extreme position among whites. But the South's effort to dissolve the Union redefined the terms of engagement. On the one hand, Lincoln was confronted by the pro-slavery Confederacy, which was willing to kill the nation before entertaining the idea of black freedom, and on the other hand, some radical abolitionists who were willing to kill slaveholders if that's what it took to emancipate the slaves, as John Brown had demonstrated. Within this context, colonization became a middle ground for Lincoln: one that neither radical abolitionists like Brown nor slaveholders like Jefferson Davis would ever support, yet one that seemed like a reasonable alternative for those who considered themselves levelheaded statesmen. Ironically, some "Radical Republicans" who embraced colonization before and during the war then changed their minds as the war concluded by supporting the end of slavery and pushing forward constitutional amendments that provided black males full legal rights.

In the fall of 1862, various newspapers reported on the president's Emancipation Proclamation in conjunction with colonization. One article explained how "it is Senator Pomeroy's intention to go with 500 able bodied negroes as the first colony . . . between the 5th and 10th of October . . . as pioneers to smooth the way for others." When the "pioneers" arrived in Chiriqui, "on the Isthmus, two hundred miles north of Aspinwall and the Panama Railroad," the men would "make the colony speedily self-supporting." President Lincoln sent Pomeroy with "a letter, charging him to 'maintain the honor of the Republic abroad.'" Chiriqui was, according to the article, "where Columbus landed on his second trip . . . and much gold is believed to be in the mountains." This area of nearly two million acres had "already been negotiated for" and the senator had been given "power to negotiate for all that is needful."[75]

Slavery had put the nation under tremendous strain, and Lincoln's colonizationist sympathies centered on the notion that the end of slavery would only come with a clear, well-thought-out plan for removing African Americans from the United States.[76] Thus, soon after entering office and within the context of the outbreak of the "War of Rebellion," Lincoln set about searching for a location for African American deportation, and this mission was boldly proclaimed in his first annual message in December 1861. Lincoln explained to Congress that there was the possibility of "the acquiring of territory and the appropriation of money" needed to make the plan succeed. Federal funds for colonization, according to Lincoln, could inspire free blacks, "so far as individuals may desire, [to] be included in such colonization"—to seek a better life somewhere else.[77]

A year later Lincoln told Congress, perhaps exaggerating a bit, that he believed free blacks whom he had spoken with seemed enthusiastic about colonization. In his 1862 "Annual Message to Congress," he claimed: "Applications have been made to me by many free Americans of African descent to favor their emigration, with view to such colonization as was contemplated in recent acts of Congress."[78] Of course, Lincoln didn't bother spelling out a specific number who had claimed to support leaving under his plan, nor did he cite any large meetings in black communities to discuss leaving, as had been the case when blacks had pondered emigration to Haiti or Liberia over the past four decades. Yet he, like so many colonizationists, believed that free blacks needed only to be provided with the opportunity to leave and they would most certainly do so. Lincoln's belief was backed by federal dollars, and in July 1862 Congress put $600,000 aside to colonize African Americans who had been set free under the Confiscation Act of July 17, 1862. An additional

$100,000 had been made available from the District of Columbia Emancipation Act, and $500,000 more was made ready to fund colonization per the Supplemental Appropriations for Sundry Civil Expenses by July 16, 1862. While each proposed colonization project provoked debate in Washington, it seemed clear that, in any case, federally funded colonization of freed African Americans remained connected to the Emancipation Proclamation.[79]

Having fought the specter of colonization for nearly four decades, black leaders came to regard Lincoln's penchant for colonization as ominous. Their struggle in opposition to colonization and their attempt to prove that African Americans deserved equal rights seemed to be ignored. For all of Lincoln's claims that he acted for the benefit of black people, African American spokespersons like Frederick Douglass were not impressed.[80] Soon, Douglass became one of Lincoln's most ardent critics as the war continued, asserting that a race treated so miserably for so long should be compensated, not with "deportation," as Douglass put it, but full citizenship and land.[81]

After the Civil War began, whites in the North, most of whom did not support abolition, called on the president to increase the federal government's effort to remove African Americans from the nation. As blacks poured into Union-occupied areas of the South by 1861, the pressure to initiate a colonization plan increased. Some worried that newly self-liberated blacks would come north and compete with whites for jobs. Others could not imagine emancipated African Americans living as equals among southern whites who had built an entire racial system rooted in slavery and oppression.[82]

While some scholars note the small numbers who left for Liberia with funding from the American Colonization Society during the Civil War, it seems clear that this is no indication that members of the ACS had given up on colonization. In fact, the ACS boasted that black Americans appeared more interested than ever in colonization to Liberia. "The Africans of the United States are beginning to see the importance of Liberia," one article explained, and others were "moving towards that point." The same article explained that "[Blacks] are inaugurating societies among themselves to promote emigration." The ACS claimed that "they had never before had so many applications for passage to the coast of Africa," and bragged that, in fact, "more emigrants will sail this year than for the last five years."[83] Articles such as these created the illusion that the ACS was as strong as ever—when in reality, between 1861 and 1865 the ACS only funded the transportation of 169 blacks to Liberia.

These figures, especially the 23 blacks who left in 1864, were some of the lowest numbers of émigrés to leave America for Liberia in the organization's history. Not until the end of the war in 1865 would the ACS send as many colonists to Liberia as they had in the early 1850s, when the organization thrived.[84]

Even with what seemed like lack of support for colonization in Liberia, Lincoln publicized his plan with the hope that it would lead to a ground-swell of support in black communities throughout the nation. But no such support was forthcoming. When newspapers published Lincoln's colonization plan, African Americans gathered throughout the nation to protest it rather than champion it. In Queens County, New York, for example, black Americans "met in a mass meeting . . . to consider the speech of Abraham Lincoln" regarding colonization. This "mistaken policy," they proclaimed, caused them to let their "views on the subject of being colonized to Central America or some other foreign country" be known. The United States was "their native country," and they explained the "strong attachment to [their] native hills, valleys, plains, luxuriant forests, flowing streams, mighty rivers, and lofty mountains, as [among] any other people." African Americans admitted feeling "a strong attach-ment to the whites with whom our blood has been commingling for the earliest days of this country." And blacks argued that Lincoln's speech "served the cause of our enemies, who wish to insult and mob us," and this caused at least one person among those gathered to complain about being "repeatedly insulted, and told that [blacks] must leave the coun-try," as a consequence of his remarks.[85]

After learning of Lincoln's colonization plan, a group of African Americans in Philadelphia came together to draft "An Appeal from the Colored Men of Philadelphia to the President of the United States." The "Appeal" claimed that "while colonization in many of its features might be advantageous to our race . . . it is doubtful whether [white] people seriously desire a depletion of this kind, however much they wish to separate from us." African Americans in Philadelphia also pointed to the material wealth blacks created in this nation as a way to defend their right to remain in America. The petition argued: "If statistics prove anything, then we constitute, including our property qualifications, almost the entire wealth of the Cotton States . . . [and] our own houses and other property, amounting, in the aggregate, to millions of dollars." Mass colonization, then, made little sense to them, and they queried, "Shall we sacrifice this, leave our homes, forsake our birth-place, and flee to a strange land, to appease the anger and prejudice of the traitors now in arms against the Government, or their aiders and abettors in this or in foreign lands?"[86]

Black individuals such as Francis E. Watkins Harper wrote open letters to Lincoln to inveigh against his "colonization scheme." Watkins Harper, a renowned black literary figure and activist during the nineteenth century, described Lincoln's colonization plan as analogous to "a man almost dying with a loathsome cancer, and busying himself about having his hair trimmed according to the latest fashion." Protest against colonization was nothing new to Watkins Harper, who had been raised by the famous black leader and anticolonizationist, William Watkins, who in turn, some claim, had convinced William Lloyd Garrison of the evils of colonization, and pushed him to take a more radical stand against slavery.[87] With the eloquence of a true poet, Watkins Harper explained, "we neither see the wisdom nor expediency of our self-exportation from a land which . . . [has been] enriched by our toil for generations." She best expressed the faith and hope that many blacks had at the start of the Civil War when she wrote: "O, be hopeful, my friend! Upon our side of the controversy stands God himself, and this gives us a solemn and sublime position. A people thus situated may lift up their heads and take courage in the hope of a sure and speedy redemption." Embedded in her condemnation of the president's colonization plan was the notion that mass colonization would undermine the nation's future prosperity. Like other black citizens who protested Lincoln's plan, Watkins Harper found colonization unrealistic and detrimental to the nation. "And even were we willing to go," she argued, "is the nation able to part with four millions of its laboring population?" Watkins Harper's practical view of the irrationality of colonization resembled the pragmatism embraced by those who gathered in Philadelphia to protest Lincoln's policy.[88]

Black community leader George Vashon explained in a letter to Lincoln, "I do not put myself in opposition to the emigration of Colored Americans, either individually, or in large masses. . . . But, entertaining these views, and almost persuaded to become an emigrant myself. . . . I am confident that, in thus feeling, I am not in sympathy with the majority of my class—not in sympathy either with the great body of them." Vashon deplored the baseless nature of the type of forced colonization that he believed Lincoln had initiated. In Vashon's view, even while "setting aside the injustice of a policy which would expatriate black Americans," it was clear that Lincoln's "scheme" had neglected the fact that "negro cultivators are absolutely required for that portion of the Union," which he worked so tirelessly to preserve. Furthermore, the impracticalities of such a venture, Vashon explained, "are such as to be termed Herculean," because "to remove entirely this 'bone of contention'" demands the expatriation of nearly one-sixth portions of the Union." Vashon imagined that such a project was unrealistic and far from solving the great problem the nation confronted with southern secession.[89]

When the Massachusetts Anti-Slavery Society met in January 1862, the well-known black doctor John S. Rock delivered an address that expressed the frustrating options available to black people seeking to change their circumstances at the start of the Civil War. "This nation is mad," Rock declared, "if you find you cannot rob the negro of his labor and of himself, you will banish him!" Rock considered colonization ridiculous, and hypocritical, pointing out that "the black man is a good fellow while he is a slave, and toils for nothing, but the moment he claims his own flesh and blood and bones he is a most obnoxious creature, and this is a proposition to get rid of him!" However, the Civil War had not ushered in a "dark hour," in Rock's opinion. Instead, he claimed, "I do not agree with those men who see no hope in this war. . . . The Government . . . while fighting for its own existence, it has obliged to take slavery by the throat, and sooner or later must choke her to death."[90]

Although Frederick Douglass continued to fight against the "spirit of colonization" among philanthropic interests in the nation, he devoted space for criticism of "our garrulous and joking President . . . [who had made] . . . two speeches, which delivered by any other than the President of the United States, would attract no more attention than the funny little speeches made in front of the arcade." Douglass dismissed Lincoln's first addresses for being "tediously long, full of repetitions, and so remarkably careless in style that it reminds one strongly of the gossiping manner in which a loquacious old woman discusses her neighbors and her own domestic affairs."

Lincoln's second speech was the "more important communication of the President," Douglass informed his readers. This time, Douglass criticized Lincoln for using "the language and arguments of an itinerant Colonization lecturer," and Douglass argued that this speech demonstrated "[Lincoln's] contempt for Negroes" and "his pride of race and blood." Colonization as federal policy was stupid in Douglass's view, and he claimed that it didn't "require any great amount of skill to point out the fallacy and expose the unfairness of the assumption" that black Americans would be better off in a distant land. According to Douglass, any man with "an ounce of brain in his head" could tell that such schemes had little merit for the nation or African Americans. The president, Douglass continued, "says to the colored people: I don't like you, you must clear out of the country," and this opinion, Douglass argued, was "in keeping with his whole course from the beginning of his administration up to this day, and confirms the painful conviction that though elected as an anti-slavery man by Republican and Abolition voters, Mr. Lincoln is quite a genuine representative of American prejudice and Negro hatred." Douglass's comments reflect his understandable frustration with what appeared to be Lincoln's pro-colonization, attitude, which Douglass believed contrasted with his self-proclaimed respect for black Americans. "This address of his leaves us less ground to hope for anti-slavery action at his hands than any of his previous utterances," Douglass lamented.[91]

A month later, Douglass wrote a letter to Postmaster General Montgomery Blair, who had been assigned to work with Lincoln on the federal colonization project. When Blair replied to Douglass's initial correspondence, one can see how closely linked colonization was to his support for the American racial ideology that denied black equality. Douglass had argued that African Americans had just as much right to remain in the United States as whites, and if whites wanted to live separately from blacks, then they were the ones who should emigrate from the continent. To this Blair replied, "The answer to that is that here the whites rule, and cannot be reasonably expected that they would voluntarily go away. As leading men in society do not abandon their old homes to seek advancement in new communities, so controlling races will not abdicate their power or surrender their country." Yet Blair argued that this colonization scheme was not based solely on what he viewed as black inferiority: "There is in fact, no question of superiority or inferiority involved in the proposed removal. When we say that society is necessarily made up of superiors and inferiors in grades of intellect, and according to the ordinary classification of employments, it is manifest that no removal of the colored race would be necessary on that account, even if it were true that the race was inferior to ours." Colonization, as he imagined, "arises not from any consideration of the relative merits of the different races, but from the distances between them which the Creator himself has made." Here, Blair placed Anglo-Saxon, Anglo-American racial superiority within the context of the wishes of the "Creator" and those of the "founding fathers," explaining that "it seems as obvious to me as it was to the benevolent and philosophical mind of Jefferson that the opinion against which you protest, is the necessary result of indelible differences thus made by the Almighty."[92]

With a final gust of arrogance, the postmaster general challenged Douglass, as well as all African Americans, to disprove his theory by creating a great black nation that could demonstrate the superiority, or at least the equality, of black people. Blair admitted that "he and those of us who have adopted his teachings may therefore be in error on this point. But if so," he wondered, "what more effective way is there to disabuse the people of the error, than for the most enlightened and enterprising of the colored race to avail themselves of the opportunity to establish for themselves an Empire. If they succeed in this enterprise it will at once free their race from bondage, because when the poor whites see that the colored race can go away they will be for emancipation, and then the opinion against which you protest, if it be as you suppose, but a prejudice produced by the enslavement of the race, will soon wear away." Had Blair concluded there, perhaps, he would not have drawn Douglass out from behind his humble posture. Instead, Blair's final comments exemplified one of the most important points Douglass had made to Delany and other emigrationists regarding the poisonous effect of emigrationism for free blacks who sought to remain in the United States. "For my own part," Blair argued, "I do not expect that the colored people will disappear from among us in many generations"; however, he believed that "even the first step will do wonders for the peace of this country. . . . If successful and I have no doubt it will be . . . we shall soon have the products of the tropics made by free labor and that puts an end to slavery and the slave trade and redeems Africa itself."[93]

Douglass responded to Blair's letter in a way that bespeaks his skill as an orator and public lecturer. "I have read your statements and reasonings," Douglass began, "with very great respect, and perhaps with a spirit of deference for your ability and position as a statesman. . . . I sincerely thank you for your letter, first because it gives me an occasion for expressing more fully than I have yet done, the sentiments I entertain respecting this new scheme, and secondly because it is a mark of consideration towards the race of which I am in part a representative." After adorning his letter with the necessary flattery most white men of power came to expect from African Americans, Douglass claimed that, since he was "writing to a statesman," he would deal with the matter "on a comprehensive basis." First, he argued that Blair's "ground is strictly ethnological" and not dependent on what Douglass found to be necessary: "I see nothing in the nature of the difference between the two races, to prevent their living peaceably and happily in the same country, under the same government." However, Douglass continued, if blacks "really wished to get away from this great Anglo-Saxon race, the plan now commended to the free colored people would be unavailing." A colonized group of black Americans could never rise up from under "the white man's hand," because, as Douglass saw it, that hand "is felt in every part of the habitable globe."[94]

As he had argued for decades, whites and blacks *could* live peaceably in the United States, and free blacks had as much right to reside in America as whites. For Blair or anyone else to argue to the contrary was to argue against those treasured American ideals expressed in the Declaration of Independence. In Douglass's opinion, the true greatness of the "Caucasian power" could only be achieved when white Americans disavowed their fear of free blacks and made a place for them here in the United States. "Different races have lived in it very comfortably, and with one exception do now manage so to live," Douglass explained. Furthermore, he asked, "Are not Americans themselves a composite race?" It was then that Douglass made his grand indictment against Blair, an indictment similar to ones he had made against Henry Clay and all colonizationists before: "It requires very little power of discrimination to detect the sympathetic relationship between the doctrines of colonization and the doctrines of slavery."[95]

Within a month, Lincoln's colonization plan would be discussed by black people throughout the nation as they wondered whether or not this president-backed plan for colonization would lead to deportation of free black Americans en masse—an action that would be on par with the Indian removal of the early 1830s, which some black abolitionists had fought against.[96] Douglass found himself battling with Delany and other emigrationists who had blurred the line between black-led initiatives and those concocted by the Colonization Society and the president. Delany was traveling from venue to venue throughout America, calling upon black people to claim their rightful role as the leaders in the quest to redeem the race. This caused Douglass to shake his head in frustration at what he considered to be Delany's misguided views. As Robert Levine notes, "in providing Delany with a platform for his African emigration program, Douglass maintains, Rochester's blacks only further encouraged racist colonizationists." Further, blacks need not leave the United States to demonstrate their "manhood," Douglass argued. African American men who seized the day and recognized the Civil War as an opportunity to assert their manhood in combat were more likely to attain equality than those who created a nation-state of expatriate black Americans. Up until the end of the war, African Americans continued to condemn Lincoln for his colonization scheme and to see the war as a chance to save the nation's soul, end slavery, and usher in a new dawn.

Epilogue

When Frederick Douglass, Henry Highland Garnet, and John Mercer Langston joined with other black leaders from all over the country at the National Convention of Colored Men of America in Washington, D.C., in January 1869, the issue of black equality and justice remained as pertinent as ever. Such issues were central to the struggle for democracy and citizenship that a generation of abolitionists, activists, and community leaders had fought for, and continued to strive for, in the aftermath of the Civil War. John Mercer Langston called on his peers to keep struggling against "the odious featurers [sic] of the Northern States, which disfranchised the colored man," and he claimed that blacks needed to "to correct public opinion, rather than to demand, or appeal to Congress." As he explained: "both Congress and the President elect . . . would be found willing and anxious to obey the will of the people." Indeed, black leaders, he claimed, had an obligation to shape public opinion in a way that would afford blacks a place in the nation, as they sought to make the fourteenth amendment meaningful.[1] This desire to convince the majority of white Americans—the general public, as it were—that black Americans deserved all of the rights and privileges bestowed to its citizens had been a central component of the struggle against the American Colonization Society and colonizationist ideology since the early 1820s.

The first two days of the convention went on without any mention of colonization or the ACS. However, rumors had spread about some antendees sympathic to colonization and Liberia, and they had planned to make a motion that ex-president J.J. Roberts be named an honorary member. When the moment finally arrived, George Downing tried to prevent rehashing the old debates, and he called for the motion to be tabled. This didn't work, however, and those in attendance with anti-colonization views seized the chance to ridicule Roberts, Liberia, and the ACS. The first to speak was a "Mr. Green," who began a "lengthy, earnest speech" on the subject. As soon as he sat down, a "Mr. Weir" of Pennsylvania commented that "he had hoped" that this would not be brought up, "thinking his friends had better sense." However, because the question had been raised, Weir took the opportunity to blast those who had made the motion, claiming that he was disappointed that "this foreign odor" had been forced "under our noses." He went on to mock Roberts, stating that "He ran away to Liberia in the time of our need, and hid himself in the swamps of Liberia, and cried Colonization." This caused members of the audience to erupt in "great laughter."

Even though the American Colonization Society and its black supporters had spent four decades defending colonization in Liberia against this exact sort of anticolonization rancor, men like Roberts could not shake their reputation as "enemies of the race" despite their best attempts. Thus, black American leaders who gathered at the National Convention of 1869 snubbed Roberts and a movement that had hoped to galvanize free blacks to link their destiny with the first black American republic: Liberia. Yet, as this episode demonstrated, Roberts's association with the ACS was toxic; black convention members felt that acknowledgment of Roberts would be interpreted as support of the ACS and colonization.[2]

On the other hand, Martin Delany's emigrationist efforts during the 1850s did not sully his reputation among black leaders who gathered for the 1869 convention. Delany, a man who once accepted funding from the New York Colonization Society, was made an honorary member. Even with his chief advisory in the room, Frederick Douglas, Delany's peers honored his past achievements despite the feuds and disagreements over emigration that animated the decade before the Civil War. Perhaps Delany's participation in the war, and his involvement in South Carolina during Reconstruction, mattered more than his role as one of the premier emigrationist leaders in the eyes of some who formed an anticolonization, anti-emigration block in the North and Midwest. Delany had emerged in the postwar world as a man worth reverence, and such respect stood in stark contrast to Roberts's denunciation. In a way, this episode underscores the central argument of this book: While black American leaders outside the slave South considered leaving the United States, and at times initiated emigration movements to Haiti, Canada, and even West Africa, they ultimately fostered negative views of Liberia and rejected the ACS-led colonization movement.

However, despite the continued slander of the ACS and Liberia among these black leaders, the American Colonization Society emerged in a position of strength in the post–Civil War era. Unlike their northern brethren, African Americans in the South pondered whether or not colonization in Liberia would provide a better alternative than life in war-torn Dixie. Although emancipation brought new opportunities, the circumstances birthed by the war challenged newly freed men and women to assert themselves in new ways. Many freed blacks, as historian Steven Hahn observes, traveled to find relatives lost in the intercontinental slave trade, which had ripped apart millions of African American families in the South.[3] Soon after reuniting with their kin, southern blacks looked to the federal government for political rights, protection from violence, and, perhaps most important, land. For African Americans the bare fact remained: former slaves were forced into social arrangements only marginally better than what they endured before emancipation. This incomplete revolution was just not enough. Nothing short of full political rights, social autonomy, and redistribution of land could be acceptable to ex-slaves who had often described the war in millenial terms. And when dreams of "forty acres and a mule" were dashed, many of them did look to the American Colonization Society and Liberia for new opportunities.

Throughout the 1860s and 1870s, these challenges prompted southern blacks to mail letters to the American Colonization Society requesting passage to Liberia in order to live free of racial discrimination and violence. Often these letters were a grim testimony to the horrible conditions that remained in the wake of slavery. Paramilitary violence that whites considered "redemption" remained a pressing concern for southern blacks who wrote to the ACS. Thus, colonization in Liberia was one of many options that they considered within the context of the harassment and violence of whites seeking to reconstitute southern power relationships similar to those that had existed before the Civil War.

This interest among southern blacks was, of course, a boon to the ACS, and Corresponding Secretary William Coppinger busied himself with trying to raise money and support to meet this fresh surge of interest. As P.J. Staudenraus has explained, "The Civil War and the sudden unleashing of thousands of slaves offered an unparalleled opportunity for mass colonization and emigration projects under government sponsorship."[4] While the ACS had never succeeded in attracting great numbers between 1817 and 1865, freedom for African Americans vastly increased the pool of potential colonists into the millions.

Yet the American Colonization Society continued to struggle to raise funds after the war. Even though the organization's donations grew from nearly $47,000 in 1865 to over $71,000.00 by 1869, it still needed an additional $9,000 to match its expenditures. These financial difficulties undermined its ability to capitalize on southern blacks' interest in leaving the United States for Liberia.[5] To raise these funds, members of the ACS renewed their attempts to gain federal support. This led to a virtual deluge of pro-colonization tracts, appeals, and pamphlets that poured down on Washington. Yet even with this support, the ACS once again failed to convince federal legislators, and the majority of Americans, that the country would benefit from colonizing freed blacks in Liberia. In addition, federal officials rejected appeals from ACS officials and their supporters because they feared that blacks who left for Liberia would do so only by violating labor contracts that had sought to keep them on plantations, procuring cotton. Even members of state branches acknowledged the challenge that the organization faced to raise money because people throughout the nation depended on cotton production, and thus northerners and southerners had a vested interest in keeping blacks on the land. For example, the New York State Colonization Society noted in its annual reports that "The changes in the civil condition of the negro in our country within the last eleven years, have effected a revolution of feeling in relation to African colonization, both among the white and the colored population. With respect to the former it is manifested in a loss of interest in the enterprise. This is shown by the falling off in contributions made in its aid."[6]

However, whatever the odds, ACS leaders refused to give up. They spread their message to various reform organizations, churches, and any and all political entities that would listen to them. In Tennessee, unionist state officials introduced a bill in December 1866 that would establish a five-member board of commissioners to be nominated by the governor and the state senate that would determine a way to fund colonization of blacks in their state. Individual donations increased in Tennessee from $1,200 in March to $10,000 in May 1868.[7] In an effort to capitalize on this upsurge of colonization sentiments, Corresponding Secretary Coppinger mailed documents to state senators and house members imploring them to consider the well-being of black Americans who were showing interest in leaving for Liberia. One such petition from blacks living in Georgia and Alabama called on federal officials to fund colonization to help end the "injustice and wrongs" that would continue "as long as we remain here." Coppinger heard statements like this as he traveled throughout the South and met with blacks in country stores and churches, trying to recruit them to leave for Liberia. While letters to the ACS office had encouraged Coppinger that blacks in the South were interested in leaving for Liberia, his organizing efforts were not as promising as he had hoped they would be. Ultimately, Coppinger came to the realization that convincing blacks to leave for colonization in Liberia was just as challenging as raising the necessary funds to send them there, to say nothing of attracting federal support.[8]

If Coppinger did not already have his hands full trying to recruit blacks and raise money, he also faced the snickering and jeers of Radical Republicans who stuck to their abolitionist-inspired views of the ACS, as well as the enduring hatred of black leaders in the North who railed against colonization and Liberia as Reconstrution came to an end. Even when Henry McNeal Turner tried to revive a colonization movement in the 1880s, he confronted hostility from black leaders such as T. Thomas Fortune, who continued to describe the colonization movement as an antiblack program, and those who supported it as traitors to the race. This of course was an exaggeration, but such impressions remained in the consciousness of most black leaders at the turn of the century. When all was said and done, and Turner had crisscrossed the land trying to initate a large-scale movement of blacks to Liberia, only about 450 black Americans left between 1886 and 1892, hardly an impressive number despite the ACS claim in 1892 that one million had shown an interest in leaving for Liberia.[9]

By the 1920s, the one individual who inspired the most interest in a black-led emigration movement was Marcus Garvey, who imagined Liberia as the beachhead for his "Africa for the African" movement.[10] Despite the warnings of Hubert Harrison, a black radical and *Negro World* associate editor, that public cries of unity with Liberia could jeapordize their efforts, Garvey continued speaking boldly about his desire to forge ties with Liberia. Although Harrison agreed to chair a delegation of UNIA members to Liberia, it wasn't long before he informed Garvey and other UNIA officials that no passports for travel to Liberia were forthcoming. The U.S. governement was not about to let Garvey's supporters create ties with Liberia, and Liberian officials, fearful of Garvey's negative reputation among U.S. political leaders, rebuffed the leader of the largest mass movement of black Americans.

While Hubert Harrison had entertained travel to Liberia under Garvey's banner, he had, ironically, previously described the Colonization

Society in a manner that illustrated that black leaders continued to hold the same nineteenth-century aversion to the ACS into the twentieth century. In fact, when criticizing white liberals in the NAACP, Harrison referenced the American Colonization Society as the "first friends" of black Americans. He wrote, "The first great 'friend' of the Negro was the Southern politician Henry Clay, who in the first half of the nineteenth century organized the American Colonization Society." He reminded his readers, sarcastically and inaccurately, that the "Society befriended the 'free men of color' by raising funds to ship them to Liberia." One hundred years had passed since the founders of the American Colonization Society had tried to convince black Americans of the sincerity of its venture, but the organization and its leaders were still being mocked for having sinister motives. Whether or not the ACS represented a heterogenous group of emancipationists and slaveholders, the majority of blacks viewed ACS leaders as those who would either "rob blacks of their labor" or "deport them to Liberia."[11]

Marcus Garvey's charismatic leadership during the 1920s illustrates most clearly the legacy of emigrationism among twentieth-century activists who rejected the American racial caste system and argued for the importance of African resettlement as an expression of black pride. As a descendant of nineteenth-century black emigrationist ideology, Garvey shared the same sort of oppositional position rooted in the notion that African Americans need not wait for white sympathy for race advancement in the wake of racial violence and the persistence of structural racial inequality. Garvey's efforts, therefore, must be placed within the context of what Delany and others attempted to initiate in the 1850s. This vision of freedom excited many more thousands of blacks all across the nation in the 1920s than it had in the 1850s, yet such linear comparisons are difficult to make, given the two different historical contexts. While resistance to racial hostility and violence continued to be a central part of the black struggle for freedom and equality in the 1920s, it would be a stretch to argue that the manifestations of white supremacy Garvey agitated against were on par with those during the 1850s, a decade when the vast majority of Africans in America were enslaved in the South.

By his quixotic, indeed grandiose, claims, Garvey had tapped into black Americans' desire to live in a land free of racial prejudice, and such dreams of freedom inspired them to imagine the formation of a black American nation in Africa. On the heels of a "great migration" from the rural South to urban centers such as New York and Chicago, Garvey had been afforded an audience much larger than Delany had seventy years before. Scholar Michael Dawson points out that "what weds Delany's nationalism to Garvey's is that both embrace the idea of a separate state as a solution to the problem of continuing black oppression," and the vision of such a solution continued to endure well after the ACS and Liberia called on black Americans to join the first black American republic.

While Garvey's nationalistic emigrationist views bothered Liberian officials who were less than thrilled about aligning with a man who once boasted that he sought to be the president of Africa, Liberia's elite remained eager for black American support, even if they rejected Garvey's advances. Although they encouraged black American investment, they were unwilling to alienate the American government by housing black American radicals of Garvey's kind.

Even if Garvey's critics, such as W.E.B. DuBois, balked at emigrationism for reasons similar to those espoused by Douglass in the 1850s, Garvey attracted tremendous attention from those black Americans who shared with nineteenth-century blacks the belief that emigration to Africa constituted the ultimate expression of black pride and self-determination inherent in the African American struggle in the United States. DuBois agreed with Douglass that the fight against white supremacy began at home, yet DuBois shared with Garvey and Delany a pan-African commitment to race advancement that linked the destiny of the African continent with that of African Americans. Thus, even if DuBois's and Garvey's ideas about race advancement diverged in specific ways, they both acknowledged that the global struggle against European colonialism in Africa, and American racism, were two sides of the same coin.

Why did African Americans continue to embrace nineteenth-century emigrationism into the early part of the twentieth century? Several explanations can be gleaned from this study. First, black Americans with no real hope of securing the basic rights of citizenship, such as safety, due process of the law, and political representation, or who were trapped in poverty and truly lacked employment opportunities, comprised a ready and willing group of recruits for emigration movements. This was the case for Europeans who arrived in North America in the late nineteenth and early twentieth centuries, as well as those individuals and groups who emigrate to the United States today. Therefore, African American emigrationists were a part of a broader movement of people, ideas, and goods that have made up the Atlantic world from the nineteenth century until today. Second, black emigrationism had, from the founding of the United States, represented a rhetorical tool of self-empowerment that remained absolutely central to those black Americans fed up with both structural racism and everyday racial slights and insults. Thus, twentieth-century black activists shared their nineteenth-century predecessors' desire to use emigrationist rhetoric and initiatives as a way to both assert their sense of racial pride, while at the same time searching for an alternative to living in a national polity that continued to fail to eradicate structural racial inequality. For this reason, Marcus Garvey, Cyril Briggs, Harry Haywood, and Malcolm X remained inspired by Delany and other emigrationists of the antebellum era who looked to Africa as an ideal location for establishing a black American nation in opposition to the United States. Liberia, however, disappeared from any serious discourse about nation building in Africa among black activists who espoused emigrationist sentiments after the 1920s. Therefore, Garvey's effort to align with Liberian officials in the early part of the decade was the final call for unity by black Americans and their Liberian kin.

The American Colonization Society ceased attempting to populate Liberia with African Americans by the time Garvey began raising money for the "Black Star Line." Suprisingly, the organization continued functioning until 1964, when it turned its assests over to the Phelps-Stokes Fund, officially disolving one of the longest-lasting philanthropic entities in American history. Even with the dream of repatriation dashed, they pressed on well into the twentieth century, funding scholarships for Liberians to attend U.S. colleges and universities, as well as providing money for specific educational efforts in Liberia. Perhaps the most notable twentieth-century initiative remained the Booker T. Washington Institute. The Institute was established in Liberia by the Phelps-Stokes Fund in 1927, which had been created a decade earlier by a large bequest from Caroline Phelps Stokes, whose family had been members of the New York Colonization Society from its inception.[12] African Americans, by the 1960s, had much more on their mind than the defunct organization that had at one time considered itself a beacon of hope for black Americans, who they believed would never receive equal treatment in America. With the passage of the Civil Rights Act of 1964 and the increased momentum of the Black Freedom Movement, the ACS Board of Directors decided it was time to let go of their Liberian dream once and for all.[13]

NOTES

Notes to the Preface

1. The early history of the American Colonization Society's formation in late 1816 and early 1817 has most often begun with Rev. Robert Finley's success at organizing whites in Washington, DC, into an organization to promote African colonization during the fall of 1816. However, more recently, historians have identified Charles Mercer as the father of the American Colonization Society because, after uncovering secret documents that revealed the Virginia General Assembly's inquiry into colonization in 1800, he began publicly promoting the cause in the spring of 1816. Nevertheless, Rev. Robert Finley was instrumental in organizing important people in Washington to attend the first meeting of the organization on December 21, 1816. See *The First Annual Report of the American Society for Colonizing the Free People of Colour of the United States* (New York: Negro Universities Press, 1969); Eric Burin, *Slavery and the Peculiar Solution: A History of the American Colonization Society* (Gainsville: University of Florida Press, 2005), 13–14.

2. P.J. Staudenraus, *The African Colonization Movement, 1816–1865* (New York: Columbia University Press, 1961), 28; Henry Noble Sherwood, "The Formation of the American Colonization Society," *The Journal of Negro History* 2, no. 3 (July 1917): 222–23; *Poulson's Daily Advertiser*, January 1, 1817.

Notes to the Introduction

1. William W. Brown, *The Anti-Slavery Harp* (Boston: Bela Marsh, 1848).

2. *Poulson's Daily Advertiser*, January 10, 1817.

3. Ibid.

4. Ibid., 21.

5. This idea was expressed at one of the first anticolonization gatherings in Philadelphia in 1817. See Richard S. Newman, *The Transformation of American Abolitionism: Fighting Slavery in the Early Republic* (Chapel Hill: University of North Carolina

Press, 2002), 96–98; Benjamin Quarles, *Black Abolitionists* (Oxford, UK: Oxford University Press, 1969), 3–4.

6. Benjamin Quarles makes this observation in his study of black abolitionists. In their edited collection of black state convention records, Phillip Foner and George E. Walker also point to the formation of the ACS as a catalyst for the creation of a national, unified struggle for racial justice, social equality, and political rights. See Benjamin Quarles, *Black Abolitionists*, 3–5; Phillip Foner and George E. Walker, eds., *Proceedings of the Black State Conventions, 1840–1865* (Philadelphia: Temple University Press, 1979), xi.

7. Staudenraus, *The African Colonization Movement*, 27–35.

8. In Winston James's biography of Russwurm, he argues that Russwurm came to accept colonization when learning of northern white philanthropic interest in African American betterment. His key argument revolves around the notion that the ACS remained a fractured organization with various discordant views among its members. James accurately points out that not all colonizationists believed in ridding the nation of free blacks in order to bolster slavery. See Winston James, *The Struggles of John Brown Russwurm: The Life and Writings of a Pan-Africanist Pioneer, 1799–1851* (New York: New York University Press, 2010).

9. "Colonization," *The North Star*, Rochester, NY, January 26, 1849.

10. For the most important recent study of the American Colonization Society, see Eric Burin, *Slavery and the Peculiar Solution: A History of the American Colonization Society* (Gainesville: University Press of Florida, 2005). Several studies of black colonization to Liberia have been written since the beginning of this century. These include Marie Tyler-McGraw, *An African Republic: Black & White Virginians in the Making of Liberia* (Chapel Hill: University of North Carolina Press, 2007); Claude A. Clegg III, *The Price of Liberty: African Americans and the Making of Liberia* (Chapel Hill: University of North Carolina Press, 2004); Alan Huffman, *Mississippi in Africa: The Saga of the Slaves of the Prospect Hill Plantation and Their Legacy in Liberia Today* (New York: Gotham Books, 2003).

11. Beverly C. Tomek, *Colonization and Its Discontents: Emancipation, Emigration, and Antislavery in Antebellum Pennsylvania* (New York: New York University Press, 2011), 130–31.

12. I define *pan-African* as the movement of African-descended people in opposition to European colonialism, American slavery, and race-based oppression throughout the world, including in Africa. See Immanuel Geiss, *The Pan-African Movement: A History of Pan-Africanism in America, Europe, and Africa* (New York: Africana Publishing Co., 1968), 3–4.

13. Richard Blackett, *Building an Antislavery Wall: Black Americans in the Atlantic Abolitionist Movement, 1830–1860* (Baton Rouge: Louisiana State University Press, 1983); see also Betty Fladeland, *Men and Brothers: Anglo-American Antislavery Cooperation* (Urbana: University of Illinois Press, 1972); Kathryn Kish Sklar and James Brewer Stewart, eds., *Women's Rights and Transatlantic Antislavery in the Era of Emancipation* (New Haven, CT: Yale University Press, 2007).

14. James Oliver Horton and Lois E. Horton, *In Hope of Liberty: Culture, Community, and Protest Among Northern Free Blacks, 1700–1860* (New York: Oxford University Press, 1997), 198.

15. By the end of the 1850s, Delany found himself in need of funds to further his trip to the Niger Valley and to promote emigration. Thus, he received money from colonizationists, such as Benjamin Coates from Philadelphia, who convinced him of their benevolent intent. See Emma J. Lapansky-Werner and Margaret Hope Bacon, eds., *Back to Africa: Benjamin Coates and the Colonization Movement in America, 1848–1880* (University Park: Pennsylvania University Press, 2005).

16. Floyd J. Miller, *The Search for a Black Nationality: Black Emigration and Colonization, 1787–1863* (Urbana: University of Illinois Press, 1975).

17. Thomas Lamont, *Rise to Be a People: A Biography of Paul Cuffe* (Urbana: University of Illinois Press, 1986), 111.

18. Howard Bell, "Negro Nationalism: A Factor in Emigration Projects, 1858–1861," *Journal of Negro History* 47, no. 1 (January 1962), and "The Negro Emigration Movement, 1849–1854: A Phase of Negro Nationalism," *Phylon Quarterly* 20, no. 2 (2nd quarter, 1959), are extremely useful for establishing a framework for understanding emigrationist ideology. Benjamin Quarles's *Black Abolitionists* is the classic study of black abolitionism; see also Jane and William H. Pease, *They Who Would Be Free: Blacks' Search for Freedom, 1830–1861* (Urbana: University of Illinois Press, 1974).

19. Anne M. Boylan, "Benevolence and Antislavery Activity among African American Women in New York and Boston, 1820–1840," in Jean Fagan Yellin and John C. Van Horne, *Abolitionist Sisterhood: Women's Political Culture in Antebellum America* (Ithaca, NY: Cornell University Press, 1994), 122–23; Julie Wench, "'You Have Talents—Only Cultivate Them': Philadelphia's Black Female Literary Societies and the Abolitionist Crusade," in Yellin and Van Horne, *Abolitionist Sisterhood*, 128–35; Beth A. Salerno, *Sister Societies: Women's Antislavery Organizations in Antebellum America* (Dekalb: Northern Illinois University Press, 2005), 13.

20. Julie Roy Jeffrey, *The Great Silent Arm of Abolitionism: Ordinary Women in the Antislavery Movement* (Chapel Hill: University of North Carolina Press, 1998), 15–17; see also Salerno, *Sister Societies*, 14. Elizabeth R. Varon's work shows that in Virginia, colonization represented "the most important charity" and was a crucial stepping stone toward political participation. See Elizabeth R. Varon, *We Mean to Be Counted: White Women and Politics in Antebellum Virginia* (Chapel Hill: University of North Carolina Press, 1998), 44–45.

21. For a more expansive examination of the theoretical issues at play regarding black masculinity and public discourse, see Gail Bederman, *Manliness and Civilization: A Cultural History of Gender and Race in the United States, 1880–1917* (London: University of Chicago Press, 1996).

22. Patrick Rael, *Black Identity and Black Protest in the Antebellum North* (Chapel Hill: University of North Carolina Press, 2002), 7.

23. For excellent studies of southern blacks who left for Liberia, see Penelope Campbell, *Maryland in Africa* (Urbana: University of Illinois Press, 1971); Randall Miller, *Dear Master: Letters of a Slave Family* (Athens: University of Georgia Press, 2004); Clegg, *The Price of Liberty*; Tyler-McGraw, *An African Republic*; Huffman, *Mississippi in Africa*.

24. Campbell, *Maryland in Africa*; Barbara Jeanne Fields, *Slavery and Freedom on Middle Ground: Maryland During the Nineteenth Century* (New Haven, CT: Yale University Press, 1985).

25. See Harvey Whitfield, *Blacks on the Border: Black Refugees in British North America, 1815–1860* (Burlington: University of Vermont Press, 2006).

26. Ibid., 49, 220–21.

27. Massachusetts Colonization Society Annual Reports, presented May 27, 1847, *Sixth Annual Report of the Board of Managers of the Massachusetts Colonization Society* (Boston: Press of T.R. Marvin), 9–11.

28. Some of the most important work on white supremacy must be credited to George Fredrickson. See his books *White Supremacy: A Comparative Study in American and South African History* (New York: Oxford University Press, 1981); and *The Black Image in the White Mind: The Debate on African American Character and Destiny, 1817–1914* (New York: Harper and Row, 1971). For black American perspectives on whites, see Mia Bay, *The White Image in the Black Mind: African American Ideas about White People, 1830–1925* (Oxford: Oxford University Press, 2000).

29. See Patrick Rael, *Black Identity and Black Protest in the Antebellum North* (Chapel Hill: University of North Carolina Press, 2002); Kwando M. Kinhasa, *Emigration v. Assimilation: The Debate in the African American Press* (Jefferson, NC: McFarland & Company, 1988); Robert S. Levine, *Martin Delany, Frederick Douglass, and the Politics of Representative Identity* (Chapel Hill: University of North Carolina Press, 1997).

30. Newman, *Transformation of American Abolitionism*, 100–1.

31. Ibid.

32. Nicholas Guyatt draws this important link, arguing that "juxtaposing Indian and black removal enables us to reconsider the relationship between colonization and race." Guyatt goes on to explain, "The parallel histories of racial removal bear out one broad generalization: White Americans were extremely uncomfortable with non-whites in their midst, and they struggled to square their consciences with the reality of a multiracial republic." See Nicholas Guyatt, "'The Outskirts of Our Happiness': Race and the Lure of Colonization in the Early Republic," *The Journal of American History*, Volume 95, No. 4 (March 2009): 986–1011.

33. Joanne Pope Melish's work on northern white attitudes is an important contribution to the history of white national identity construction. Melish builds on Winthrop Jordan's *White Over Black: American Attitudes toward the Negro, 1550–1812* (Chapel Hill: University of North Carolina Press, 2012) and George Fredrickson's *The Black Image in the White Mind*. See Joanne Pope Melish, *Disowning Slavery: Gradual Emancipation and "Race" in New England* (Ithaca, NY: Cornell University Press, 1998); see also James Brewer Stewart, "The Emergence of Racial Modernity and the Rise of the White North," *Journal of the Early Republic* 18, no. 2 (Summer 1998): 181–217.

34. Staudenraus, *The African Colonization Movement, 1816–1865*, 1–5. Staudenraus's book is the foundational text on the American Colonization Society, and colonization generally.

35. For example, see *Petitions of African Americans to Massachusetts General Court to Abolish Slavery and to the Massachusetts Legislature*, "That your petitioners apprehend that they have, in common with all other men, a natural and inalienable right to that freedom, which the great Parent of the universe hath bestowed equally on all mankind, and which they have never forfeited by any compact or agreement whatever," in John H. Bracey Jr. and Manisha Sinha, eds., *African American Mosaic: A Documentary History from the Slave Trade to the Twenty-First Century, Volume One to 1877* (Upper Saddle River, NJ: Prentice Hall, 2004), 53–57. For African American

petitions to state and federal officials, see Herbert Aptheker, ed., *A Documentary History of the Negro People in the United States* (New York: Citadel Press, 1951).

36. Melish, *Disowning Slavery*, 2.

37. While the origins of these two means of racial exclusion coincide with state-issued mandates denying blacks access to education, as well as other social and economic rights, Leonard L. Richards explains that whites embraced colonization as an expression of white supremacy. Richards argues that "The New York City rioters of July, 1834, shouted colonization vows in Chatham Street Chapel. The Utica mob of October, 1835, included leading local colonizationists. The Cincinnati mob of July, 1836, included most of the city's prominent colonizationists. The rioters who killed Elijah Lovejoy at Alton, Illinois, in November, 1837, identified openly with African colonization." See Leonard L. Richards, *"Gentlemen of Property and Standing": Anti-Abolition Mobs in Jacksonian America* (London: Oxford University Press, 1970), 30.

38. Alexander Saxton, *The Rise and Fall of the White Republic: Class Politics and Mass Culture in Nineteenth-Century America* (New York: Verso Press reprint, 2003); Theodore Allen, *The Invention of the White Race* (New York: Verso Press, 2012); David Rodiger, *Wages of Whiteness: Race and the Making of the American Working Class* (New York: Verso Press, 1999). For a critique of Saxton and Rodiger's analysis, see Bruce Laurie, *Beyond Garrison: Antislavery and Social Reform* (New York: Cambridge University Press, 2005), 84–88.

39. Eric Foner, *The Fiery Trial: Abraham Lincoln and American Slavery* (New York: W.W. Norton, 2010), 17. Despite recent scholarship that shows a diverse range of emancipationists and humanitarians, some of whom did not depise blacks, most historians share Foner's basic assessment of colonization ideology. For instance, Eric Burin writes that earlier scholars failed to look at colonization on a local level, and thus they dismissed the more complex motives of those who conducted their work away from the organizational leaders based in Washington, DC. However, Burin asserts that, overall, "the American Colonization Society (ACS) hoped to rid the United States of both slavery and black people," pointing out that "As sectional tensions heightened during the antebellum era, colonizationists became more vocal, pleading that only emancipation and deracination could solve the country's troubles" See Burin, *Slavery and the Peculiar Solution*, 1; Charles I. Foster, "The Colonization of Free Negroes, in Liberia, 1816–1835," *Journal of Negro History* 38, no. 1 (January 1953): 46–47.

Notes to Chapter 1

1. Saunders, "Memoir Presented to the American Convention for Promoting the Abolition of Slavery, and Improving the Condition of the African Race," December 11, 1818. In Prince Saunders, *Haytian Papers: A Collection of the Very Interesting Proclamations and other Official documents; Together with Some Account of the Rise, Progress, and Present State of The Kingdom of Hayti* (London: W. Reed, Law Bookseller, No. 17, Fleet Street, 1816), 12–13.

2. Paul Gilroy situates the Haitian Revolution in an ideological context, underscoring its importance in the formation of an African diasporic identity as a "global phenomenon." He asserts that "In periodising modern black politics it will require fresh thinking about the importance of Haiti and its revolution for the development of African American political thought and movements of resistance." Paul Gilroy, *The*

Black Atlantic: Modernity and Double-Consciousness (Cambridge, MA: Harvard University Press, 1993), 17.

3. Leon D. Pamphile, *Haitians and African Americans: A Heritage of Tragedy and Hope.* Gainesville: University Press of Florida, 2001), 44.

4. While African Americans lauded Haitian independence, the movement pushing for emigration to Haiti did not begin until after the birth of the American Colonization Society in 1816–1817. See Miller, *The Search for a Black Nationality*, 74.

5. Julie Winch, *A Gentleman of Color: The Life of James Forten* (New York: Oxford University Press, 2002), 209.

6. For a discussion of the ideological underpinnings of black nationalism, see Dean E. Robinson, *Black Nationalism in American Politics and Thought* (New York: Cambridge University Press, 2001), 9–15; and Ronald W. Walters, *Pan Africanism in the African Diaspora: An Analysis of Modern Afrocentric Political Movements* (Detroit: Wayne State University Press, 1997).

7. Rael, *Black Identity and Black Protest*, 209–13; Laurent Dubois, *Haiti: The Aftershocks of History* (New York: Henry Holt & Company, 2012), 83–86; Wim Klooster, *Revolutions in the Atlantic World: A Comparative History* (New York: New York University Press, 2009), 115.

8. Laurent Dubois, *Avengers of the New World: The Story of the Haitian Revolution* (Cambridge, MA: Harvard University Press, 2005), 302–5.

9. White, "Prince Saunders: An Instance of Social Mobility among Antebellum New England Blacks," *Journal of Negro History* 60 (1975), 526–27.

10. Saunders's trip reflects the transnational nature of African American agitation against slavery and racial oppression, and it illustrates how Cuffe's groundwork had opened a dialogue between African American leaders and renowned British abolitionists such as William Wilberforce and Thomas Clarkson. The press covered Cuffe's visit extensively, gushing over his physical presence, intelligence, and manner of speaking. The directors of the African Institution in London met Cuffe on August 27, 1811, and after a brief introduction by William Allen, Cuffe explained African American interest in emigrating to West Africa to settle and thereby work towards spreading Christian civilization and challenging the coastal slave trade. Cuffe argued that a strong African American nation in Africa could help end slave trading, and would demonstrate black people's ability to create a society equal to white societies in Europe and America. While scholars often note the importance of American abolitionists' forging ties with their European peers after 1830, rarely do they cite the pioneering work of Cuffe or Saunders. Black leaders are infrequently presented as the *progenitors* of transnational antislavery activism. See Blackett, *Building an Antislavery Wall*.

11. Chris Dixon asserts: "Historians have disagreed over Cuffe's motivations for supporting colonization.... [However,] it is clear that Cuffe betrayed the cultural and hierarchical assumptions that were characteristic of African American emigrationism.... his scheme aroused little support within the free black community, and ended with his death in September 1817." See Chris Dixon, *African America and Haiti: Emigration and Black Nationalism in the Nineteenth Century* (Westport, CT: Greenwood Press, 2000), 20. While Dixon's claim seems, on the surface, plausible, it fails to take into account the fact that free black leaders such as Prince Saunders, Daniel Coker, and James Forten supported Cuffe's plan, at least initially. It was with the rise of the ACS that they turned against African colonization and looked, instead,

to Haiti. As Julie Winch writes, "Despite his growing antagonism toward the ACS, James Forten had been careful not to denounce 'all plans of colonization.' Even as late as August, he had not apparently given up on the Sierra Leone scheme." Winch, *A Gentleman of Color*, 197.

12. Several useful studies of Haitian independence and African Americans' opinions about Haiti include Dubois, *Avengers of the New World*; Sibylle Fischer, *Modernity Disavowed: Haiti and the Cultures of Slavery in the Age of Revolution* (Durham: Duke University Press, 2004); David P. Geggus, ed., *The Impact of the Haitian Revolution in the Atlantic World* (Columbia: University of South Carolina Press, 2001); and Alfred N. Hunt, *Haiti's Influence on Antebellum America* (Baton Rouge: Louisiana State University Press, 1988).

13. "African Institution, Philadelphia, September 6, 1816," *The Yankee*, September 13, 1816, vol. V, no. 38, 2.

14. "From the British Monitor: Memoirs of Henry 1, Late King of Hayti," *The Watch-Tower*, May 13, 1822, vol. IX, 1.

15. Ibid.

16. This account of Christophe's early years can be found in the introduction of Earl Leslie Griggs and Clifford H. Prator, eds., *Henry Christophe and Thomas Clarkson: A Correspondence* (New York: Greenwood Press, 1968), 39–41.

17. Ibid., 62.

18. Ibid.

19. Rayford Logan, *The Diplomatic Relations of the United States with Haiti, 1776–1891* (New York: Kraus Reprint, 1941 [originally University of North Carolina Press, 1941]), 314.

20. The sum of $25,000 would be the equivalent of approximately $495,000 in 2011. See "Measuring Worth," www.measuringworth.com/aboutus.php.

21. "Manifesto of the King," in Prince Saunders, *Haytian Papers*.

22. White, "Prince Saunders," 528.

23. As reported by Winston James in his *The Struggles of John Brown Russwurm*, 13; White, "Prince Saunders," 530.

24. White, "Prince Saunders," 529.

25. Horton and Horton, *In Hope of Liberty*, 192–93.

26. Ibid.

27. "Necessity of a Colony of Free Blacks Supercede," *New England Palladium*, February 11, 1817.

28. Saunders, *The Haytian Papers*, vii.

29. An article in *The Yankee* (September 13, 1816) expressed William Wilberforce's support of King Christophe: "Mr. Wilberforce rose, and made a most fulsome eulogium on Christophe, the black king of Hayti, whom he extolled as combining every princely quality, and holding his 'golden circle' by a right more legitimate than the ex-emperor of France, or the kings of Spain and Naples." See also "Philadelphia, Sept. 6, African Institution," *The Yankee*, September 9, 1816. Saunders's support of Christophe is featured in his Memoir to the American Convention, and again in a letter he wrote on August 13, 1816. See Saunders, *The Haytian Papers*, 18–19.

30. Saunders, *The Haytian Papers*, vii–xi.

31. Prince Saunders, "An Address, Delivered at Bethel Church, Philadelphia; on the 30th of September, 1818, Before the Pennsylvania Augustine Society, for the Education of People of Colour," 4, in Saunders, *The Haytian Papers*.

32. White, "Prince Saunders," 531–32; see also Miller, *The Search for a Black Nationality*, 74.

33. "People of Color," *Niles' Weekly Register*, October 17, 1818.

34. Brenda Gayle Plummer, *Haiti and the United States: The Psychological Moment* (Athens: University of Georgia Press, 1992) 29–30; Sayre, "The Evolution of Early American Abolitionism," 81.

35. "The American Convention for Promoting the Abolition of Slavery and Improving the Condition of the African Race" was the largest early antislavery organ in America. Established in 1794 in Pennsylvania, with the cooperation of the Pennsylvania Abolition Society and the New York Manumission Society, the American Convention provided various abolitionists across the United States with a forum for discussing tactics and the progress of abolition. The American Convention created its constitution in 1801, and the organization become an official entity in 1803. It petitioned Congress about the slave trade, sought to protect the legal rights of blacks, and organized programs for educating blacks. Sayre's dissertation, "The Evolution of Early American Abolitionism," remains the most thorough examination of the organization. See Paul J. Polgar, "'To Raise Them to an Equal Participation': Early National Abolitionism, Gradual Emancipation, and the Promise of African American Citizenship," *Journal of the Early Republic* 31, no. 2 (Summer 2011): 229–58; Prince Saunders, "An Address Delivered at Bethel Church, Philadelphia, 1818"; "A Memoir Presented to the American Convention for Promoting the Abolition of Slavery, 1819 [1818], Haytian Papers.

36. Saunders, like Forten, considered emigration to be a viable option for blacks but rejected the American Colonization Society. Saunders read a petition to the American Convention calling its members to, as Richard S. Newman puts it, "mount a blistering attack on a proposal that surrendered the moral high ground of abolitionism and legitimized whites' worst racial assumptions." See Newman, *The Transformation of American Abolitionism*, 98.

37. Sayre, "The Evolution of Early American Abolitionism," 202.

38. Ibid., 195–96.

39. Ibid., 197.

40. Ibid., 198.

41. Ibid., 199–200.

42. Ibid., 201.

43. Ibid., 202. Beverly C. Tomek does an excellent job showing how black resistance to colonization played a major role in shaping the views of its members. See Tomek, *Colonization and Its Discontents*, 37–42.

44. Ibid.

45. Saunders, "Memoir Presented to the American Convention," December 11, 1818, 16–17.

46. Ibid. Paul Gilroy identifies this transnational and diasporic movement of ideas regarding black nationalism, racial uplift, and "movements of resistance," broadly defined, as an important feature of a "Black Atlantic" sensibility. Thus, Gilroy asserts, "the histories of Africans in the diaspora must include an evaluation of movement— voluntary and forced—to and from Africa, Europe, and North and South America." See Gilroy, *The Black Atlantic*, 17. This is a central argument in James Sidbury's

trenchant study of African Americans in the Atlantic world. See James Sidbury, *Becoming African in America* (New York: Oxford University Press, 2007), 8–13.

47. White, "Prince Saunders," 534.

48. Logan, *The Diplomatic Relations*, 191.

49. Burr, "Mulatto Machiavelli," 324–28.

50. See: "Colonization of the Blacks," *Newport Mercury*, June 26, 1824; see also Boyer's letters to Loring D. Dewey in Loring D. Dewey, *Correspondence Relative to the Emigration to Hayti, of the Free People of Colour, in the United States, Together with Instructions to the Agent Sent Out by President Boyer* (New York: Mahlon Day Press, 1824). This episode is recounted in several texts, and most clearly in Julie Winch's book, *Philadelphia's Black Elite* (Philadelphia: Temple University Press, 1988), 52.

51. See *American Advocate and Kennebee Advertiser*, June 6, 1818.

52. "Hayti," *Columbian Sentinel*, July 4, 1821.

53. This article from the *Portland Gazette* was reprinted in *The Farmer's Cabinet*, December 11, 1819; see also "Colonization," *New Bedford Mercury*, December 3, 1819.

54. "Haytian Company of Maryland," *City of Washington Gazette*, February 24, 1821.

55. Reprinted from the *Boston Gazette* as "From Hayti" in the *Newburyport Herald*, August 24, 1821.

56. *The Sixth Annual Report of the American Society for Colonizing the Free People of Colour of the United States*, 67–70.

57. Staudenraus, *The African Colonization Movement*.

58. Dewey, *Correspondence Relative to the Emigration to Hayti*, 2.

59. Ibid., 28.

60. "New York Colonization Society," *New-Bedford Mercury*, July 2, 1824.

61. This announcement was printed in the *Providence Gazette*, May 26, 1824.

62. "The Journal Saturday, July 3, 1824," in the *Portsmouth Journal of Literature and Politics*, July 3, 1824.

63. Ibid.

64. Dewey, *Correspondence Relative to the Emigration to Hayti*, 29–31.

65. Leslie M. Harris, *In the Shadow of Slavery: African Americans in New York City, 1626–1863* (Chicago: University of Chicago Press, 2003), 61.

66. Harris, *In the Shadow of Slavery*, 141.

67. Dewey, *Correspondence*, 31.

68. Portions of this letter, dated January 10, 1825, were printed in the *Pittsfield Sun* on April 7, 1825, under the title, "Emigration to Hayti."

69. Horton and Horton, *In Hope of Liberty*, 191–95.

70. "Emigration to Hayti," *Columbian Star*, as reported in the *Vermont Gazette*, August 3, 1824.

71. Ibid.

72. *Independent Chronicle and Boston Patriot*, July 3, 1824.

73. "Colonization of the Blacks," *Newport Mercury*, June 26, 1824. This article was written on June 19, 1824, in New York.

74. "Agent from Hayti," *Eastern Argus*, June 19, 1824. Boyer's letter to Dewey explains that "Those come, being children of Africa, shall be Haytiens [*sic*] as soon as they put their feet upon the soil of Hayti: they will enjoy happiness, security,

tranquility, such as we ourselves possess, however our defamers declare the contrary." Dewey, *Correspondence Relative to the Emigration to Hayti*, 10.

75. *Genius of Universal Emancipation*, vol. IV, no. 2, November 1824, 17.

76. *Genius of Universal Emancipation*, November 1824, 28.

77. "Haytien Mission," *Genius of Universal Emancipation*, December 1824, 34–35.

78. "Letters from Hayti," *Genius of Universal Emancipation*, January 1825, 58.

79. "The Emigrants to Hayti," *Genius of Universal Emancipation*, January 1825, 49.

80. Lundy argued, "In the course of my observations, I have remarked that the best informed among the advocates of Universal Emancipation, are, generally, in favour of the removal of our coloured population to Hayti." See "Emigration to Hayti—No. III," *The Genius of Universal Emancipation*, January 1825, 52.

81. This diatribe against Lundy touches on several issues, which reinforce Lundy's claim that ACS members failed to understand that motives and intentions count more than finances. African Americans, according to Lundy, rejected colonization in Africa because some ACS members believed in the perpetuation of slavery in America, and ACS recruitment strategies included the denigration of the free black press in their effort to gain support and donations in the white community. See "To the Editor of the Genius of Universal Emancipation," *Genius of Universal Emancipation*, February 1825, 69–71.

82. Ibid.

83. "Emigration to Hayti—No. IV," *Genius of Universal Emancipation*, February 1825, 72.

84. *Freedom's Journal*, edited by Samuel Cornish and John Russwurm, was the first black newspaper in the United States. See Horton and Horton, *In Hope of Liberty*.

85. Ibid., 73.

86. American Colonization Society, *Ninth Annual Report*, 8.

87. Pamphile, *Haitians and African Americans*, 45.

88. Miller, *In Search of a Black Nationality*, 81.

89. Ibid., 101.

90. Miller, *In Search of a Black Nationality*, 80.

91. "Latest from Hayti," *Boston Commercial Gazette*, June 6, 1826.

92. Ibid.

93. This statement was a response to a previous article citing "verbal accounts" regarding the tranquility of the island and the prosperous conditions of the emigrants. Benjamin Lundy, according to the article, found that "Respectable and industrious blacks will . . . always find a home in Hayti, and sincere friendship and protection in the government." See "Latest from Hayti," *Boston Commercial Gazette*, June 6, 1826.

94. Dillon, *Benjamin Lundy*, 99.

95. According to historian Ludwell Lee Montague, "It is not difficult to perceive how the idea of an independent negro nationality in America would affect the antebellum planter, to whom public order and private fortune were alike based on the premise that negroes were unfit for self-government." Montague, *Haiti and the United States, 1714–1938*, 25.

96. Dillon, *Benjamin Lundy*, 99–100.

97. Staudenraus, *The African Colonization Movement*, 83–87.

98. *Norwich Courier*, vol. V, no. 26, September 27, 1826, 3. John B. Russwurm has often been acknowledged as the first African American to graduate from a college

in the United States, but Edward Jones actually graduated from Amherst College right before Russwurm completed his studies at Bowdoin College. Russwurm is listed as receiving his B.A. in an article entitled "At the Late Commencement at Bowdoin College the following Young Gentlemen Received the Degree of Bachelor of Arts," in *Eastern Argus*, vol. II, no. 209, September 12, 1826, 2; William B. Brewer, "John B. Russwurm," *Journal of Negro History* 13, no. 4 (October 1928): 413.

99. John B. Russwurm, "The Condition and Prospects of Hayti," Commencement Address of Bowdoin College, September 6, 1826, reprinted with editorial comments by Philip S. Foner in *The Journal of Negro History* 54, no. 4 (October 1969). For biographical information on Russwurm, see Winston James, *The Struggles of John Brown Russwurm: The Life and Writings of a Pan-Africanist Pioneer, 1799–1851* (New York: New York University Press, 2010), and Amos J. Beyan, *African American Settlements in West Africa: John Brown Russwurm and the American Civilizing Efforts* (New York: Palgrave, 2005).

100. *Norwich Courier*, vol. V, no. 26, September 27, 1826, 3.

101. Beyan, *African American Settlements in West Africa*, 4.

102. For a discussion of transnational black identity, see James Sidbury, *Becoming African in America: Race and Nation in the Early Black Atlantic* (New York: Oxford University Press, 2006).

103. Winston James, *John Brown Russwurm: The Life and Writings of a Pan African Pioneer, 1799–1851* (New York: New York University Press, 2010), 24–25.

104. See Jacqueline Bacon, *Freedom's Journal* (Lanham, MD: Lexington Press, 2007), 56–59; Winston James, *The Struggles of John Brown Russwurm*, 38–42; Beyan, *African American Settlements in West Africa*, 27.

105. James, *The Struggles of John Brown Russwurm*, 46.

106. For a thorough analysis of Russwurm's decision and its impact on his legacy and career, see Sandra Sandiford Young, "John Brown Russwurm's Dilemma," in Timothy Patrick McCarthy and John Stauffer, eds., *Prophets of Protest: Reconsidering the History of American Abolitionism* (New York: The New Press, 2006), 90–113. Winston James treats Russwurm's decision to leave in extraordinary detail. He shows that most scholars who have come to believe that Russwurm had "fallen under the spell of colonization" in the absence of Cornish have not marshalled enough evidence to prove that contention. See James, *The Struggles of John Brown Russwurm*, 44–54.

107. Leslie Harris writes, "A few blacks supported colonization, but the vast majority of New York City blacks opposed it, and many heaped scorn on its supporters, white and black." Soon, Russwurm would be one of the scorned few who drifted in that direction for reasons still debated among scholars. See Leslie Harris, *In the Shadow of Slavery: African Americans in New York City, 1626–1863* (Chicago: University of Chicago Press, 2002), 141; see also James, *The Struggles of John Brown Russwurm*, 46–51.

108. "Our Vindication," *Freedom's Journal*, March 7, 1829.

109. "To Our Patrons, and the Publick Generally," *The Rights of All*, May 29, 1829.

110. Ibid. Winston James points out that by 1838 Cornish would denounce Russwurm in ways that resembled the onslaught of criticism in the late 1820s. See James, *The Struggles of John Brown Russwurm*, 51.

111. "Candid Acknowledgment of Error," *African Repository*, February 1829; Bacon, *Freedom's Journal*, 59–64; James, *John Brown Russwurm*, 43.

112. *Freedom's Journal*, February 21, 1829. See James, *John Brown Russwurm*, 45.

113. Ibid.

114. Bruce Rosen, "Abolition and Colonization, the Years of Conflict: 1829–1834," *Phylon* 33, no. 2, (2nd Quarter, 1972): 177–92.

115. Julie Winch, *A Gentleman of Color*, 205–6.

116. Peter P. Hinks, ed., *David Walker's Appeal to the Coloured Citizens of the World* (University Park: Pennsylvania State University Press, 2008), 46–82.

Notes to Chapter 2

1. Maria W. Stewart, "An Address Delivered at the African Masonic Hall, Boston, February 27, 1833," reprinted in Dorothy Porter, ed., *Early Negro Writing, 1760–1837* (Boston: Beacon Press, 1971), 133–35.

2. "A Lecture by Maria W. Stewart, given at Franklin Hall, Boston, September 21, 1832," reprinted in Porter, ed., *Early Negro Writings*, 136–38.

3. Marilyn Richardson, "'What If I Am a Woman?': Maria W. Stewart's Defense of Black Women's Political Activism," in Donald M. Jacobs, ed., *Courage and Conscience: Black and White Abolitionists in Boston* (Bloomington: Indiana University Press, 1993), 191–206; see also Yee, *Black Women Abolitionists*, 115–16.

4. "An Address to the Citizens of New York," *The Liberator*, February 12, 1831, Volume 1, No. 7 Boston. For a much more nuanced study of black political activism in New York City, see Leslie M. Alexander, *African or American? Black Identity and Political Activism in New York City, 1789–1861* (Urbana: University of Illinois Press, 2008), 8.

5. Stephen Kantrowitz points out that the quest for citizenship remained central to black struggles against racism, violence, and colonization. See Stephen Kantrowitz, *More Than Freedom: Fighting for Black Citizenship in a White Republic, 1829–1889* (New York: Penguin Press, 2012), 2–6.

6. Richard S. Newman, *The Transformation of American Abolitionism: Fighting Slavery in the Early Republic* (Chapel Hill: University of North Carolina Press, 2002), 106; Paul Goodman, *Of One Blood: Abolitionism and the Origins of Racial Equality* (Berkeley: University California Press, 1998), 1–3.

7. Garrison, quoted in Horton and Horton, *In Hope of Liberty*, 211.

8. Peter P. Hinks, ed., *David Walker's Appeal to the Coloured Citizens of the World* (University Park: Pennsylvania State University Press, 2000), xxiii.

9. Ibid., xxv.

10. Herbert Aptheker, *A Documentary History of the Negro People*, vol. I (New York: Citadel Press, 1969), 100; Hezekiah Grice was also a leader of the Haitian emigration movement. See Leon D. Pamphile, *Haitians and African Americans: A Heritage of Tragedy and Hope* (Gainesville: University Press of Florida, 2001), 34.

11. Peter Hinks, ed., *David Walker's Appeal to the Coloured People of the World* (University Park: Pennsylvania State University Press, 2000).

12. Ibid., 70.

13. Ibid., 71.

14. Ibid., 58.

15. Newman, *The Transformation of American Abolitionism*, 96.

16. Ibid., 96–97. See William Hamilton, senate president of the Conventional Board, "Address to the Fourth Annual Convention of the Free People of Color of the United States, Delivered at the Opening of Their Session in the City of New York, June

2, 1834," reprinted in Dorothy Porter, ed., *Negro Protest Pamphlets* (New York: Arno Press and the *New York Times*, 1969), 5.

17. Howard H. Bell, *A Survey of the Negro Convention Movement, 1830–1861* (New York: Arno Press, 1969), 10–37.

18. Bell, *Negro Convention Movement*, 27.

19. Aptheker, *A Documentary History*, 106.

20. Ibid., 16–17.

21. Ibid.

22. Horton and Horton, *In Hope of Liberty*, 209; Staudenraus, *African Colonization Movement*, 198; "To the Free Colored Inhabitants of these United States," Second Annual Negro Convention, 1832, in Aptheker, *A Documentary History*, 134.

23. William Lloyd Garrison to Simeon C. Jocelyn, Boston, MA, May 30, 1831, in Walter M. Merrill, ed., *The Letters of William Lloyd Garrison*, vol. I—*I Will Be Heard!* 1822–1835 (Cambridge, MA: Harvard University Press, 1971), 119.

24. "Immediate Abolition" editorial, *The Liberator*, January 7, 1832; "To Rev. Isaac Oar, Letter I," *The Liberator*, January 7, 1832.

25. Richard Newman points out that many blacks appreciated the efforts of paternalistic white members of antislavery organizations, such as the Pennsylvania Abolitionist Society (PAS). Likewise, Bruce Laurie argues that blacks often gravitated toward communities and organizations led by paternalistic white antislavery activists rather than those dominated by white exclusionists, or segregationists. And, when paternalistic white antislavery advocates were a minority, blacks often found life much more challenging. See Newman, *The Transformation of American Abolitionism*, 31–37; see also Laurie, *Beyond Garrison*, 87–89.

26. Henry Mayer argues that "Thoughts captured the attention of the humanitarian public with a force unmatched in American journalism since Tom Paine's *Common Sense*. . . . Garrison intended to make his Thoughts into 'a textbook for abolitionists,' and he succeeded." Henry Mayer, *All on Fire: William Lloyd Garrison and the Abolition of Slavery* (New York: St. Martin's Press, 1998), 138. Garrison's work was not alone, and several other works published during the nineteenth century examined colonization in the same way that Garrison did in *Thoughts on African Colonization*. One notable example is G.B. Stebbins's *Facts and Opinions Touching the Real Origin, Character, and Influence of the American Colonization Society: Views of Wilberforce, Clarkson, and Others, and the Opinions of the Free People of Color of the United States* (Boston: John P. Jewett, 1853; reprinted by Negro Universities Press, 1969). Stebbins structured his critique in the same manner as Garrison. Thus, his work is presented as an "objective" study of ACS resolutions, letters, and statements, as well as black opposition to colonization. Also, see Garrison, *Thoughts on African Colonization*, 3–4.

27. Margaret Hope Bacon, *"I Speak for My Slave Sister": The Life of Abby Kelley Foster* (New York: Cromwell, 1974), 17–19.

28. Julie Roy Jeffrey, *The Great Silent Army of Abolitionism: Ordinary Women in the Antislavery Movement* (Chapel Hill: University of North Carolina Press, 1998), 31.

29. Lydia Maria Child, *An Appeal in Favor of That Class of Americans Called Africans*, ed. Carolyn L. Karcher (Amherst: University of Massachusetts Press, 1996), 121–27.

30. Sarah H. Southwick, *Reminiscences of Early Anti-Slavery Days* (Cambridge, MA: The Riverside Press and H.O. Houghton and Company, 1893), 5–12.

31. Beth A. Salerno, *Sister Societies: Women's Antislavery Organizations in Antebellum America* (DeKalb: Northern Illinois University Press, 2005), 28.

32. Shirley Yee, *Black Women Abolitionists: A Study in Activism, 1828–1860* (Knoxville: University of Tennessee Press, 1992), 114––15.

33. Martha S. Jones, *All Bound Together: The Woman Question in African American Public Culture, 1830–1900* (Chapel Hill: University of North Carolina Press, 2007); Debrah Gray White, *Ar'n't I a Woman? Female Slaves in the Plantation South* (New York: W.W. Norton & Company, 1999).

34. Shirley Yee, *Black Women Abolitionists*, 88; Jeffrey, *The Great Silent Army of Abolitionism*, 41–43; *The Liberator*, vol. 2, no. 46, November 17, 1832 (American Periodicals Series Online, 183).

35. *Turning the World Upside Down: The Anti-Slavery Convention of American Women, Held in New York City, May 9–12, 1837* (New York: The Feminist Press at the City University of New York, 1987), 18–19.

36. Jean Fagan Yellin and John C. Van Horne, eds., *The Abolitionist Sisterhood: Women's Political Culture in Antebellum America* (Ithaca, NY: Cornell University Press, 1994), 11.

37. Jeffrey, *The Great Silent Army of Abolitionism*, 44–45.

38. Yee, *Black Women Abolitionists*, 88–90.

39. For a discussion of Gerrit Smith's conversion from colonization to immediatism, see John Stauffer, *The Black Hearts of Men: Radical Abolitionists and the Transformation of Race* (Cambridge, MA: Harvard University Press, 2002), 97–103.

40. "The Seventeenth Annual Report of the American Society for Colonizing the Free People of Colour of the United States," January 20, 1834, iv–ix, in *The Annual Reports of the American Society for Colonizing the Free People of Colour of the United States*, vols. 11–20, 1828–1836 (New York: Negro Universities Press, 1969).

41. Stauffer, *The Black Hearts of Men*, 100.

42. Frederick J. Blue, *No Taint of Compromise: Crusaders in Antislavery Politics* (Baton Rouge: Louisiana State University Press, 2005), 32; Bruce Laurie, *Beyond Garrison: Antislavery and Social Reform* (New York: Cambridge University Press, 2005), 150–51; Richard H. Sewell, *Ballots of Freedom: Antislavery Politics in the United States, 1837–1860* (New York: Oxford University Press, 1976), 20–23; Gerald Sorin, *The New York Abolitionists: A Case Study of Political Radicalism* (Westport, CT: Greenwood Publishing, 1971), 32–33.

43. Sorin, *The New York Abolitionists*, 34.

44. Stanley Harrold, *American Abolitionists* (New York: Pierson Education, 2001), 66.

45. *Proceedings of the National Convention of Colored People, and Their Friends*, held in Troy, NY, October 6–9, 1847, reprinted in Howard H. Bell, ed., *Minutes of the National Negro Conventions* (New York: Arno Press, 1969).

46. *Proceedings of National Convention, 1848*, in Bell, ed. *Minutes of the National Negro Conventions*.

47. Bruce Laurie explains: "Never an inspiring speaker, Garrison was a forceful if not lyrical writer and a shrewd tactician, at least regarding civil action. He appeared inconsistent and hypocritical, however, when it came to translating demands into public policy because of his aversion to politics." Laurie, *Beyond Garrison*, 101.

48. This is the central point of Frederick Cooper's important essay, "Elevating the Race: The Social Thought of Black Leaders, 1827–50." I agree with Cooper's basic premise that self-improvement and social reform remained a crucial part of black activism in the nineteenth century and beyond. However, he dismisses the importance of race to white social reformers, and thus does not fully develop their views on those free blacks living in their midst. For this study, white reformers' views about blacks are crucial. Thus, it is important that, even if "race" had not been central to social reform discourse, those white social reformers who did consider the racial realities actually believed that the best way to "deal" with blacks was through reform. Laurie and Fredrickson have accordingly shown the centrality of blacks to discourses on reform.

Yet such social reform discourse assumed that the cause of black depravity was environmental rather than biological. This, of course, was not the dominant view among white reformers, most of whom held a colonizationist view that black self-perfection would not change the basic facts of American society. Thus, when the most educated and moral in the black community had driven all of the vices and immoral behavior from every last free black in the North, black leaders most likely would still have come to the conclusion of John Russwurm–that white Americans had no plans for including black people in American society, and so colonization remained the best alternative. See Frederick Cooper, "Elevating the Race: The Social Thought of Black Leaders, 1827–50," in Patrick Rael, ed., *African-American Activism before the Civil War: The Freedom Struggle in the Antebellum North* (New York: Routledge Press, 2008).

49. Graham Russell Gao Hodges's biography of Ruggles points out that Ruggles offers an essential perspective on the struggle for black rights and against white violence, slavery, and colonization. As Hodges illustrates, Ruggles's "practical abolition" focused the attention of black reformers and abolitionists in the North on the pressing need for a militant core, able to meet each blow of the rioter or slave catcher with an equal blow, if blacks in the North were to achieve any measure of freedom. For Ruggles's quote, see Graham Russell Gao Hodges, *David Ruggles: A Radical Black Abolitionist and the Underground Railroad in New York City* (Chapel Hill: University of North Carolina Press, 2010), 91.

50. Patrick Rael, *Black Identity and Black Protest in the Antebellum North* (Chapel Hill: University of North Carolina Press, 2002), 179–206; Robert S. Levine, *Martin Delany and Frederick Douglass and the Politics of Representative Identity* (Chapel Hill: University of North Carolina Press, 1997), 22–23.

51. Laurie, *Beyond Garrison*, 102.

52. This vow to avoid liquor united white reformers such as Smith, who also believed that abolition and temperance went hand in hand. Black leaders often faced an uphill battle in combating alcohol, which was very popular among African Americans and working class people generally. Yet, as Benjamin Quarles explains, "again and again Negro reformers declared that the free colored man owed it to his brother in chains to join in the cold water army." Quarles, *Black Abolitionists*, 92–100.

53. "Ruggles magnified his impact on an emerging abolitionist movement by pushing a radical abolitionist agenda further than the founding fathers of the movement." See Hodges, *David Ruggles*, 6.

54. Bell, *The Negro Convention Movement*, 44–60.

216 / NOTES

Notes to Chapter 3

1. Betty Fladeland's pioneering work on British and American antislavery reform remains the definitive study of the interconnected history of antislavery reform across the Atlantic during the forty years before the Civil War. Yet Richard Blackett's study of black abolitionists abroad positions the activism of African American leaders at the center of his narrative, thus offering a nuanced perspective on the transatlantic antislavery movement missing in Fladeland's study. See Betty Fladeland, *Men and Brothers: Anglo-American Antislavery Co-operation* (Urbana: University of Illinois Press, 1972); and: Richard Blackett, *Building an Antislavery Wall: Black Americans in the Atlantic Abolitionist Movement, 1830–1860* (Ithaca, NY: Cornell University Press, 1983).

2. David Turley, *The Culture of English Antislavery, 1780–1860* (London: Routledge Press, 1991), 199.

3. Blackett, *Building an Antislavery Wall*, 40; Betty Fladeland, *Men and Brothers*, 168, 214; Tomek, *Colonization and Its Discontents*, 117–18.

4. In the introduction to Ripley's edited volume of the *Black Abolitionist Papers*, he explains the significance of Paul's mission to England and places Paul's work in a broader perspective of transcontinental reform. See: C. Peter Ripley, ed., *The Black Abolitionist Papers, Vol. I, The British Isles, 1830–1865* (Chapel Hill: University of North Carolina Press, 1985), 7.

5. Fladeland, *Men and Brothers*, 214.

6. William H. Pease and Jane Pease, *Black Utopia: Negro Communal Experiments in America* (Madison: Wisconsin Historical Society, 1963); Fladeland, *Men and Brothers*, 214.

7. Mary Reckord, "The Jamaica Slave Rebellion of 1831," *Past and Present* 40 (1968): 108–25.

8. Gad Heuman, "From Slavery to Freedom: Blacks in Nineteenth-Century British West Indies," in Philip D. Morgan and Sean Hawkins, eds., *Black Experience and the Empire* (New York: Oxford University Press, 2004), 146–47.

9. Stanley Harrold, *American Abolitionists* (Edinburgh, UK: Pearson Education Limited, 2001), 73–76; Better Fladeland, *Men and Brothers*, 168.

10. Burin, *Slavery and the Peculiar Solution*, 85.

11. Several of the founding members of "The Society for the Mitigation and Gradual Abolition Throughout the British Dominions," most notably James Cropper and Zachary Macaulay, became ardent anticolonizationists. Other members, however, such as Thomas Clarkson and even William Wilberforce, were initially persuaded to accept the goodwill of the ACS. For an in-depth examination of the Anti-Slavery Society and British abolition before the 1830s, see Wayne Ackerson, *The African Institution (1807–1827) and the Anti-slavery Movement in Great Britain* (Lewiston, UK: Edwin Mellen Press, 2005).

12. Gad Heuman, "From Slavery to Freedom: Blacks in Nineteenth-Century British West Indies," in Philip D. Morgan and Sean Hawkins, eds., *Black Experience and the Empire* (Oxford: Oxford University Press, 2004), 146–47.

13. Nathaniel Paul, *An Address, Delivered on the Celebration of the Abolition of Slavery in the State of New York, July 5, 1827* (Albany, NY: John B. Van Steenbergh, 1827), 17; reprinted in Dorothy Porter, *Negro Protest Pamphlets* (New York: Arno Press, 1969).

14. Nathaniel Paul, "The Truth and Nothing but the Truth," *The Rights of All*, September 18, 1829.

15. "Speech by Nathaniel Paul" delivered at the Trade's Hall, Glasgow, Scotland, December 2, 1834, in Ripley, *The Black Abolitionist Papers*, 53–57.

16. Nathaniel Paul to William Lloyd Garrison, London, July 3, 1832, printed in *The Liberator*, August 25, 1832; see Carter G. Woodson, ed., *The Mind of the Negro as Reflected in Letters Written During the Crisis, 1800–1860* (Washington, DC: Association for the Study of Negro Life and History, 1926), 163–65; Blackett, *Building an Antislavery Wall*, 53.

17. Nathaniel Paul to William Lloyd Garrison, Bristol, UK, April 10, 1833, published in *The Liberator*, June 22, 1833; also see Woodson, *The Mind of the Negro*, 165–67.

18. Speeches Delivered at the Anti-Colonization Meeting in Exeter Hall, London, July 13, 1833, by James Cropper et al. (Boston: Garrison and Knapp, 1833). Nathaniel Paul's speech is reprinted in Dorothy Porter, *Early Negro Writing, 1760–1837* (Boston: Beacon Press, 1971), 286–91.

19. Nathaniel Paul to William Lloyd Garrison, Bristol, UK, April 10, 1833, in *The Liberator*, June 22, 1833; printed in Woodson, *The Mind of the Negro*, 165–67.

20. For a summary of Cresson's trip, see "Agency of Elliott Cresson in England," *African Repository and Colonial Journal*, May 1832, vol. 8, no. 3, 77.

21. Fladeland, *Men and Brothers*, 214–16; P.J. Staudenraus explains how that debate caused a schism among the ACS members. Some members from the North, who came into colonization from Christian missionary work or who were social reformers, argued against slavery. On the other hand, colonizationists from the South hoped to encourage free blacks to leave, and they had no intention of freeing their own slaves. See Staudenraus, *The African Colonization Movement*, 204–5.

22. Blackett, *Building an Antislavery Wall*, 52.

23. *The Fifteenth Annual Report of the American Society for the Colonizing of Colored Americans in Africa* (New York: Negro Universities Press, 1969), 49.

24. In Eric Burin's recent study on the emancipation and colonization in the South, he points out how few emancipations were directly related to colonization. See Burin, *Slavery and the Peculiar Solution*, 5; for the number of African Americans sent to Liberia, see Staudenraus, *The African Colonization Movement, 1816–1865*, appendix, 251.

25. Blackett, *Building an Antislavery Wall*, 56.

26. For commentary on Wilberforce and Cresson, see Fladeland, *Men and Brothers*, 210; for the Wilberforce quotation, see *Fifteenth Annual Report of the American Colonization Society*, 14–15.

27. This letter was published in Benjamin Lundy's *Genius of Universal Emancipation* newspaper and the New England Anti-Slavery Society's *The Abolitionists*. See "English Opinions of The Colonization Society," *Genius of Universal Emancipation*, February 1833, vol. 3, no. 4, 53; see also "A Letter from James Cropper to Thomas Clarkson," *The Abolitionist or Record of the New England Anti-Slavery Society*, March 1833, vol. 1, no. 3, 39.

28. P.J. Staudenraus explains: "By May 1833, Cresson was thoroughly weary of his private war. . . . Everywhere he went insult and accusation mocked him." Staudenraus, *African Colonization Movement*, 217.

29. *Second Annual Report of the New-England Anti-Slavery Society*, January 15, 1834. Samuel May recalled that "Garrison remained in England three or four

months . . . with the execrations of the leading Colonizationists, and all the proslavery partisans of our country upon his head." See Samuel J. May, *Recollections of Our Anti-Slavery Conflict* (Boston: Fields, Osgood, & Co., 1869), 72–79.

30. *Second Annual Report*, 32.

31. William Lloyd Garrison, "Mission to England," *Second Annual Report of the Board of Managers of the New-England Anti-Slavery Society*, January 15, 1834, appendix, 32–48.

32. Garrison, *Mission to England*, 38; Fladeland, *Men and Brothers*, 215.

33. Ibid.

34. Betty Fladeland points out that Wilberforce "paid tribute to [Cresson's] spirited benevolence" in crossing the Atlantic on behalf of his long-neglected fellow creatures. It was to Cresson that Wilberforce expressed his great faith in the efficacy of Anglo-American cooperation, dramatically quoting a passage from Scripture, "And there shall be no more sea." See Fladeland, *Men and Brothers*, 210–11.

35. Speech by Nathaniel Paul, delivered at Exeter Hall, London, England, July 13, 1833, in C. Peter Ripley et al., eds., *The Black Abolitionist Papers, vol. I, The British Isles, 1830–1865* (Chapel Hill: University of North Carolina Press, 1985), 47.

36. Ibid., 49.

37. "The American Colonization Society: Sentiments of Daniel O'Connell," Anti-Colonization Meeting in Exeter Hall, July 13, 1833, in *Daniel O'Connell upon American Slavery: With Other Irish Testimonies* (New York: American Anti-Slavery Society, Anti-Slavery Tracts, no. 5, 1860), 43–47.

38. Garrison, "Mission to England," *Second Annual Report of the New-England Anti-Slavery Society*, 46–47.

39. Blackett, *Building an Antislavery Wall*, 75.

40. Mayer, *All on Fire*, 163; for this letter, see: G.B. Stebbins, *Facts and Opinions Touching the Real Origin, Character, and Influence of the American Colonization Society: Views of Wilberforce, Clarkson, and Others, and Opinions of the Free People of Color of the United States* (Boston: John P. Jewett & Company, 1853), reprinted by Negro Universities Press, 1969, 215–24.

41. Samuel J. May, *Some Recollections of Our Antislavery Conflict* (Boston: Fields, Osgood, & Co., 1869), 80.

42. G.B. Stebbins, *Facts and Opinions Touching the Real Origin, Character, and Influence of the American Colonization Society*, 213–14.

43. Staudenraus, *African Colonization Movement*, 216.

44. Ibid., 218–20.

45. Ibid., 64.

46. For example, Zachary Macaulay had been the governor of Sierra Leone, and Cresson claimed that Macaulay had envied Liberia's progress. See Staudenraus, *African Colonization Movement*, 216; also see Fladeland, *Men and Brothers*, 23.

47. Blackett, *Building an Antislavery Wall*, 60–61.

48. Ibid., 224.

49. Tomek, *Colonization and Its Discontents*, 124–31.

50. Richards, *Men of Property and Standing: Anti-Abolitionist Mobs in Jacksonian America* (Oxford: Oxford University Press, 1971).

51. Mayer, *All on Fire*, 166–67.

52. Nathaniel Paul to William Lloyd Garrison, London, January 22, 1834, printed in *The Liberator*, April 12, 1834, reprinted in Woodson, *The Mind of the Negro*, 168–70.

53. Margaret Hope Bacon, *But of One Race: The Life of Robert Purvis* (Albany, NY: State University of Albany Press, 2007), 43; Fladeland, *Men and Brothers*, 237.

54. See *The Liberator*, March 8, 1834, vol. 4, no. 10, 38.

55. Robert Purvis to William Lloyd Garrison, London, July 13, 1834, printed in *The Liberator*, August 23, 1834, reprinted in Woodson, *The Mind of the Negro*, 175–76.

56. Virtually all studies of the abolitionist movement analyze the different reasons for the movement's fracturing near the end of the 1830s and in the early 1840s. For an excellent summary of the various debates within the movement, see Stanley Harold, *American Abolitionists*; for African American perspectives on these debates, see Horton and Horton, *In Hope of Liberty*, 240–44.

57. Ralph R. Gurley, *Mission to England in Behalf of the American Colonization Society* (Washington, DC: W. M. Morrison, 1841), 1.

58. Fladeland, *Men and Brothers*, 276; Blackett, *Building an Antislavery Wall*, 70.

59. Ralph R. Gurley to the Executive Committee of the American Colonization Society, London, August 17, 1840, in Gurley, *Mission to England*, 15–16.

60. Gurley, *Mission to England*, 19.

61. Ibid., 22.

62. Ibid., 92.

63. Gurley, *Mission to England*, 61–68; see also the editorial in *The Colored American* on February 27, 1841, which acknowledges Buxton as an associate of Charles Lenox Remond and American abolitionists.

64. "The African Civilization Society and the American Colonization Society, from Sir Thomas Fowell Buxton, Baronet, to the Rev. R. R. Gurley, Secretary of the American Colonization Society," printed in *The Colored American*, New York, February 27, 1841 (reprinted from the *London Patriot*).

65. Gurley, *Mission to England*, 61–68; "Buxton to Gurley," *The Colored American*, New York, February 27, 1841.

66. Ibid.; for the often-cited "Protest," see G.B. Stebbins, *Facts and Opinions*, 213–14.

67. Staudenraus, *African Colonization Movement*, 277.

68. Ibid., 233.

69. Gurley, *Mission to England*, 47–48.

70. Ibid., 49; Gurley, *Mission to England*, 57.

71. Quarles, *Black Abolitionists*, 131–33.

72. See Horton and Horton, *In Hope of Liberty*, 227; Blackett, *Building an Antislavery Wall*, 71–72.

73. See Donald R. Kennon, "'An Apple of Discord': The Women Question at the World's Anti-Slavery Convention of 1840," in John R. McKivigan, ed., *Abolitionism and Issues of Race and Gender* (New York: Garland Publishers, 1999). This work has several useful essays that explore race and gender in the abolition movement. For African American responses to these issues within the mainstream abolition movement, see Horton and Horton, *In Hope of Liberty*, 241–42.

74. Charles Lenox Remond to William Lloyd Garrison, October 1840, published in *The Liberator*, November 13, 1840; this is also printed in Ripley et al., *The Black Abolitionist Papers*, 80–81.

75. Ibid.

76. "R.R. Gurley," *The Liberator*, November 13, 1840.

77. Ibid.

78. Charles Lenox Remond to William Lloyd Garrison, *The Liberator*, May 21, 1841; also printed in Ripley, *Black Abolitionists Papers*, 92–94.

79. "Prejudice in England," *The Colored American*, October 3, 1840.

80. Fredrickson, *The Black Image in the White Mind*, 321; Leslie M. Harris, *In the Shadow of Slavery: African Americans in New York City, 1626–1863* (Chicago: University of Chicago Press, 2003), 247–50.

81. Blackett, *Building an Antislavery Wall*, 75–77.

82. "Colonizationist Measures: An Address Delivered in New York, New York, April 24, 1849," in John Blassingame, ed., *The Frederick Douglass Papers: Series One: Speeches, Debates, Interviews*, vol. 2: 1847–54 (New Haven: Yale University Press, 1982), 158–67.

83. "Letter from the Editor," *The North Star*, May 4, 1849; see "Colored Americans, Come Home!" *Frederick Douglass Papers*, July 31, 1851.

84. "Colonization," *The Liberator*, February 8, 1850.

85. Ibid.

86. Ibid.

87. "African Colonization," *The North Star*, February 22, 1850.

88. "Colonization of Free Blacks," *The Farmers' Cabinet*, August 29, 1850.

89. "Senatorial Sensibility," *The National Era*, January 23, 1851, Washington, DC, vol. V., no. 212, 14.

Notes to Chapter 4

1. "Massachusetts Colonization Society," *Christian Watchman*, June 4, 1847, 1.

2. See "To the Editor of the Abolitionist," *The Abolitionist*, New England Anti-Slavery Society, vol. I, 124–25, reprinted in Louis Ruchames, ed., *The Abolitionists* (New York: Capricorn Books, 1964), 71–72.

3. "The Colonization Conspiracy," *The Liberator*, June 25, 1847, 106; for an account of Humphrey's tenure at Amherst College and a brief overview of the events discussed here, see: W.S. Tyler, *A History of Amherst College during the Administrations of the First Five Presidents: From 1821–1891* (New York: F. Hitchcock, 1895).

4. "Massachusetts Colonization Society, Sixth Annual Report," *Christian Register*, June 24, 1847, 119.

5. Historian Eric Burin points out that "[t]he antimanumission campaign, though foiled in some states, had impaired the colonization movement in the South, or so ACS spokespersons claimed." Burin, *Slavery and the Peculiar Solution*, 130.

6. "The Colonization Conspiracy," *The Liberator*, June 18, 1847, 98.

7. Ibid.

8. "The Colonization Cause," *The North Star*, July 13, 1849.

9. Stebbins, *Facts and Opinions*, 206.

10. P.J. Staudenraus argues that the Colonization Society transformed itself into an emigration agency after 1847. Yet, as this chapter attempts to demonstrate, the line between "emigration agency" and "colonization enterprise" appears blurred. In fact, after 1847 the organization continued with its erstwhile intent, sending agents to hustle throughout the nation in search of donors and emigrants

for colonization to Liberia. See Staudenraus, *The African Colonization Movement*, 242–49.

11. See: *American Colonization Society, Fifty-Second Annual Report*, January 19 and 20, 1869.

12. Ibid.

13. "Colonization—An Urgent Appeal," *Pittsfield Sun*, December 16, 1847, vol. XLVIII, 1.

14. Interestingly, the ACS raised $39,900.43 in 1847, which, in comparison to the fundraising of other benevolent organizations, seems quite impressive, especially if you consider that Frederick Douglass and other abolitionists had believed the organization dead. According to a January 1847 article in *Zion's Herald and Wesleyan Journal*, the breakdown of receipts for major philanthropic organizations for 1846 was as follows: the American Temperance Union raised $1,522, the American Anti-Slavery Society and American and Foreign Anti-Slavery Society combined raised only $21,432, the Board of Missions of the Presbyterian Church $95,628, and the American Protestant Society $19,709. See: "Benevolent Operations," *Zion's Herald and Wesleyan Journal*, June 9, 1847, 90.

15. "The American Colonization Society in Need of Funds," *Daily Ohio Statesman*, November 20, 1848.

16. Julia Griffiths, Frederick Douglass's assistant secretary, recounted this speech by Thompson in *The North Star*. See "Mass Anti-Slavery Convention in Rochester," *The North Star*, March 20, 1851.

17. Ibid.

18. "Illinois Conference of the Methodist Episcopal Church on Colonization," *African Repository and Colonial Journal*, November 1847, 344.

19. Ibid.

20. "Chicago Discussion," B.T. Kavanaugh, *African Repository and Colonial Journal*, November 1847, 346.

21. Ibid.

22. An untitled document in the *African Repository* lists "Agents" of the Colonization Society, and the Reverend R.S. Finley is given the title "Secretary [of the] Missouri State Colonization Society." See *African Repository and Colonial Journal*, June 1847, 162.

23. "Funeral of General Hardin—Convention, Etc.," *The National Era*, August 5, 1847, 4.

24. J.J. to Fredrick Douglass, Chicago, February 4, 1848, reprinted in *The North Star*, June 23, 1848.

25. "Colonization and Illinois," *African Repository and Colonial Journal*, May 1848, 157.

26. "Liberia," *North Star*, April 13, 1849.

27. "Extracts," *North Star*, April 20, 1849.

28. "Colonization Meeting in Indiana," *African Repository and Colonial Journal*, November 1848, 349.

29. Gwendolyn J. Crenshaw, "'Bury Me in a Free Land': The Abolitionist Movement in Indiana, 1816–1865," Indiana Historical Bureau, www.in.gov/history.

30. *Corydon Indiana Gazette*, February 10, 1820, transcription, in "Extracts from Corydon Newspapers, 1820–1838," bound typescript in Indiana Division, Indiana State Library. See Crenshaw, "Bury Me in a Free Land."

31. Ibid.

32. "Report of a Meeting of the Colored Citizens of Indiana," January 17, 1842, in Foner and Walker, *Proceedings of the Black State Conventions*, 173–75.

33. Ibid. Colonizationists had for decades sought out free blacks to travel to Liberia and return with favorable reports. But whenever a disgruntled black American returned from Liberia, the ACS was compelled to attempt to counter the criticism. See Burin, *Slavery and the Peculiar Solution*, 68.

34. "Indiana," *The Colonizationist*, Indianapolis, May 1847, vol. II, no. 2.

35. "No Colonization," *The North Star*, August 17, 1849.

36. Nikki M. Taylor, *Frontiers of Freedom: Cincinnati's Black Community, 1802–1868* (Athens: Ohio University Press, 2005), 118–26.

37. "Colonization," *The Palladium of Liberty*, August 28, 1844, vol. I, no. 29, 3.

38. Ibid.

39. "Colonization Society Meeting," *Tri-Weekly Ohio Statesman*, November 27, 1846, 2.

40. "Liberian Colonization," *The North Star*, September 8, 1848.

41. "Great Colonization Meeting," *Christian Observer*, July 29, 1848, 122.

42. "To the Citizens of Ohio," Minutes and Address of the State Convention of the Colored Citizens of Ohio, Convened at Columbus, January 10–13, 1849, reprinted in Foner and Walker, *Proceedings of the Black State Convention*, 231–34.

43. Eric Foner, *Free Soil, Free Labor, Free Men: The Ideology of the Republican Party before the Civil War* (London: Oxford University Press, 1970), 262. Nikki Taylor points out that the Free Soil Party in Ohio made important gains in 1848 and 1849 as a result of a partisan struggle between Whigs and Democrats, thus allowing for a repeal of the Black Laws and a separate school system. This did not mean, however, that blacks no longer endured racial discrimination and violations of their civil rights. See Taylor, *Frontiers of Freedom*, 165.

44. Foner, *Free Soil, Free Labor, Free Men*, 225.

45. Stephen Middleton, *The Black Laws: Race and the Legal Process in Early Ohio* (Athens: Ohio University Press, 2005), 121–22.

46. David Christy was quite a prolific writer. He published three major volumes addressing slavery, the slave trade, and colonization. *Cotton Is King* explores the basis of slavery as rooted in economic realities of the nation, while his second work, *Ethiopia: Her Gloom and Glory*, discusses the importance of Liberia in the progress of ending the slave trade and setting Africa on the path towards Christian salvation. His third work, *Pulpit Politics*, explores the "moral progress of the African race." See David Christy, *Pulpit Politics; or, Ecclesiastical Legislation on Slavery, in its Disturbing Influences on the American Union* (New York: Negro Universities Press, 1869); and *Ethiopia: Her Gloom and Glory, As Illustrated in the History of the Slave Trade and Slavery, the Rise of the Republic of Liberia, and the Progress of African Missions* (New York: Negro Universities Press, 1969).

47. "The Republic of Liberia," *African Repository and Colonial Journal*, June 1848, 177.

48. "Memorial," in the *Thirty Second Annual Report of the American Colonization Society*, 37–39.

49. "Ohio in AfricaPrincely Liberality," *Massachusetts Ploughman and New England Journal of Agriculture*, December 16, 1848, 1. This article was originally printed

in the *Cincinnati Gazette*. *Niles' National Register* also carried a short blurb sum-marizing Christy's efforts to create "Ohio in Africa"; see "The States," *Niles' National Register*, October 4, 1848, 211.

50. "To the Citizens of Ohio," Minutes and Address of the State Convention of the Colored Citizens of Ohio, Convened at Columbus, January 10–13, 1849, reprinted in Foner and Walker, *Proceedings of the Black State Convention*, 231–34.

51. "Meeting of the Colored Freemen of Columbus," *The North Star*, June 29, 1849.

52. "Operations in Ohio," *African Repository and Colonial Journal*, December 1849, 379.

53. David Carl Shilling, "Relation of Southern Ohio to the South During the Decade Preceding the Civil War," *Quarterly Publication of the Historical and Philo-sophical Society of Ohio*, vol. VIII, no. 1, January–March 1913 (Cinicinnati: Jennings and Graham Press, 1913): 9.

54. "Colonization," from the *Presbyterian Herald*, reprinted in *African Repository and Colonial Journal*, February 1847, 55.

55. "Convention of the Free Negroes of Kentucky!," *New Hampshire Sentinel*, August 5, 1847, 2.

56. "Colonization and Gradual Emancipation," *Presbyterian Herald*, Louisville, KY, reprinted in *African Repository and Colonial Journal*, November 1848, 321.

57. "Project of Colonization," Thirtieth Congress, Second Session, Wednesday, January 10, 1849, *The National Era*, January 18, 1849, 9.

58. Horton and Horton, *In Hope of Liberty*, 252–53.

59. Wilson Jeremiah Moses, *Alexander Crummell: A Study of Civilization and Dis-content* (New York: Oxford University Press, 1989), 65.

60. Hollis R. Lynch, *Edward Wilmot Blyden: Pan-Negro Patriot, 1832–1912* (Lon-don: Oxford University Press, 1967), 4–5.

61. "Speech of Mr. Clay," *The National Era*, December 2, 1847, 4.

62. "Mr. Clay's Speech," *The North Star*, December 3, 1847.

63. "Henry Clay," *The North Star*, January 28, 1848.

64. "Colonization Meeting," *Boston Recorder*, January 28, 1848, 15; see also "Selec-tions" from *The Liberator*, "Henry Clay and African Colonization," *The North Star*, February 11, 1848.

65. "To Henry Clay," *The Liberator*, March 16, 1849.

66. "Henry Clay," *The North Star*, March 23, 1849.

67. "Colonizationist Measures: An Address Delivered in New York, New York, on April 24, 1849," in John W. Blassingame, ed., *The Frederick Douglass Papers, Series One: Speeches, Debates, and Interviews*, vol. 2: 1847–54 (New Haven, CT: Yale Univer-sity Press, 1982), 165.

68. Waldo E. Martin Jr., *The Mind of Frederick Douglass* (Chapel Hill: University of North Carolina Press, 1984), 74.

69. "Illinois," *The Harbinger*, February 26, 1848, 136.

70. "The Black Laws of Illinois," *The National Era*, March 17, 1853, 42.

71. "Convention in Southern Illinois," *The National Era*, November 4, 1847, 4.

72. "Exclusion of Negroes from Indiana," *The Christian Observer*, August 30, 1851, 240. Emma Lou Thornbrough places pro-colonizationism within the context of such laws, writing: "In Indiana proposals both for preventing Negroes from settling in the state and for persuading or compelling those already resident there to go to Liberia

found a receptive audience. They resulted first in a law adopted in 1831 which limited the right of settlement and later in an article in the second state Constitution which completely prohibited Negroes from seeking residence in the state. The white population showed considerable interest in the colonization movement, which received a blessing in the Constitution of 1851 and which was given some financial support by the state." Emma Lou Thornbrough, *The Negro in Indiana Before 1900: A Study of a Minority* (Bloomington: Indiana University Press, 1993), 55.

73. "Proscription of Colored People," *The National Era*, February 13, 1851, 26.

74. Stephen Middleton, *The Black Laws in the Old Northwest: A Documentary History* (Westport, CT: Greenwood Publishing Group, 1993), 217–24.

75. Michael J. McManus, *Political Abolitionism in Wisconsin, 1840–1861* (Kent, OH: Kent State University Press, 1998), 161–63.

76. Ibid.

77. Interestingly, the *African Repository and Colonial Journal* also reprinted this article back in October 1847. It was nearly two years later that Douglass reprinted it as well, acknowledging the rise of colonization sentiment in the West. See "Condition of the Free People of Color in the Free States," *African Repository and Colonial Journal*, October 1847, 304; "Folly of Our Adversaries. Arguments for Colonization," *The North Star*, March 2, 1849.

78. "German Emigration," *Niles' Register*, May 8, 1847, 155.

79. "Oppressive Legislation—Colonization," *The National Era*, vol. VI, no. 282, 86.

80. "New Phases," *New York Observer and Chronicle*, December 29, 1859, 410.

81. "Proceedings of the State Convention of Colored People Held in Albany, New York, July 22–24, 1851," in Foner and Walker, *Proceedings of the Black State Conventions*, 69; also quoted in Stebbins, *Facts and Opinions*, 198–99.

82. Ibid.

83. "New-York State Colonization Society," *New York Daily Times*, May 14, 1852, 1.

84. "Position of the Colored Race in the United States," *Christian Inquirer*, February 21, 1852, 2.

85. "New York Legislature," *New York Daily Times*, February 11, 1852, 1; "New York Legislature. Senate. Colonization. Wednesday March 3," *New York Observer and Chronicle*, March 11, 1852, 86.

86. "Gov. Hunt on Colonization," *German Reformed Messenger*, January 21, 1852, 3415; "Gerrit Smith to NY Gov. Hunt, on Colonization," *The Liberator*, March 5, 1853.

87. "Congress," *Christian Watchman and Reflector*, January 29, 1852, 19.

88. Ibid.

89. "Colored People Acting," *The Liberator*, March 5, 1852, 38.

90. The State Convention of Colored Citizens of New York met at City Hall in Albany, New York, on January 20, 1852, with J.W.C. Pennington presiding. The quotes above are drawn from the statement derived by the members, which was reprinted in *The Liberator*. See "Colored People of New York," *The Liberator*, March 5, 1852, 1.

91. "The Colored Voters of New York," *The National Era*, February 5, 1852, 23; see also an untitled article in the *National Era*, February 19, 1852, 29.

92. "Anti-Colonization Meeting," *The Liberator*, May 14, 1852, 78.

93. Be Done for the Colored Man?," *New York Evangelist*, February 12, 1852, 1.

94. Ibid.

95. Frederick Douglass to Gerrit Smith, January 21, 1851, in Phillip S. Foner, ed., *Frederick Douglass: Selected Speeches and Writings* (Chicago: Lawrence Hill Books, 1999), 170–72. For a more nuanced discussion of Gerrit Smith and Frederick Douglass, see John Stauffer, *The Black Hearts of Men: Radical Abolitionists and the Transformation of Race* (Cambridge, MA: Harvard University Press, 2002).

96. "Letter from Gerrit Smith to Governor Hunt, of New York, on African Colonization," *The Liberator*, March 5, 1852, 38.

97. "A Liberian's Reply to Gerrit Smith," *The African Repository and Colonial Journal*, January 1853, 10.

98. Quoted in Stebbins, *Facts and Opinions*, 200; see also "Anti-Colonization Meeting," *Frederick Douglass' Paper*, August 27, 1852.

99. "Colonization Meeting in New York," *African Repository and Colonial Journal*, November 1852, 334.

100. Ibid.

101. Ibid.; see also "Colonization Meeting," *New York Observer and Chronicle*, October 7, 1852, 322.

102. "Great Anti-Colonization Meeting in Philadelphia, August 20," *The Liberator*, October 7, 1853.

103. "Proceedings of the Convention, of the Colored Freemen of Ohio," in Foner and Walker, *Proceedings*, 279; reprinted in Stebbins, *Facts and Opinions*, 196–97.

104. "Proceedings of the Colored National Convention Held in Rochester, July 6th, 7th, and 8th, 1853," in Howard Holman Bell, ed., *Minutes of the Proceedings of the National Negro Conventions, 1830–1864* (New York: Arno Press, 1969), 39.

105. Ibid., 47.

106. Ibid., 56.

107. "Committee on Colonization, Proceedings of the Colored National Convention, held in Rochester July 6th, 7th and 8th, 1853," in Bell, *Minutes of the Proceedings of the National Negro Conventions, 1830–1864*.

108. Fredrickson, *The Black Image in the White Mind*, 47.

Notes to Chapter 5

1. Quarles, *Black Abolitionists*, 221.

2. William J. Wilson to "My Dear Cousin M_____," October 1855, in C. Peter Ripley et al., eds., *The Black Abolitionist Papers, vol. IV: The United States, 1847–1858* (Chapel Hill: University of North Carolina Press, 1991), 313.

3. Ibid., 314.

4. For example, Wilson Moses refers to the National Emigration Convention of 1854 as "an 1854 colonization convention in Cleveland," while also acknowledging elsewhere that the convention "took a strong stand against colonization, and while taking an occasional interest in emigration, was careful to disassociate itself from the aims of the [American Colonization] Society." See Wilson Jeremiah Moses, *Afrotopia: The Roots of African American Popular History* (New York: Cambridge University Press, 1998), 25; Wilson Moses, *The Golden Age of Black Nationalism, 1850–1925* (New York: Oxford University Press, 1978), 34–35. More recently, historians have been more careful to distinguish emigration, colonization, and the aims of ACS. For example, see James Oakes, *The Radical and the Republican: Frederick Douglass, Abraham Lincoln, and the Triumph of Antislavery Politics* (New York: W.W. Norton & Company, 2007), 31.

5. See Patrick Rael, "A Common Nature, A United Destiny: African-American Response to Racial Science from the Revolution to the Civil War," in Proceedings of the Fifth Annual Gilder Lehrman Center International Conference at Yale University, Collective Degradation: Slavery and the Construction of Race, November 7–8, 2003, Yale University, New Haven, Connecticut, 2.

6. Waldo Martin points out that Douglass himself even considered leaving America for Haiti in 1861 in response to his growing frustration over the oppression of blacks. But the Civil War offered blacks new opportunities to prove themselves, and he reconsidered his plan to leave. See Waldo Martin, *The Mind of Frederick Douglass* (Chapel Hill: University of North Carolina Press, 1984), 74. Also see David W. Blight, *Frederick Douglass' Civil War: Keeping Faith in Jubilee* (Baton Rouge: Louisiana State University Press, 1989), 132–33.

7. Ibid., 168–69.

8. Dean Robinson, *Black Nationalism in American Politics and Thought* (New York: Cambridge University Press, 2001), 20–21.

9. "The Colonizationist Revival: An Address Delivered in Boston, Massachusetts, May 31, 1849," in Blassingame, *The Frederick Douglass Papers*, 210–11.

10. Russwurm took on the role of governor of Maryland of Liberia, which had been established by The Maryland Colonization Society. The MCS was one of the first auxiliaries to establish an independent colony in Liberia. For more on this, see Penelope Campbell, *Maryland in Africa: The Maryland State Colonization Society, 1831–1857* (Urbana: University of Illinois Press, 1971); James, *The Struggles of John Brown Russwurm*, 87.

11. Floyd Miller, *The Search for a Black Nationality*, 130; see also Hollis Lynch, Edward Wilmot Blyden: Pan-Negro Patriot, 1832–1912 (London: Oxford University Press, 1967).

12. Robert Campbell, Martin Delany, and Howard Holman, eds., *Search for a Place: Black Separatism and Africa, 1860* (Ann Arbor: University of Michigan Press, 1969), 7.

13. Lamin Sanneh, *Abolitionists Abroad: American Blacks and the Making of Modern West Africa* (Cambridge, MA: Harvard University Press, 1999).

14. For a more complete examination of black American attitudes toward Africans, see Tunde Adeleke, *UnAfrican Americans: Nineteenth Century Black Nationalists and the Civilizing Mission* (Lexington: University Press of Kentucky, 1998). Wilson Moses also devotes great attention to analyzing Alexander Crummell's ideas about indigenous Africans; see Wilson Moses, *Alexander Crummell: A Study of Civilization and Discontent* (New York: Oxford University Press, 1989).

15. Delany, *The Condition of the Colored People*, 209.

16. Robert Young's Ethiopian Manifesto expresses some of Delany and Holly's ideas. David Walker's *Appeal* also suggests the important role of racial destiny and redemption. Floyd Miller claims that "Lewis Woodson formulated an ideology which fused emigrationism and nationalism and set the intellectual basis for the development after mid-century of a cohesive movement advocating emigration for basically nationalistic purposes." Miller then goes on to trace Delany's views back to Woodson to show that these earlier works sowed the seeds of black nationalism. This attempt to place Delany's "conversion" to emigrationism as rooted in his interactions with Woodson appears tenuous. For many years after his tutelage under Woodson, Delany regarded emigration as an ineffective method for race advancement. See John Bracey,

Elliot Rudwick, and August Meier, eds., *Black Nationalism in America* (Indianapolis: Bobbs-Merrill, 1970); the entire introduction of Sterling Stuckey's *The Ideological Origins of Black Nationalism* (Boston: Beacon Press, 1972); and Miller, *The Search for a Black Nationality*, xi.

17. Floyd Miller has come the closest to writing a comprehensive study of black emigration, and his specific interest is the 1850s, which he considers the most important decade for emigrationism. For more on the debates of that decade, see Wilson J. Moses, *Creative Conflict in African American Thought: Frederick Douglass, Alexander Crummell, Booker T. Washington, W.E.B. Du Bois, and Marcus Garvey* (Cambridge, UK: Cambridge University Press, 2004), 56.

18. For a useful presentation of these debates, see Frederick Douglass, ed., *Arguments Pro and Con, on the Call for a National Emigration Convention to Be Held in Cleveland, Ohio, August, 1854* (Cornell University Library Collections). For Loring Dewey's account of Haitian movement, see L.D. Dewey, *Correspondence Relative to the Emigration to Hayti of the Free People of Colour in the U.S. Together with Instructions to the Agent Sent Out by President Boyer* (New York: Mahlon Day, 1924); Chris Dixon, *African America and Haiti: Emigration and Black Nationalism in the Nineteenth Century* (Westport, CT: Praeger Publishers, 2000).

19. Robert Breckinridge, "The Black Race: Some reflections on its position and destiny, as connected with our American dispensation. A discourse delivered before the Kentucky Colonization Society at Frankfort, on the 6th of February, 1851," reprinted in *The African Repository and Colonial Journal*, May 1851, 129.

20. Liberia's Declaration of Independence was printed in *The North Star* without commentary from Douglass. "Republic of Liberia. Declaration of Independence," *North Star*, January 14, 1848.

21. "Inaugural Address," *African Repository and Colonial Journal*, April 1848, 120.

22. *The North Star*, January 14, 1848. William Lloyd Garrison complained that Douglass did not go far enough in condemning Liberia, writing in July 1851 that Douglass had written editorials that showed "him now disposed to perceive that some good may grow out of [the] Colonization scheme." See "Frederick Douglass," *The Liberator*, July 11, 1851, 111.

23. "The American Colonization Society," *The North Star*, March 24, 1848.

24. "Movements Among the Colored People," *African Repository and Colonial Journal*, September 1848, 261; "Great Colonization Meeting," *Christian Observer*, July 29, 1848, 122.

25. "Letter from the President of the Republic of Liberia to the President of the New York Colonization Society," *American Quarterly Register and Magazine*, March 1849, 277.

26. "Extracts from the Proceedings of the Board of Directors of the American Colonization Society," *African Repository and Colonial Journal*, March 1848, 89.

27. "Colonization Meeting," *African Repository and Colonial Journal*, October 1849, 295.

28. "Liberia," *The North Star*, March 2, 1849.

29. "Convention of Congregational Ministers of Massachusetts on Colonization," *African Repository and Colonial Journal*, October 1849, 313.

30. "Eighth Annual Report of the Massachusetts Colonization Society," *African Repository and Colonial Journal*, September 1849, 257.

31. "Sympathy Meeting in Philadelphia," *African Repository and Colonial Journal*, July 1848, 217.

32. Murdo J. MacLeod, "The Solouque Regime in Haiti, 1847–1859: A Reevaluation," *Caribbean Studies* 10, no. 3 (1970–71): 35–48.

33. "Go ye and do likewise, LIBERIA NOW AN INDEPENDENT STATE," *Chambers's Edinburgh Journal*, December 1848, 259, 395.

34. Penelope Campbell, *Maryland in Africa: The Maryland State Colonization Society, 1831–1857* (Urbana: University of Illinois Press, 1971), 61–63. Between 1831 and 1857, the Maryland Colonization Society sent approximately 1,200 people to Liberia from Maryland out of a combined slave and free African American population of between 155,000 and 168,000. In that same time period, the American Colonization Society claimed to have sent approximately 7,000 colonists to Liberia. Nearly 5,125 African Americans sailed to Liberia in the ten-year span of 1848–1857. Thus, the obvious concern over the growing influence of the American Colonization Society by 1851 seems quite justified, although this upsurge was still quite meager, considering the entire free black population in the nation. The total number of African Americans who left for Liberia between 1820 and 1899 is now estimated to be 15,386. See Staudenraus, *The African Colonization Movement*, appendix.

35. Maryland Free Colored People's Convention, July 27–28, 1852, in Foner and Walker, *Proceedings of Black State Conventions*, vol. II, 43.

36. Ibid., 44–45.

37. Ibid., 46.

38. Ibid.

39. Ibid., 47–48.

40. Ibid., 44.

41. Victor Ullman, *Martin R. Delany: The Beginnings of Black Nationalism* (Boston: Beacon Press, 1977), 142–43; Robert S. Levine, *Martin Delany, Frederick Douglass, and the Politics of Representative Identity* (Chapel Hill: University of North Carolina Press, 1997), 63.

42. See Martin R. Delany, *The Condition, Elevation, Emigration, and Destiny of the Colored People of the United States* (New York: Arno Press, 1969), 199.

43. Delany had claimed that "to know a people, it is only necessary to know the condition of their females; and despite themselves they cannot rise above their level." Delany, *The Condition*, 199; Anna Julia Cooper would point out that Delany's notion of race representation was inaccurate. Her argument is best expressed by her oft-quoted remark, "Only the black woman can say, 'when and where I enter, in the quiet, undisputed dignity of my womanhood, without violence and without suing or special patronage, then and there the whole Negro race enters with me.'" See Cooper, *A Voice from the South*, 31; Robert Levine, *Martin Delany, Frederick Douglass, and the Politics of Representative Identity* (Chapel Hill: University of North Carolina Press, 1997).

44. Delany, *Conditions*, 208.

45. Ibid., 160.

46. Ibid., 156.

47. Martin R. Delany to Frederick Douglass, July 10, 1852, reprinted in *Frederick Douglass' Paper*, Rochester, NY, July 23, 1852, in Ripley, *The Black Abolitionist Papers*, 127.

48. Levine, *The Politics of Representative Identity*, 148.

49. Ibid., 187–88.

50. Robert Levine's work comparing Douglass and Delany goes into great detail about this debate. Douglass applauded Stowe's novel, even with all of its imperfections, as an indispensable tool in the struggle over the nation's conscience, while Delany chastised Stowe for presenting Uncle Tom as a meek, undignified black man. In Delany's view, Stowe was nothing short of a colonizationist for calling upon George to leave America for Africa. See Robert Levine, *The Politics of Representative Identity*.

51. See introduction in Harriet Beecher Stowe, *Uncle Tom's Cabin* (Oxford: Oxford University Press, 2002), xi.

52. Fredrickson, *The Black Image in the White Mind*, 115–17.

53. See: Susan Marie Nuernberg, "The Rhetoric of Race," in Mason I. Lowance Jr. et al., eds., *The Stowe Debate: Rhetorical Strategies in* Uncle Tom's Cabin (Amherst: University of Massachusetts Press, 1994), 260–61.

54. Robert Levine's trenchant study of Martin Delany and Frederick Douglass offers an important and insightful examination of the debate over Stowe's novel. Still, his work characterizes Stowe's novel as "colonizationist," and this is an example of how the two concepts, colonization and emigration, are often misinterpreted. Interestingly, when it comes to Levine's discussion of Delany's emigrationism, he shows how his program differs from that of colonizationists, writing, "In [Delany's] advocacy of black emigration, which he presented, as opposed to colonizationism, as black-led and a matter of free choice. . . ." See Robert Levine, *The Politics of Representative Identity*, 58–60.

55. Stowe, *Uncle Tom's Cabin*, 440.

56. This is an important element of Levine's analysis of the struggle between Douglass and Delany over the legitimacy of being considered the "representative black leader" in America. See Levine, *The Politics of Representative Identity*, 2.

57. Stowe, *Uncle Tom's Cabin*, 441.

58. Ibid.

59. Samuel Otter, "Stowe and Race," in Cindy Weinstein, ed., *The Cambridge Companion to Harriet Beecher Stowe* (New York: Cambridge University Press, 2004), 20.

60. Stowe, *Uncle Tom's Cabin*, 442.

61. This position on Stowe's novel goes against recent scholarship which accepts Delany's view that Stowe's novel advocates colonization. Robert Levine writes that "the fact that many of the novel's former slaves end up going to Africa suggests that Stowe uses George Harris as a mouthpiece to forward her own colonizationist views that blacks belong in Africa, whites in America." Levine, *The Politics of Representative Identity*, 58.

62. Jane Rhodes, *Mary Ann Shadd Cary: The Black Press and Protest in the Nineteenth Century* (Bloomington: Indiana University Press, 1998), 119.

63. Josephine Donovan, *Uncle Tom's Cabin: Evil, Affliction, and Redemptive Love* (Boston: Twayne Publishers, 1991), 17–18.

64. Levine, *The Politics of Representative Identity*, 72.

65. Ibid., 82.

66. David Blight, *Frederick Douglass' Civil War: Keeping Faith in Jubilee* (Baton Rouge: Louisiana State University Press, 1989), 129–30.

67. "A Nation in the Midst of a Nation: An Address Delivered in New York, New York, May 11, 1853, in Blassingame," *The Frederick Douglass Papers*, 2.

68. "The Present Condition and Future Prospects of the Negro People, speech at annual meeting of the American and Foreign Anti-Slavery Society, New York City, May, 1853," in Phillip S. Foner, ed., *The Life and Writings of Frederick Douglass, vol. II, Pre-Civil War Decade, 1850–1860* (New York: International Publishers, 1950), 243–54.

69. Ibid.

70. Mary Ann Shadd Cary, *A Plea for Emigration, or Notes of Canada West, in its Moral, Social, and Political Aspect: with Suggestions Respecting Mexico, West Indies, and Vancouver Island, for the Information of Colored Emigrants* (Detroit: George W. Pattison, 1852), in Richard Newman et al., eds., *Pamphlets of Protest: An Anthology of Early African-American Protest Literature, 1790–1860* (New York: Routledge, 2001), 176–98.

71. Ibid., 212.

72. Rev. James T. Holly, *A Vindication of the Capacity of the Negro Race for Self-Government and Civilized Progress, as Demonstrated by Historical Events of the Haytian Revolution and the Subsequent Acts of that People Since their National Independence* (New Haven, CT: Afric-American Printing Co., 1857), 5.

73. Ibid., 65.

74. James T. Holly, *Vindication of the Capacity of the Negro Race*, in Richard Newman, *Pamphlets of Protest*, 279.

75. Leon Litwack, *North of Slavery: The Negro in the Free States, 1790–1860* (Chicago: University of Chicago Press, 1961), 261. Quarles's *Black Abolitionists* offers little analysis of the National Emigration Convention and conflates emigration with colonization; see Quarles, *Black Abolitionists*, 215–18. Lois and James Horton are no more generous in their treatment of black emigration and the National Emigration Conventions in 1854 and 1855; see Horton and Horton, *In Hope of Liberty*, 263–65. Jane and William Pease, on the other hand, devote considerable space to analyzing the successes and failures of emigration, concluding that the charge of abandoning those who were still enslaved posed the most vexing question that emigrationists needed to answer. See Pease and Pease, *They Who Would Be Free*, 266–72.

76. Michael C. Dawson, *Black Visions: The Roots of Contemporary African-American Political Ideologies* (Chicago: University of Chicago Press, 2001), 94–95.

77. Levine's work on Delany and Douglass points to the importance of this convention for the broader struggle for freedom and equality in America. Delany, as he argues, caused Douglass to develop more specific goals for black advancement and defend the view that African Americans were better off fighting for rights in the United States. See Levine, *The Politics of Representative Identity*, 90–98.

78. Robert Levine, *Martin R. Delany: A Documentary Reader* (Chapel Hill: University of North Carolina Press, 2003), 241.

79. Levine makes this point in his short introduction to the document "Call for a National Emigration Convention of Colored Men to Be Held in Cleveland, Ohio, on the 24th, 25th, and 26th of August, 1854," ibid., 240.

80. Ibid.

81. "New Bedford, September 23, 1853," *Frederick Douglass' Paper*, September 30, 1853.

82. State Convention of Colored People of Massachusetts, Convention January 2, 1854, in Foner and Walker, *Proceedings*, 93.

83. "Illinois Convention," *Frederick Douglass' Paper*, November 18, 1853; reprinted in Levine, *Martin Delany*, 243–44.

84. This letter, signed by Delany, was written on November 22, 1853, and published under the heading, "Frederick Douglass and John Jones, of Illinois," in *Frederick Douglass' Paper*, December 2, 1853.

85. "Correspondence," *Frederick Douglass' Paper*, March 31, 1854.

86. Foner and Walker, *Proceedings of State Conventions*, 46–47.

87. "National Emigration Convention of Colored Men," from the *Cleveland Leader*, as reprinted in *The Liberator*, September 29, 1854.

88. "Political Destiny of the Colored Race on the American Continent," in Levine, *Martin Delany: A Documentary Reader*, 245–90.

89. Ibid., 253.

90. Delany, "Political Destiny," in Levine, *Martin Delany*, 252–53.

91. For the importance of violence and masculinity as expressed in Delany's work, see Robert Reid-Pharr's essay in *Representing Black Men*, 246.

92. Maurice Wallace argues that Delany's notions of racial destiny and masculinity originate in his association with freemasonry. See Maurice Wallace, "'Are We Men?': Prince Hall, Martin Delany, and the Masculine Ideal in Black Freemasonry, 1775–1865," *American Literary History* 9, no. 3 (Autumn 1997): 396–424.

93. Lois and James Horton reiterate the importance of "self-assertion and aggression" among these leaders in their essay "Violence, Protest, and Identity: Black Manhood in Antebellum America." As we shall see, both emigrationists and anti-emigrationists associated these two masculine traits when justifying their positions. See James and Lois Horton, "Violence, Protest, and Identity: Black Manhood in Antebellum America" in Darlene Clark Hine and Earnestine Jenkins, eds., *A Question of Manhood: A Reader in U.S. Black Men's History and Masculinity, vol. 1, "Manhood Rights": The Construction of Black Male History and Manhood, 1750–1870* (Bloomington: Indiana University Press, 1999).

94. Shadd was, in the words of her biographer, "visibly absent from the meeting," and had struggled to win male acceptance throughout her career as an abolitionist and leader. See Rhodes, *Mary Ann Shadd Cary*, 95 and 216; Ullman, *Martin R. Delany*, 163–64.

95. Shirley J. Yee, *Black Women Abolitionists: A Study in Activism, 1828–1860* (Knoxville: University of Tennessee Press, 1992), 144–45.

96. "Proceedings of the Colored National Convention held in Franklin Hall, Sixth Street, Below Arch, Philadelphia, October 16–18, 1855," reprinted in Bell, *Minutes of the National Negro Convention*, 10.

97. David Howard-Pitney, *Afro-American Jeremiad: Appeals for Justice in America* (Philadelphia: Temple University Press, 1990), 20.

98. Patrick Rael, "Black Theodicy: African Americans and Nationalism in the Antebellum North," *The North Star: A Journal of African American Religious History* 3, no. 2 (Spring 2000): 8; David Blight, *Frederick Douglass' Civil War: Keeping Faith in Jubilee* (Baton Rouge: Louisiana State University Press, 1989), 101–21.

Notes to Chapter 6

1. James McCune Smith to Henry Highland Garnet, *Weekly Anglo-African*, New York, January 12, 1861, reprinted in C. Peter Ripely et al., eds., *The Black Abolitionist Papers, vol. V, The United States, 1859–1865* (Chapel Hill: University of North Carolina Press, 1992), 103–9.

2. *Weekly Anglo-African*, New York, January 26, 1861.

3. For a recent examination of this perspective, see Patrick Rael, "The Market Revolution and Market Values in Antebellum Black Protest Thought," in Patrick Rael, ed., *African American Activism Before the Civil War: The Freedom Struggle in the Antebellum North* (New York: Routledge, 2008), 276–78. Rael's arguments build on Paul Goodman and Leon Litwack's examination of free blacks' struggle for citizenship. See Paul Goodman, *Of One Blood: Abolitionism and the Origins of Racial Equality* (Berkeley: University of California Press, 1998), 52; and: Leon Litwack, *North of Slavery: The Negro in the Free States, 1790–1860* (Chicago: University of Chicago Press, 1961), 262–78.

4. African American leaders had feared a state-sponsored plan of mass colonization since the ACS's founding in 1817. Lincoln's colonization plan has been analyzed in numerous works on the Civil War and African American history. Most recently, Eric Foner's essay "Lincoln and Colonization" challenges the view that Lincoln's penchant for colonization during the war illustrates that he was "racist." See Eric Foner, "Lincoln and Colonization," in *Our Lincoln: New Perspectives on Lincoln and His World,* Eric Foner, ed. (New York: W.W. Norton & Company Inc., 2008), 166; James D. Lockett, "Abraham Lincoln and Colonization: An Episode That Ends in Tragedy at L'Ile a Vache, Haiti, 1863–1864," *Journal of Black Studies* 21, no. 4 (June 1991): 428–44; George Fredrickson, "A Man but Not a Brother: Abraham Lincoln and Racial Equality," *The Journal of Southern Studies* 41, no. 1 (February 1975): 39–58; James M. McPherson, "Abolitionist and Negro Opposition to Colonization during the Civil War," *Phylon* 26, no. 4 (Fourth Quarter, 1965): 391–99; and Paul J. Scheips, "Lincoln and the Chiriqui Colonization Project," *Journal of Negro History* 37, no. 4 (October 1952): 418–53.

5. Willis Boyd has provided an excellent survey of colonization during the Civil War and Reconstruction. Several leading scholars on free blacks and abolition, most notably Benjamin Quarles, Jane Pease and William H. Pease, and James Oliver Horton and Lois E. Horton, have contextualized emigration and colonization during the Civil War era. See also Floyd J. Miller, *The Search for a Black Nationality: Black Emigration and Colonization, 1787–1863* (Urbana: University of Illinois Press, 1975); Willis D. Boyd, "Negro Colonization in the Reconstruction Era, 1865–1870," *Georgia Historical Quarterly* 40 (December 1956); Jane Pease and William H. Pease, *They Who Would Be Free: Blacks' Search for Freedom, 1830–1861* (Urbana: University of Illinois Press, 1974); Benjamin Quarles, *Black Abolitionists* (New York: Oxford University Press, 1969); James Oliver Horton and Lois E. Horton, *In Hope of Liberty: Culture, Community and Protest Among Northern Free Blacks, 1700–1860* (Oxford, UK: Oxford University Press, 1997).

6. Miller, *The Search for a Black Nationality*, 181–83.

7. Holly later left the movement to pursue his own Haitian emigration ambitions. See: Leon D. Pamphile, *Haitians and African Americans: A Heritage of Tragedy and Hope* (Gainesville: University Press of Florida, 2001), 48–53; Miller, *The Search for a Black Nationality*, 181.

8. Rutledge M. Dennis, "Social Darwinism, Scientific Racism, and the Metaphysics of Race," *Journal of Negro Education* 64, no. 3 (1995): 243–52; George M. Fredrickson, *Racism: A Short History* (Princeton, NJ: Princeton University Press, 2002); Michael Stanton, *The Leopard's Spots: Scientific Attitudes toward Race in America, 1815–1859* (Chicago: University of Chicago Press, 1960).

9. This commentary responded to an article that had been cut-and-pasted above it describing the "recent meeting of the Executive Committee of the National Colored Convention." See "A New Movement," *The National Era*, Washington, D.C, September 23, 1858, vol. XII, no. 612, 151.

10. "Iowa and Free Negroes," *Pittsfield Sun*, September 9, 1857, vol. LVIII, no. 2973.

11. Speech by Charles L. Remond, Mozart Hall, New York, May 13, 1858, in Ripley, *The Black Abolitionist Papers*, vol. 4, 382–88.

12. "Resolutions by Lloyd H. Brooks, Delivered at the Third Christian Church, New Bedford, Massachusetts, June 16, 1858," in Ripley, *The Black Abolitionist Papers*, 391–97.

13. Henry Highland Garnet, "An Address to the Slaves of the United States," 1843, in Herbert Aptheker, *A Documentary History of the Negro People*, 226–33.

14. "An Address to the Slaves of the United States of America," Buffalo, NY, 1843, reprinted in Earl Ofari Hutchison, *"Let Your Motto Be Resistance": The Life and Thought of Henry Highland Garnet* (Boston: Beacon Press, 1972), 144–53.

15. Henry Highland Garnet, *The Past and the Present Condition, and the Destiny, of the Colored Race*, discourse delivered at the Fifteenth Anniversary Convention of the Female Benevolent Society of Troy, NY, February 14, 1848 (Miami, FL: Mnemosyne Publishing, 1969), 29.

16. Schor's interpretation is derived from Floyd Miller and Howard Bell's analysis of Garnet's shift toward emigration. See Joel Schor, *Henry Highland Garnet*, 154–55; Earl Ofari Hutchison, *"Let Your Motto Be Resistance,"* 79; Martin B. Pasternak, *Rise Now and Fly to Arms: The Life of Henry Highland Garnet* (New York: Garland Press, 1995), 89.

17. Emma J. Lapsansky-Werner and Margaret Hope Bacon, eds., *Back to Africa: Benjamin Coates and the Colonization Movement in America, 1848–1880* (University Park: Pennsylvania State University Press, 2005), 32–33.

18. Schor, *Henry Highland Garnet*, 154–55; Crummell is quoted on page 155.

19. Frederick Douglass to Benjamin Coates, Rochester, NY, May 2, 1859, in Lapsansky-Werner and Bacon, *Back to Africa*, 126–27.

20. Henry Highland Garnet to Benjamin Coates, New York, September 9, 1859, in Lapsansky, *Back to Africa*, 145–46.

21. Mary Ann Shadd Cary to Benjamin Coates, Chatham, Canada West, November 20, 1858, in Lapsansky, *Back to Africa*, 110–14.

22. Benjamin Coates to Ralph R. Gurley, Philadelphia, January 13, 1859, in Lapsansky, *Back to Africa*, 116–18.

23. "African Civilization Society," *Douglass Monthly*, February, 1859, in Foner, *The Life and Writings of Frederick Douglass*, vol. II, 442–47; Blight, *Frederick Douglass' Civil War*, 130–31; also see Joel Schor, "The Rivalry Between Frederick Douglass and Henry Highland Garnet," *Journal of Negro History* 64, no. 1 (Winter 1979): 30–38.

24. "African Civilization Society," *Douglass Monthly*, February 1859, in Foner, *The Life and Writings of Frederick Douglass*, vol. II, 442–47.

25. Ibid.; see also Blight, *Frederick Douglass' Civil War*, 130–32. Also see the article by Joel Schor mentioned previously, "The Rivalry Between Frederick Douglass and Henry Highland Garnet."

26. While I offer a more complete discussion of Lincoln's plan later in this chapter, it is important to point out that one of the central goals of the ACS had been to get

federal funding for free black colonization in Africa. ACS leaders had never convinced a president to support colonization to Africa. Yet Lincoln did support settling free blacks and those emancipated during the war in Latin America. See: George Fredrickson, "A Man but Not a Brother: Abraham Lincoln and Racial Equality," *Journal of Southern Studies* 41, no. 1 (February 1975): 39–58.

27. "New England Colored Citizens' Convention, August 1, 1859," in Foner and Walker, *Proceedings of the Black State Conventions, 1840–1865*, 208–9; Schor, *Henry Highland Garnet*, 160–61.

28. *New England Convention*, 220.

29. Ibid., 222–23.

30. Ibid., 222.

31. Ibid., 223.

32. "Enthusiastic Meeting of Colored Citizens of Boston," *Weekly Anglo-African*, September 10, 1859; "Henry Highland Garnet's Speech at an Enthusiastic Meeting of the Colored Citizens of Boston," *Weekly Anglo-African*, September 19, 1859, reprinted in Sterling Stuckey, *The Ideological Origins of Black Nationalism* (Boston: Beacon Press, 1972), 174–94.

33. "Meeting in Joy Street Church," *The Liberator*, September 2, 1859.

34. Ibid.

35. Ibid.

36. Ibid., 188. (Italics in the original source text.)

37. *Weekly Anglo-African*, September 17, 1859.

38. "Meeting in New Bedford," *The Liberator*, Boston, March 25, 1859, 47.

39. This article was reprinted from the *Evening News* in the *National Anti-Slavery Standard*, September 17, 1859.

40. Miller, *In Search of a Black Nationality*, 184–85; Schor, *Henry Highland Garnet*, 154–56; Ofari, *Let Your Motto Be Resistance*, 79–83.

41. Miller, *In Search of a Black Nationality*, 192.

42. *The Farmers' Cabinet*, August 11, 1858, vol. 57, no. 2, 2.

43. African Civilization Society constitution, in Howard Brotz, ed., *African-American Social and Political Thought, 1850–1920* (New Brunswick, NJ: Transaction Publishers, 1993), 191–93.

44. "Cotton in Africa," *The Independent*, January 20, 1859, 2.

45. Miller, *The Search for a Black Nationality*, 218–20.

46. African News, *Weekly Anglo-African*, September 3, 1859.

47. "The Congregational Union of England," *Times* (London), September 20, 1859, no. 23416, 5; "The Congregational Union of England and Wales," *The Independent*, October 13, 1859, 3.

48. "African Civilization Society. —A Meeting," *Times* (London), September 22, 1859, no. 23418, 7.

49. "Cotton Growing in Africa," *Weekly Anglo-African*, September 3, 1859.

50. Dorothy Porter, "Sarah Parker Remond, Abolitionist and Physician," *Journal of Negro History* 20, no. 3 (July 1835): 293.

51. "American Slavery and African Colonisation [*sic*]," *Anti-Slavery Advocate*, November 1, 1859.

52. Richard Blackett, *Building an Antislavery Wall*, 179; "Speech by Sarah P. Remond, Delivered at the Athenaeum, Manchester, England, September 14, 1859," in Ripley, *The Black Abolitionist Papers*, 457–61.

53. Blackett, *Building an Antislavery Wall*, 179.

54. Floyd Miller concurs, writing, "Delany had railed against Bourne and maintained that his own expedition had no relationship at all to Bourne's activities." Yet, not even a year later, Delany would change his tune and join the African Civilization Society.

55. Ibid.

56. Richard Blackett, "Martin R. Delany and Robert Campbell: Black Americans in Search of an African Colony," *Journal of Negro History* 62, no. 1 (January 1977): 1–25.

57. *Weekly Anglo-African* published a letter from Campbell describing the success of the trip, as well as the treaty from "his majesty O'kuem Alake" and others. See "Prof. Campbell and that Treaty &c." *Weekly Anglo-African*, January 26, 1861.

58. Edward Blyden to John B. Pinney, Monrovia, July 29, 1859, reprinted in *Maryland Colonization Journal*, October 1859.

59. *Report of the Select Committee on Emancipation and Colonization with an Appendix* (Washington, DC, 1862), 37–59.

60. "Garnet and Brown," *Weekly Anglo-African*, October 22, 1859.

61. See John Stauffer, *The Black Hearts of Men*, 265.

62. Lerone Bennett, *Forced Glory: Abraham Lincoln's White Dream* (Chicago: Johnson Publishing, 2000). For a challenge to Bennett's contention, see David W. Blight, "The Theft of Lincoln in Scholarship, Politics, and Public Memory," in Eric Foner, ed., *Our Lincoln: New Perspectives on Lincoln and His World* (New York: W.W. Norton, 2008). For recent efforts to analyze Lincoln's views on race, see the introduction to Henry Louis Gates Jr., ed., *Lincoln on Race and Slavery* (Princeton, NJ: Princeton University Press, 2009).

63. Eric Foner, "Lincoln and Colonization," in *Our Lincoln*, 135–36.

64. Richard H. Sewell, *Ballots of Freedom: Antislavery Politics in the United States, 1837–1860* (New York: Oxford University Press, 1976), 99.

65. Eric Foner, *Free Soil, Free Labor, Free Men*, 267; Richard Sewell, *Ballots of Freedom*, 171–72; George Fredrickson, *The Black Image in the White Mind*, 130–31.

66. Foner, *Free Soil, Free Labor, Free Men*, 267.

67. George Fredrickson, *The Black Image in the White Mind*, 138–39.

68. Ibid., 140.

69. Just as it is important to remember that not all colonizationists favored forced expulsion of blacks, one must be cognizant of those within the Free Soil Party who advocated in behalf of African American rights based on principles such as anticolonization, which was the backbone of the Liberty Party. See Richard Sewell, *Ballots of Freedom*, 170–201.

70. George M. Fredrickson, *Big Enough to Be Inconsistent: Abraham Lincoln Confronts Slavery and Race* (Cambridge, MA: Harvard University Press, 2008), 58.

71. Foner, *Free Soil, Free Labor, Free Men*, 267–93.

72. Several articles have outlined Lincoln's colonization programs. The purpose here is to establish that African American anticolonizationists faced the prospects that Lincoln's advocacy of colonization represented the potential for a federally sponsored program that had been sought by the ACS since its founding in 1816. For the Chiriqui, Mexico scheme, see Paul J. Scheips, "Lincoln and the Chiriqui Colonization Project," *Journal of Negro History* 37, no. 4 (October 1952): 418–53. The L'Ile a Vache, Haiti, project is examined in James D. Lockett, "Abraham Lincoln and Colonization:

An Episode That Ends in Tragedy at L'Ile a Vache, Haiti, 1863–1864," *Journal of Black Studies* 21, no. 4 (June 1991): 428–44.

73. "Speech of H. Ford Douglass," *The Liberator*, July 13, 1860, 1.

74. Eric Foner devotes considerable attention to analyzing the various facets of colonization and the Republican Party in his crucial study *Free Soil, Free Labor, Free Men*, 267–80; see also W.E.B. DuBois, *Black Reconstruction in America* (New York: Simon and Schuster, 1935); Eric Foner, *Reconstruction: America's Unfinished Revolution, 1863–1877* (New York: Harper & Row, 1988).

75. "The Negro Colonization Scheme," *The Farmers' Cabinet*, vol. 61, no. 8, September 18, 1862.

76. Lind, *What Lincoln Believed*, 197–200.

77. "Annual Message to Congress," December 3, 1861, in Roy P. Basler, ed., *The Collected Works of Abraham Lincoln*, vol. V (New Brunswick, NJ: Rutgers University Press, 1953), 35–53.

78. Ibid., 520.

79. Scheips, "Lincoln and the Chiriqui Colonization Project," 418–53; Lockett, "Abraham Lincoln and Colonization," 428–44.

80. See James Oakes, *The Radical and the Republican*; Frederick Douglass, Abraham Lincoln, and the Triumph of Antislavery Politics (New York: W.W. Norton & Company, Inc., 2007), 89–95; George M. Fredrickson, "A Man but Not a Brother," 39–58.

81. James M. McPherson, "Abolitionist and Negro Opposition to Colonization during the Civil War," *Phylon* 26, no. 4 (fourth quarter, 1965): 392–93.

82. James D. Lockett, "Abraham Lincoln and Colonization: An Episode That Ends in Tragedy at L'Ile a Vache, Haiti, 1863–1864," *Journal of Black Studies* 21, no. 4 (June 1991): 428–30.

83. "Colonization," *The Farmers' Cabinet*, vol. 58, no. 52 (July 25, 1860).

84. All these statistics are from Staudenraus, *The African Colonization Movement*. See appendix for the "Annual Receipts and Colonists Sent to Liberia by the American Colonization Society."

85. "Reply to Lincoln's Colonization Plans, 1862," in Aptheker, *A Documentary History of the Negro People*, 471–73.

86. Ibid., 473–75.

87. Shirley J. Yee, *Black Women Abolitionists*, 26.

88. "Mrs. Francis E. Watkins Harper on the War and the President's Colonization Scheme," *The Christian Recorder*, September 27, 1862.

89. "George B. Vashon to Abraham Lincoln," September 1862, in Ripley, *The Black Abolitionist Papers*, vol. V, 152–55.

90. "Speech of John S. Rock, ESQ, at the annual meeting of the Massachusetts Anti-Slavery Society, Thursday Evening, January 23," *The Christian Recorder*, Philadelphia, February 22, 1862.

91. "The President and His Speeches," *Douglass' Monthly*, September 1862, reprinted in Foner, *The Life and Writings of Frederick Douglass*, 266–70.

92. Postmaster General Blair and Frederick Douglass. Correspondence regarding the new colonization scheme for Central America, Blair to Douglass, Washington DC, September 11, 1862, in Foner, *Life and Writings of Frederick Douglass*, 281–83.

93. Ibid.

94. Frederick Douglass to Hon. Montgomery Blair, Rochester, September 16, 1862, in *Douglass' Monthly*, October 1862, reprinted in Foner, *The Life and Writings of Frederick Douglass*, 283–90.

95. Ibid.

96. Levine, *The Politics of Representative Identity*, 218.

Notes to the Epilogue

1. Proceedings of the National Convention of Colored Men of America, held in Washington, DC, on January 13, 14, 15, and 16, 1869, p. 4.

2. Proceedings of the National Convention of Colored Men of America, Washington, DC, January 13, 14, 15 and 16, 1869 (Washington, 1869), 18, 26.

3. Steven Hahn, *A Nation Under Our Feet: Black Political Struggles in the Rural South from Slavery to the Great Migration* (Cambridge, MA: Belknap Press of Harvard University Press, 2003); Joel Williamson, *After Slavery: The Negro in South Carolina During Reconstruction, 1861–1877* (Chapel Hill: University of North Carolina Press, 1965).

4. Staudenraus, *The African Colonization Movement*, 246.

5. Boyd, "Negro Colonization in the Reconstruction Era," 382.

6. Proceedings at the Fortieth Annual Meeting of the New York State Colonization Society, May 1872 (New York: Baker & Godwin, Printers, 1872), 5.

7. Willis Boyd, "Negro Colonization in the Reconstruction Era, 1865–1870," *Georgia Historical Quarterly* 40, no. 4 (December 1956): 371.

8. Ibid., 380.

9. Hahn, *A Nation Under Our Feet*, 453–54.

10. Ibrahim Sundiata, *Brothers and Strangers: Black Zion, Black Slavery, 1914–1940* (Durham, NC: Duke University Press, 2003).

11. Jeffrey Perry, ed., *A Hubert Harrison Reader* (Middleton, CT: Wesleyan University Press, 2001), 143–44.

12. Edward H. Berman, "Tuskegee-In-Africa," *The Journal of Negro Education* 41, no. 2 (Spring 1972): 99.

13. Brenna W. Greer, "Selling Liberia: Moss H. Kendrix, the Liberian Centennial Commission, and the Post–World War II Trade in Black Progress," *Enterprise & Society* 14, no. 2 (June 2013): 304.

Index

ABOUT THE AUTHOR

Ousmane K. Power-Greene is an assistant professor of history at Clark University in Worcester, Massachusetts.

Early American Places

Colonization and Its Discontents: Emancipation,
Emigration, and Antislavery in Antebellum Pennsylvania
Beverly C. Tomek

Empire at the Periphery: British Colonists, Anglo-Dutch Trade, and the
Development of the British Atlantic, 1621—1713
Christian J. Koot

Slavery before Race: Europeans, Africans, and Indians
at Long Island's Sylvester Manor Plantation, 1651–1884
Katherine Howlett Hayes

Faithful Bodies: Performing Religion and Race in the Puritan Atlantic
Heather Miyano Kopelson

Against Wind and Tide: The African American Struggle
against the Colonization Movement
Ousmane K. Power-Greene